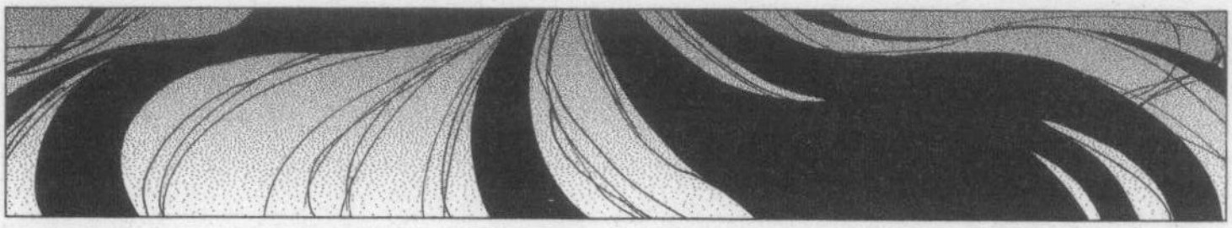

There is no difference between living and being allowed to live
Just like there is no difference between dying and being killed

BLEACH 63 | HEAR, FEAR, HERE

Shonen Jump Manga

ALL STARS AND

マスク・ド・マスキュリン

MASK DE MASCULINE

ROUJURO OTORIBASHI

鳳橋楼十郎
オオトリバシロウジュウロウ

六車拳西
ムグルマケンセイ

KENSEI MUGURUMA

plot

Ichigo Kurosaki meets Soul Reaper Rukia Kuchiki and ends up helping her eradicate Hollows. After developing his powers as a Soul Reaper, Ichigo enters battle against Aizen and his dark ambitions! Ichigo finally defeats Aizen in exchange for his powers as a Soul Reaper.

With the battle over, Ichigo regains his normal life. But his tranquil days end when he meets Ginjo, who offers to help Ichigo get his powers back. But it was all a plot by Ginjo to steal Ichigo's new powers! Ginjo, who was the first ever Deputy Soul Reaper, then reveals to Ichigo the truth behind the deputy badge. However, even after learning the Soul Society's plans for him, Ichigo chooses to continue protecting his friends and defeats Ginjo.

As the invasion of the Soul Society by the Quincies continues, Urahara contacts Mayuri with news of a method to retrieve the Soul Reaper's stolen bankai. But now the Quincies begin to release their true powers...!

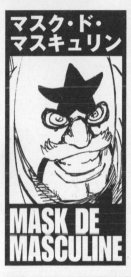

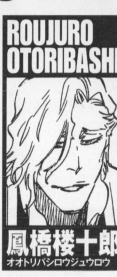

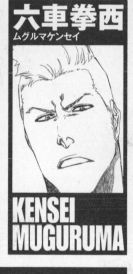

BLEACH

RENJI ABARAI

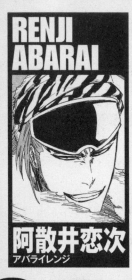

阿散井恋次
アバライレンジ

朽木ルキア
クチキルキア

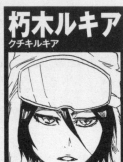
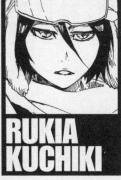

RUKIA
KUCHIKI

Äs Nödt

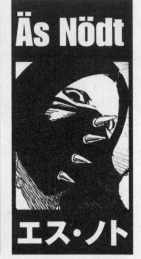

エス・ノト

STORIES

BLEACH 63

HEAR, FEAR, HERE

CONTENTS

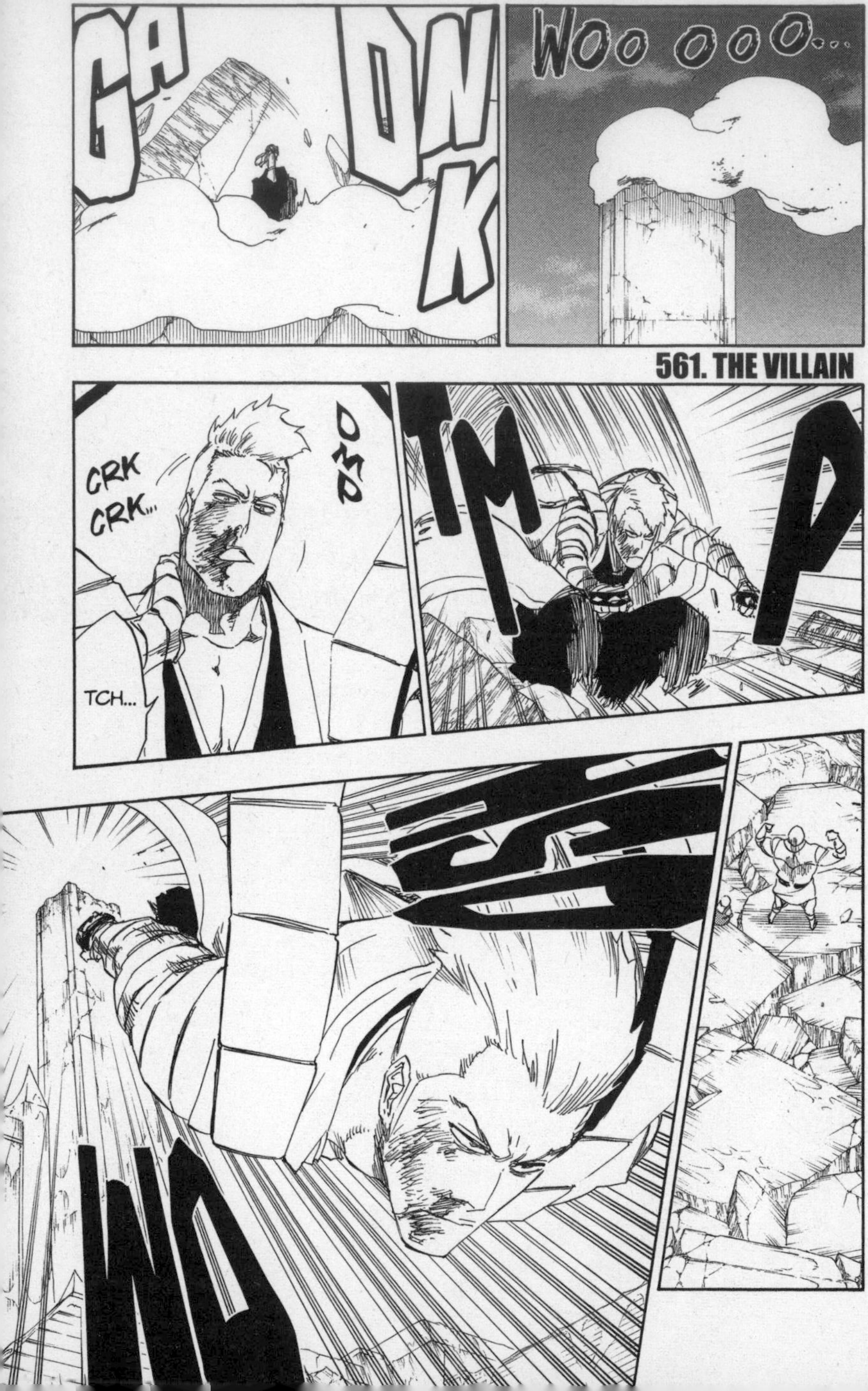
WOO OOO...
GA DN K
561. THE VILLAIN
TMP
CRK CRK...
DMR
TCH...

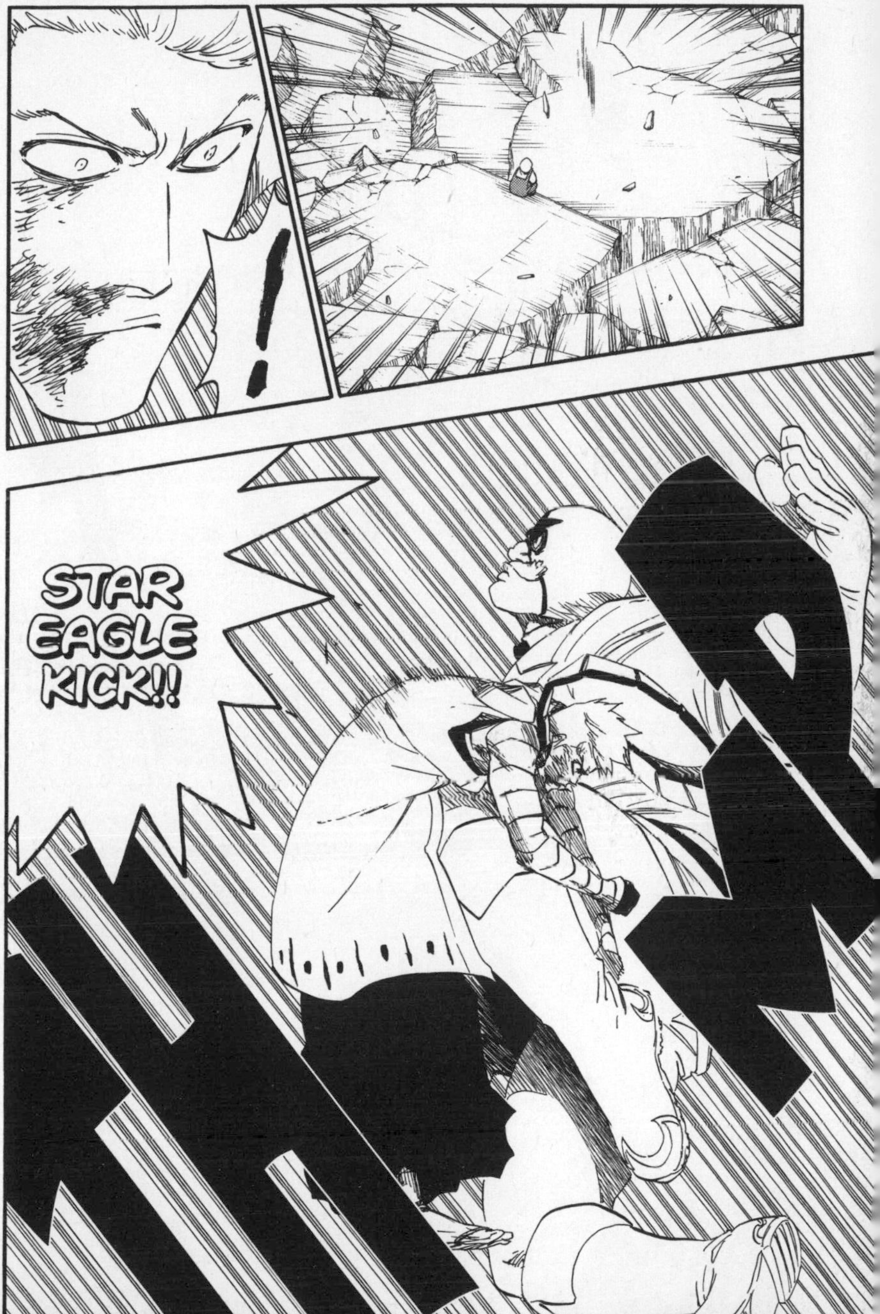
!
STAR EAGLE KICK!!

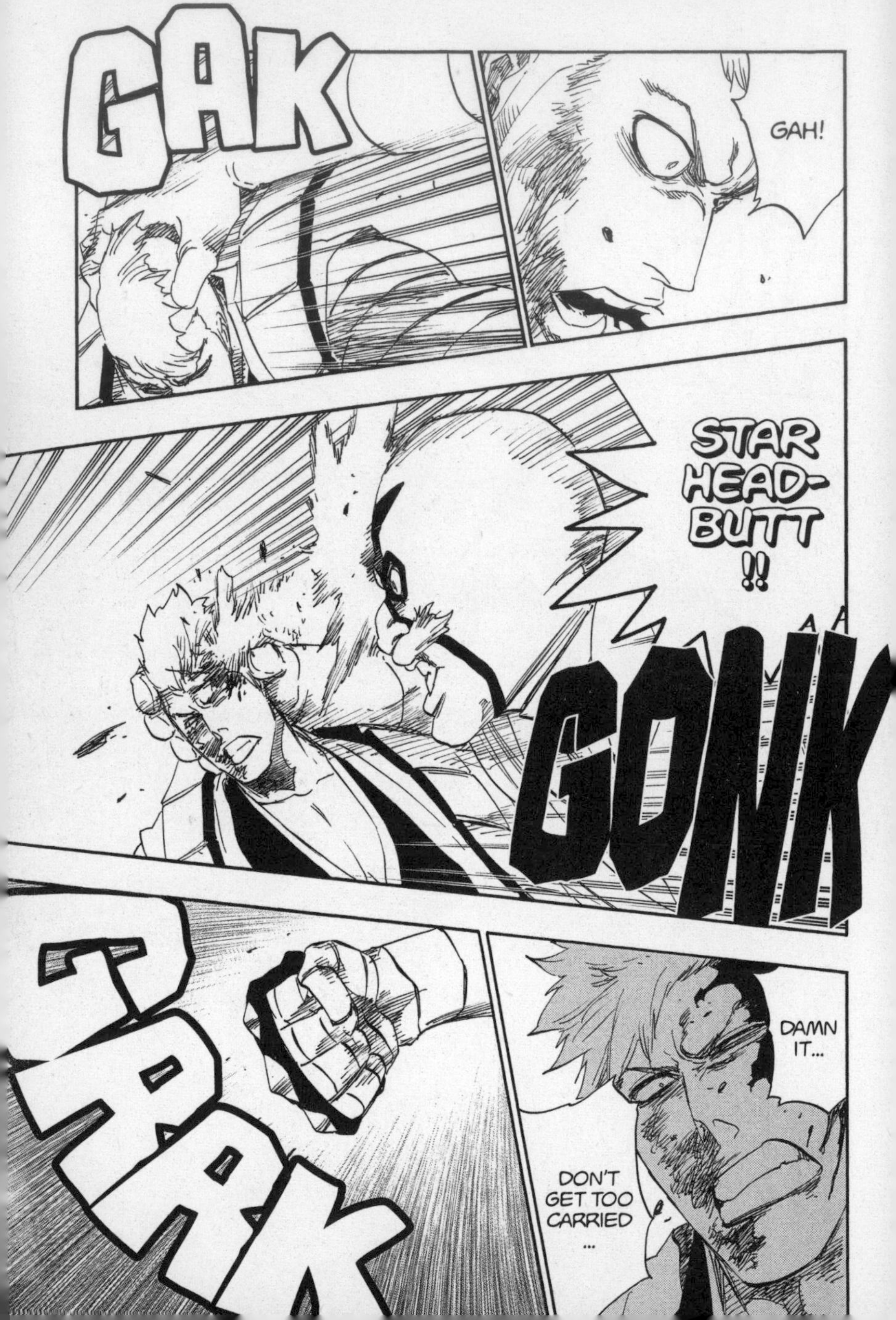
GAH!
GAK
STAR HEAD-BUTT!!
GONK
DAMN IT...
DON'T GET TOO CARRIED ...
CRAK

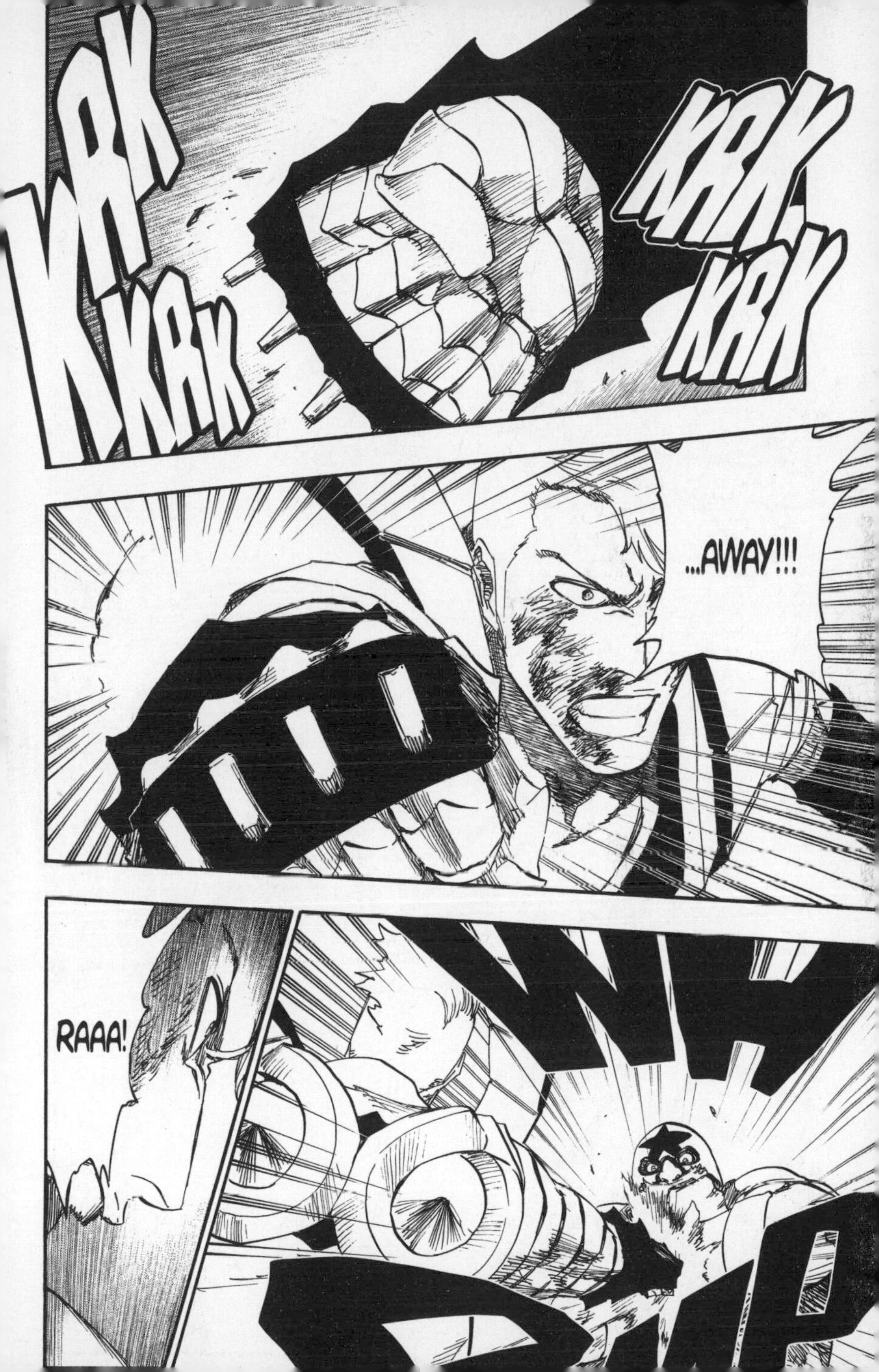
KRK KRK
KRK KRK
...AWAY!!!
RAAA!

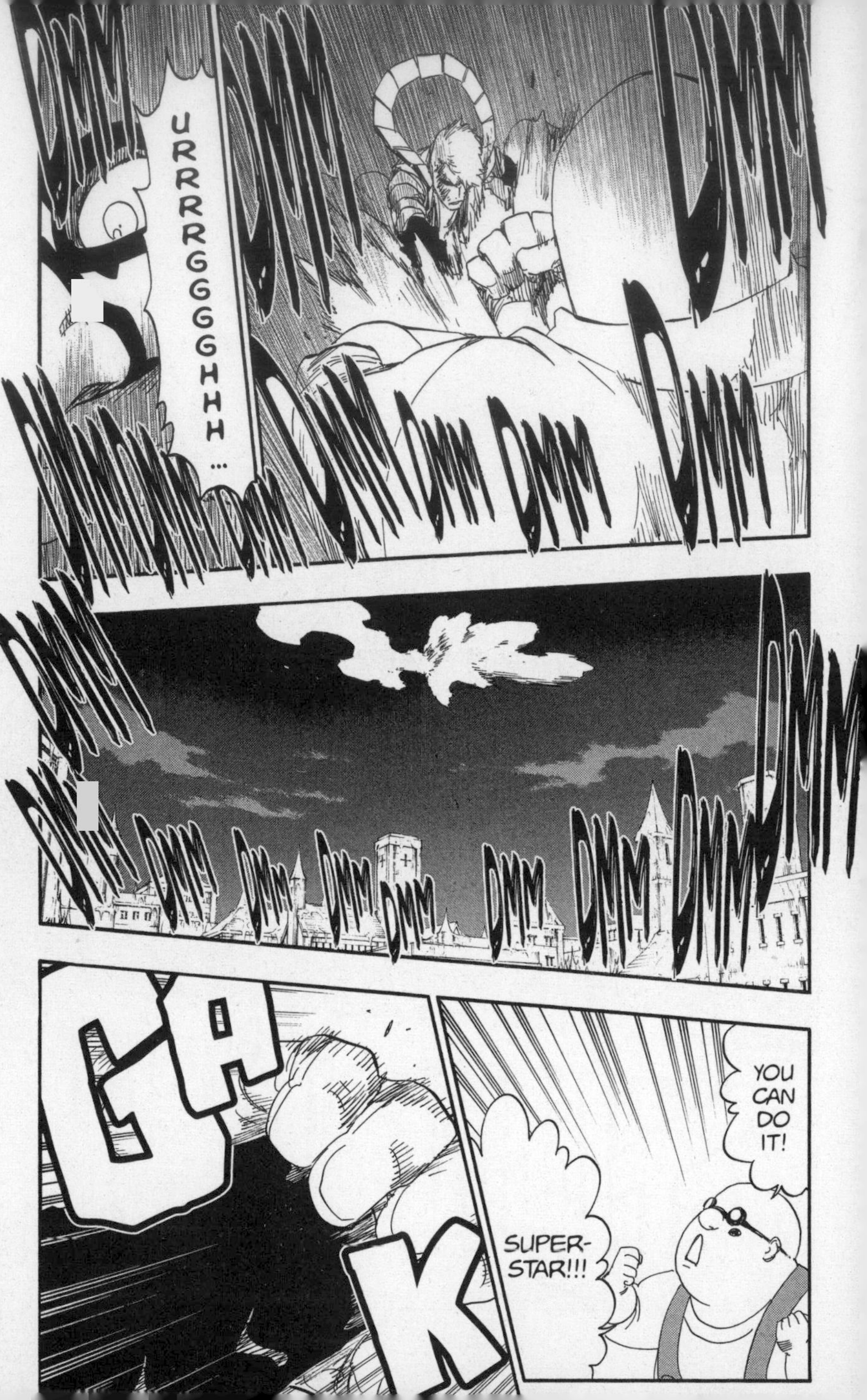
URRRRGGGGHHH...
DMM DMM DMM DMM
DMM DMM DMM DMM DMM
YOU CAN DO IT!
SUPER-STAR!!!
GA
K

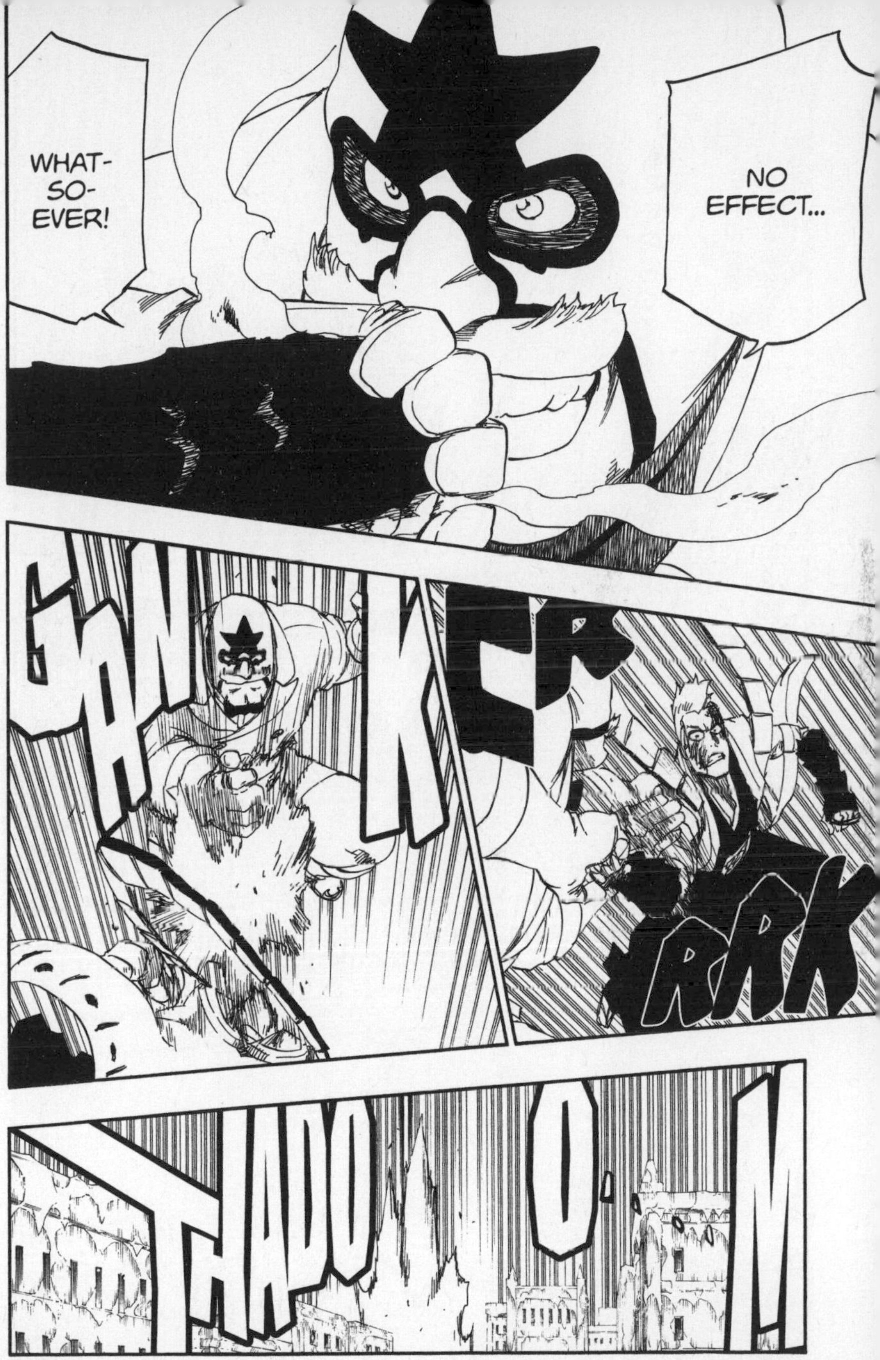
NO EFFECT...
WHAT-SO-EVER!
RRK
GANK
THADOOM

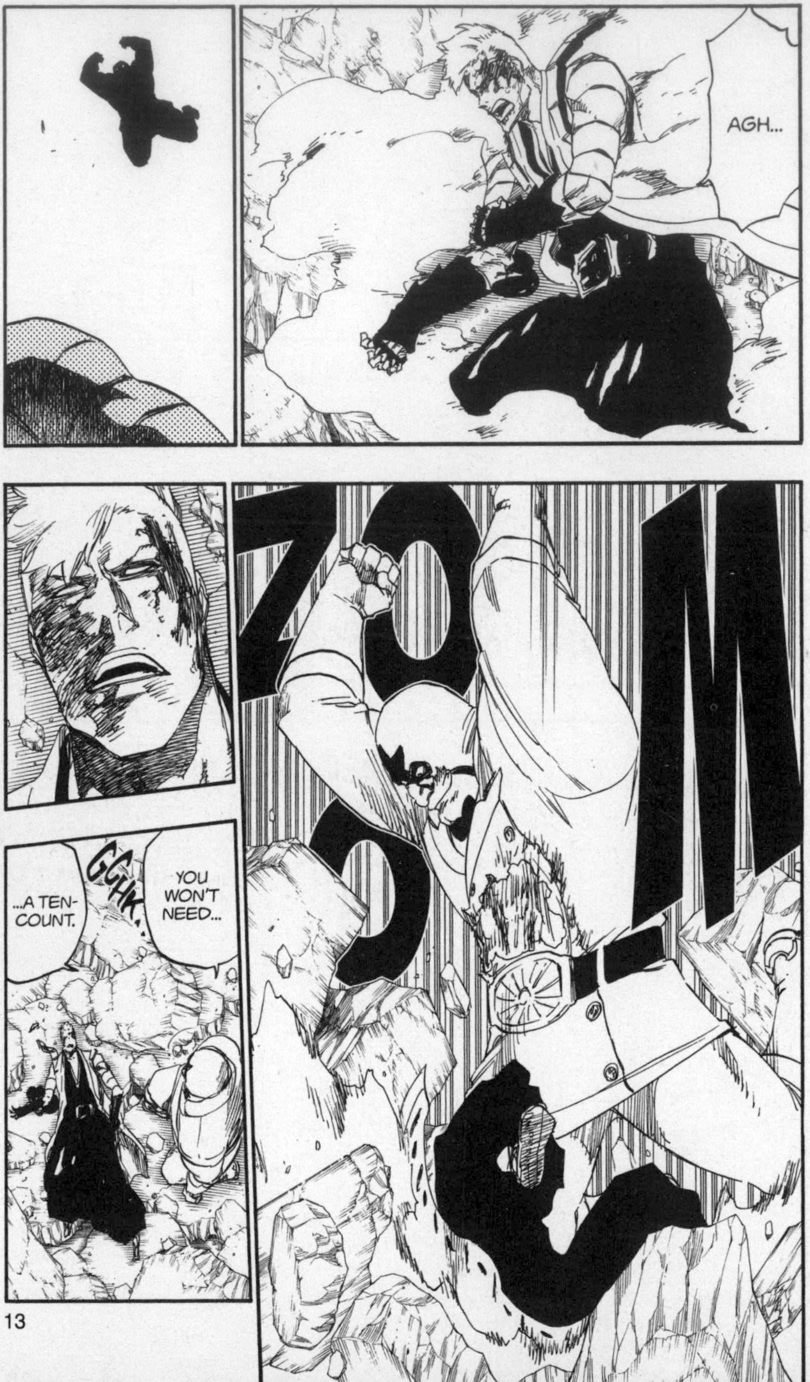

AGH...
ZOOM
YOU WON'T NEED...
GGHK
...A TEN-COUNT.

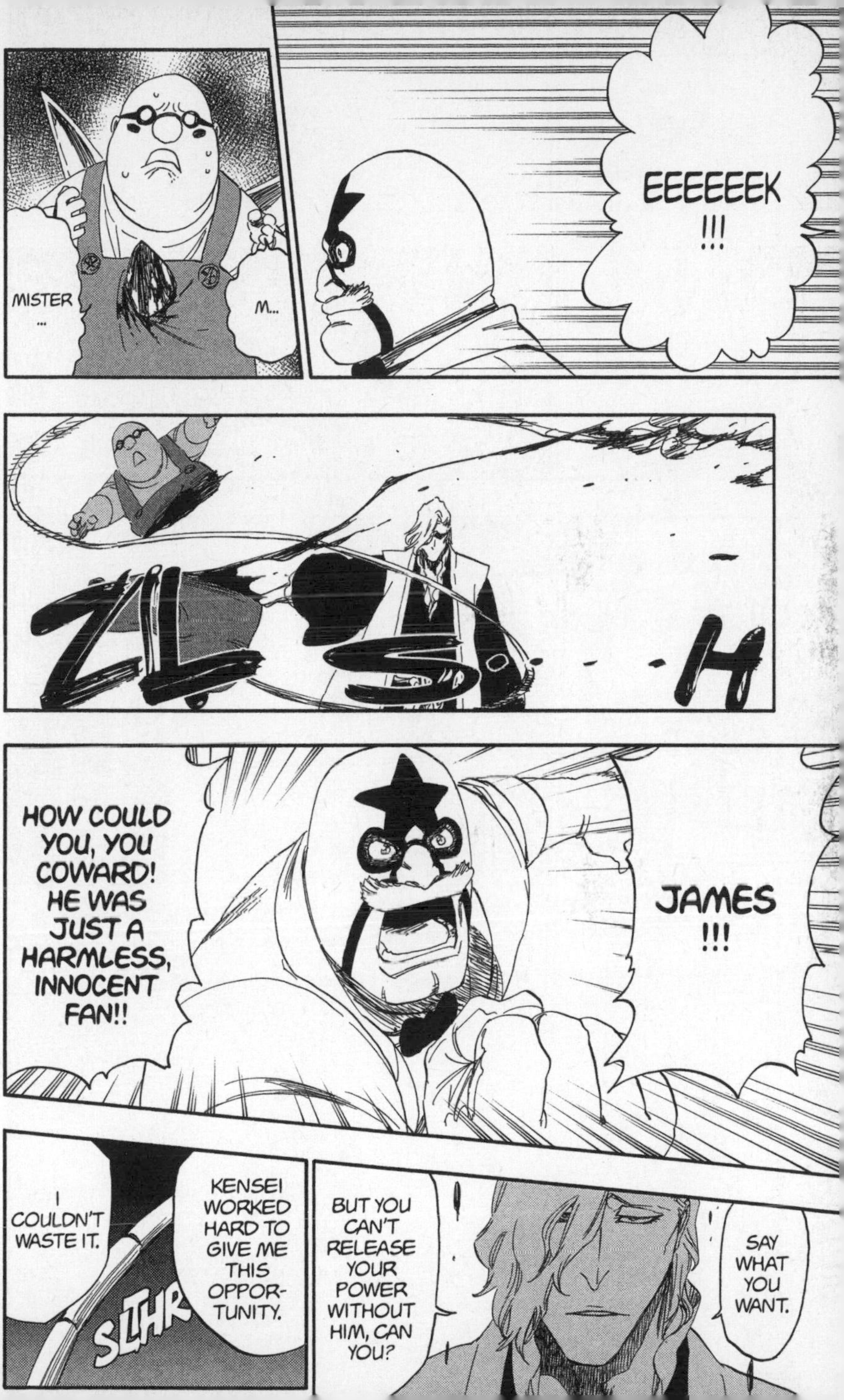
EEEEEEK !!!
MISTER ...
M...
ZLSH
JAMES !!!
HOW COULD YOU, YOU COWARD! HE WAS JUST A HARMLESS, INNOCENT FAN!!
SAY WHAT YOU WANT.
BUT YOU CAN'T RELEASE YOUR POWER WITHOUT HIM, CAN YOU?
KENSEI WORKED HARD TO GIVE ME THIS OPPOR-TUNITY.
I COULDN'T WASTE IT.
SLTHR

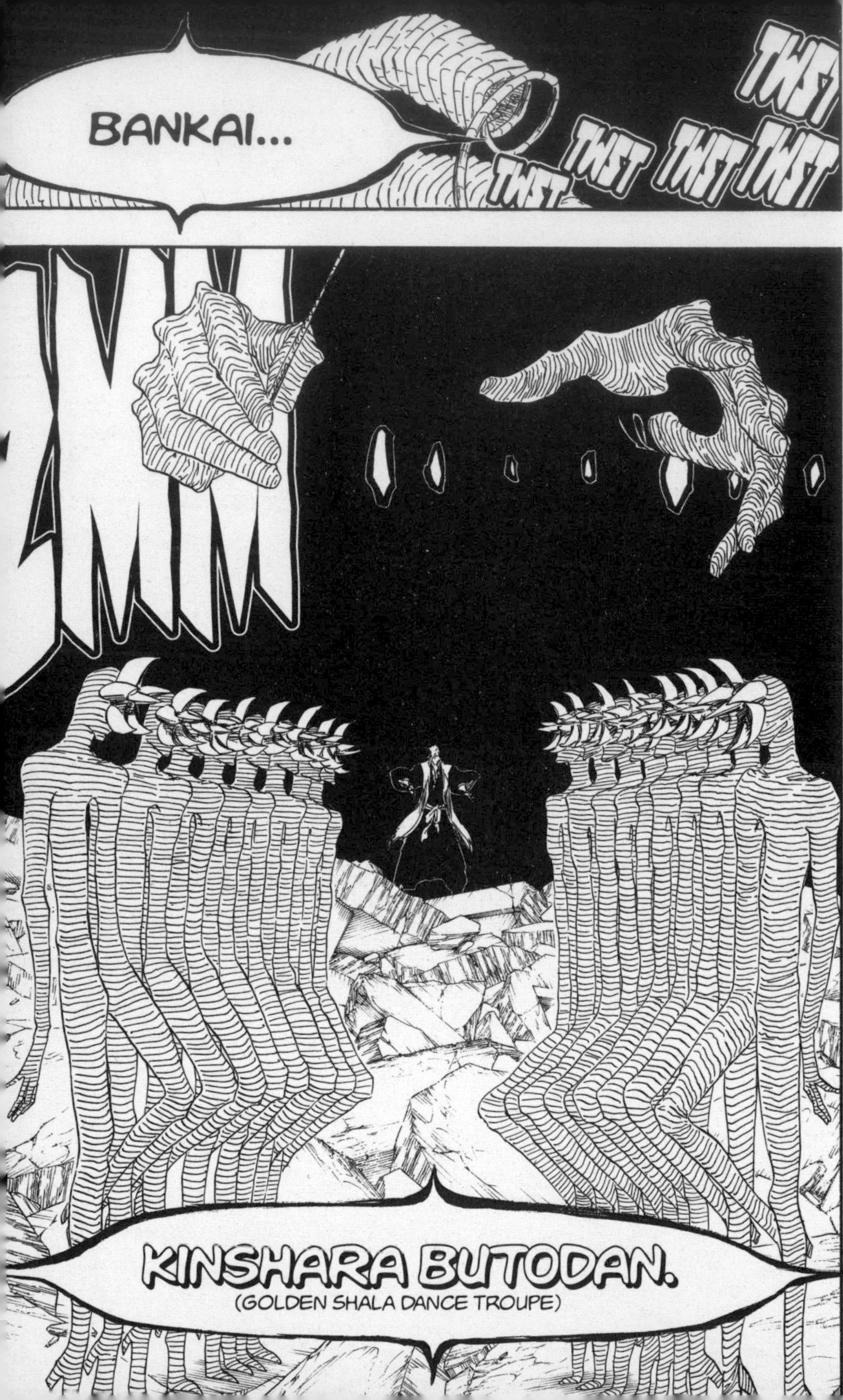
TWST
TWST TWST TWST
TWST
BANKAI...
KINSHARA BUTODAN.
(GOLDEN SHALA DANCE TROUPE)

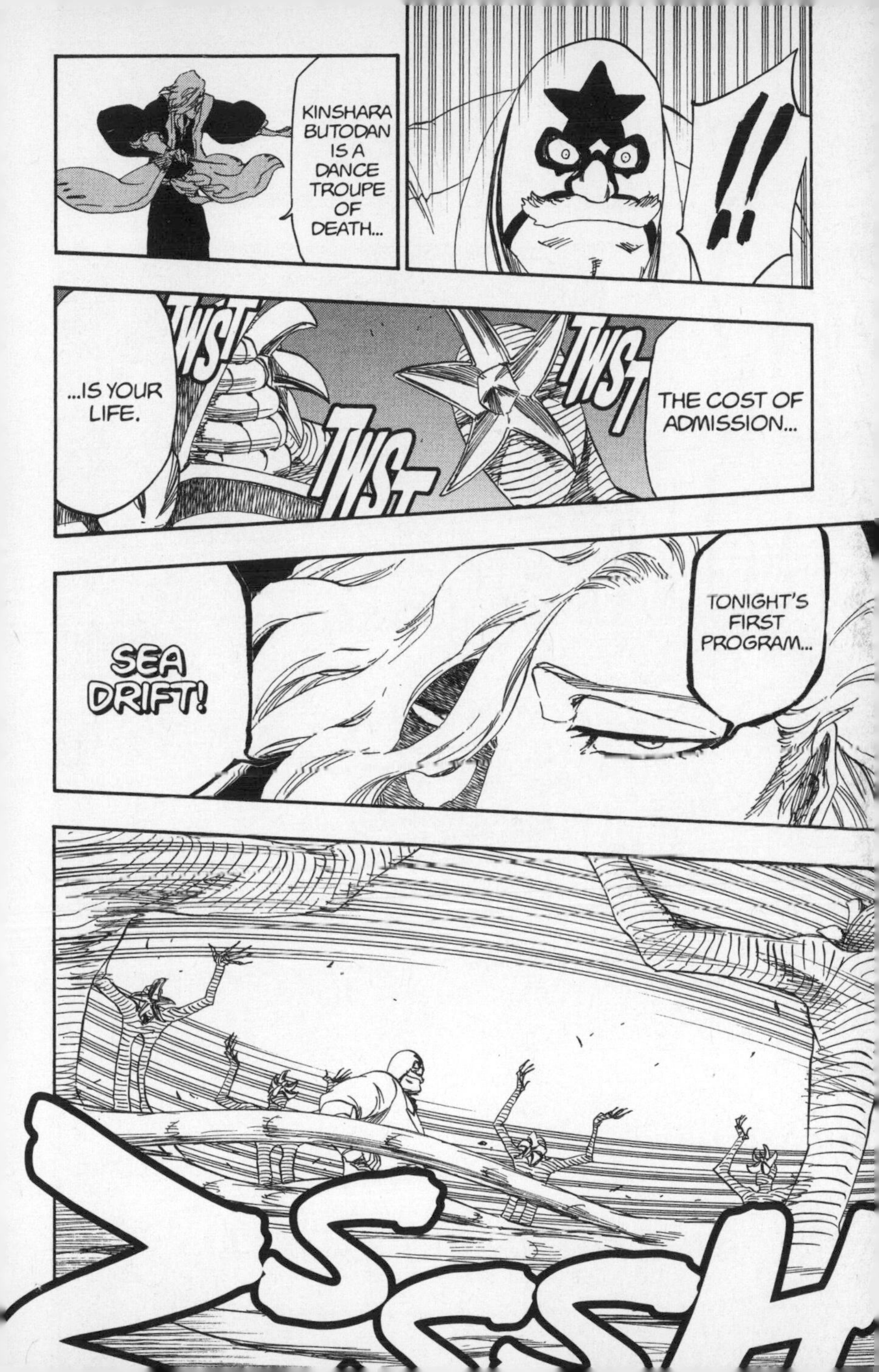
!!
KINSHARA BUTODAN IS A DANCE TROUPE OF DEATH...
THE COST OF ADMISSION...
TWST
TWST
TWST
...IS YOUR LIFE.
TONIGHT'S FIRST PROGRAM...
SEA DRIFT!

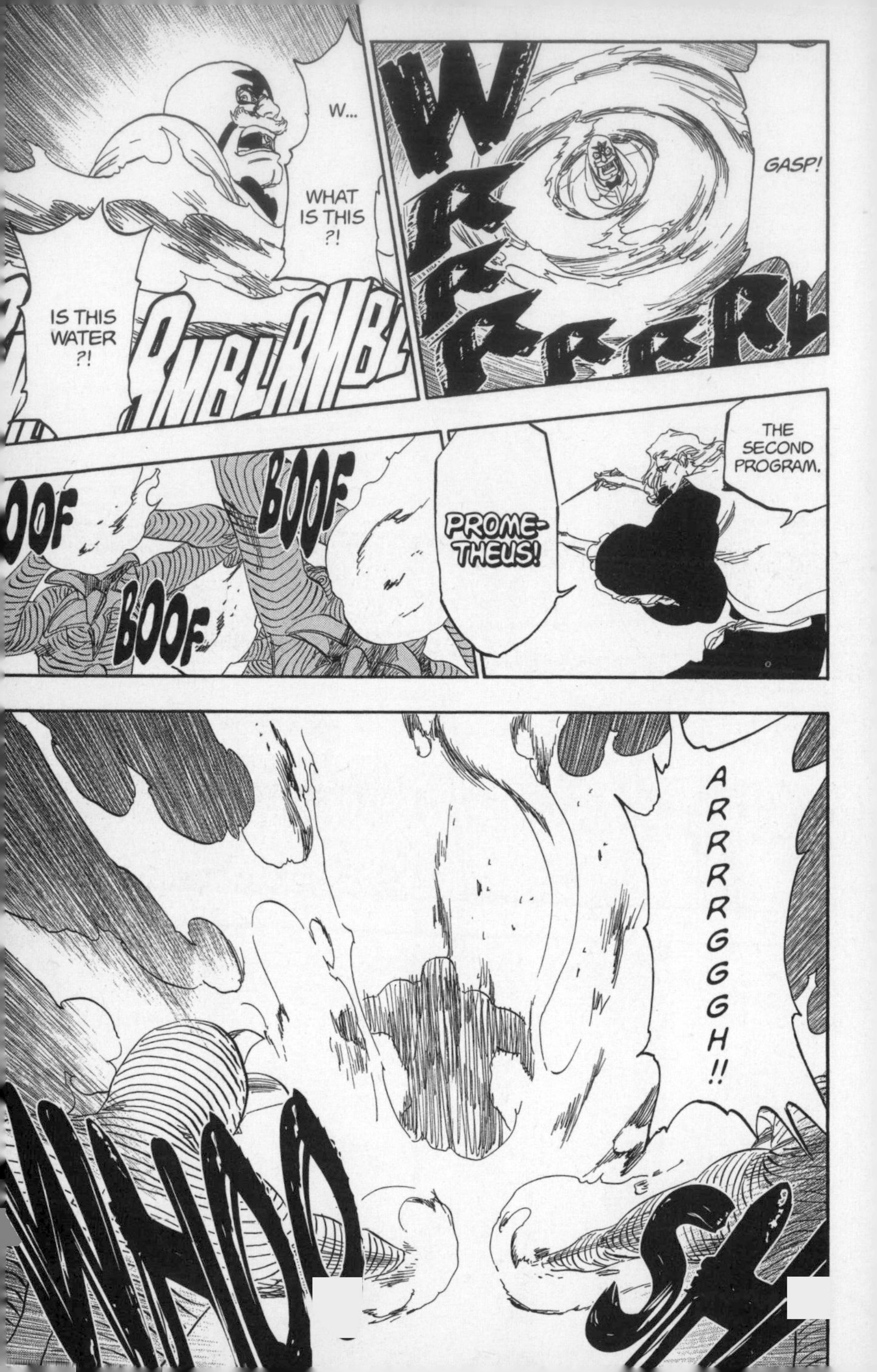
GASP!
W...
WHAT IS THIS ?!
IS THIS WATER ?!
THE SECOND PROGRAM.
PROMETHEUS!
BOOF
BOOF
BOOF
ARRRRGGGH!!

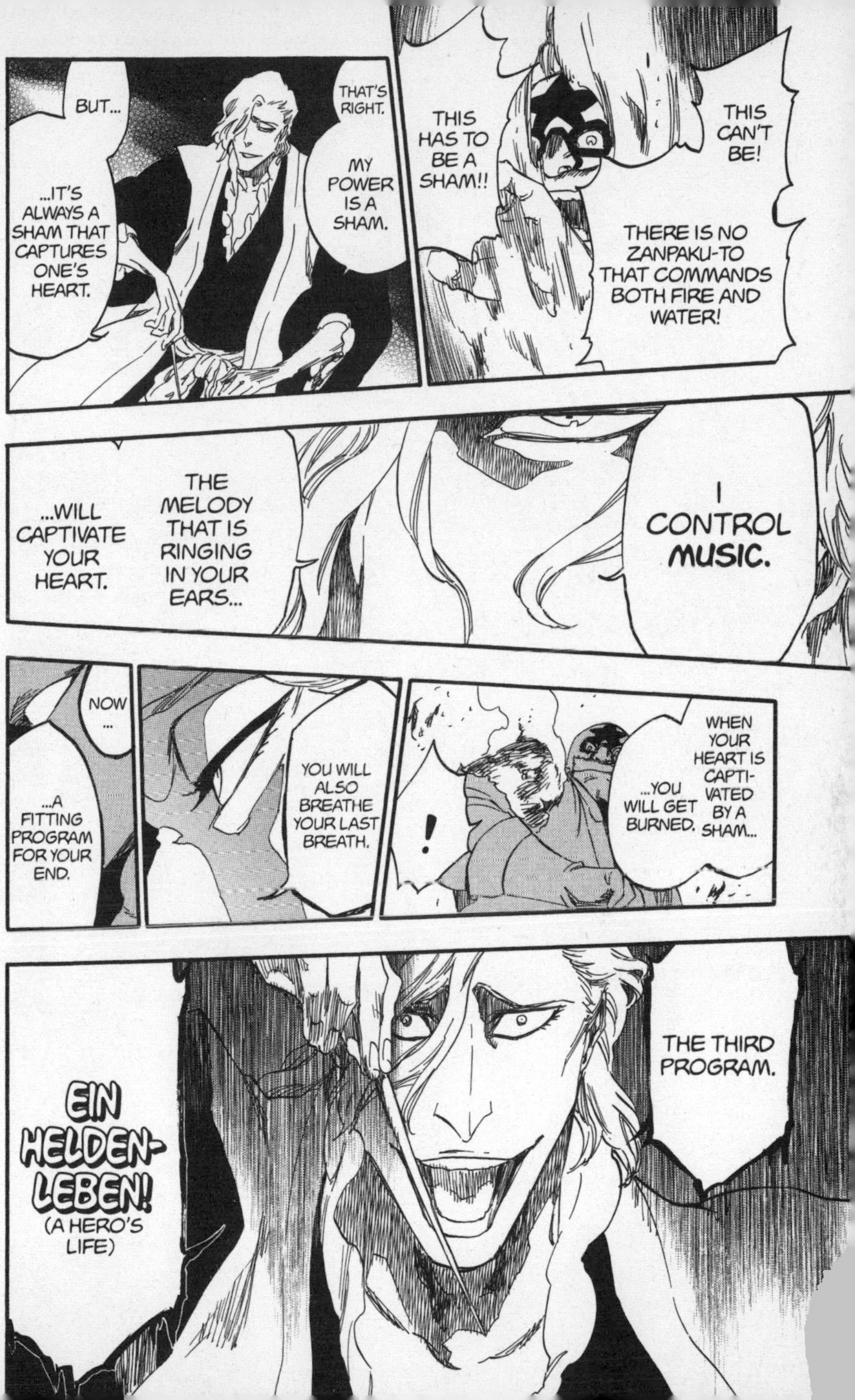
THIS CAN'T BE!
THERE IS NO ZANPAKU-TO THAT COMMANDS BOTH FIRE AND WATER!
THIS HAS TO BE A SHAM!!
THAT'S RIGHT.
MY POWER IS A SHAM.
BUT...
...IT'S ALWAYS A SHAM THAT CAPTURES ONE'S HEART.
I CONTROL MUSIC.
THE MELODY THAT IS RINGING IN YOUR EARS...
...WILL CAPTIVATE YOUR HEART.
WHEN YOUR HEART IS CAPTI-VATED BY A SHAM...
...YOU WILL GET BURNED.
!
YOU WILL ALSO BREATHE YOUR LAST BREATH.
NOW ...
...A FITTING PROGRAM FOR YOUR END.
THE THIRD PROGRAM.
EIN HELDEN-LEBEN!
(A HERO'S LIFE)

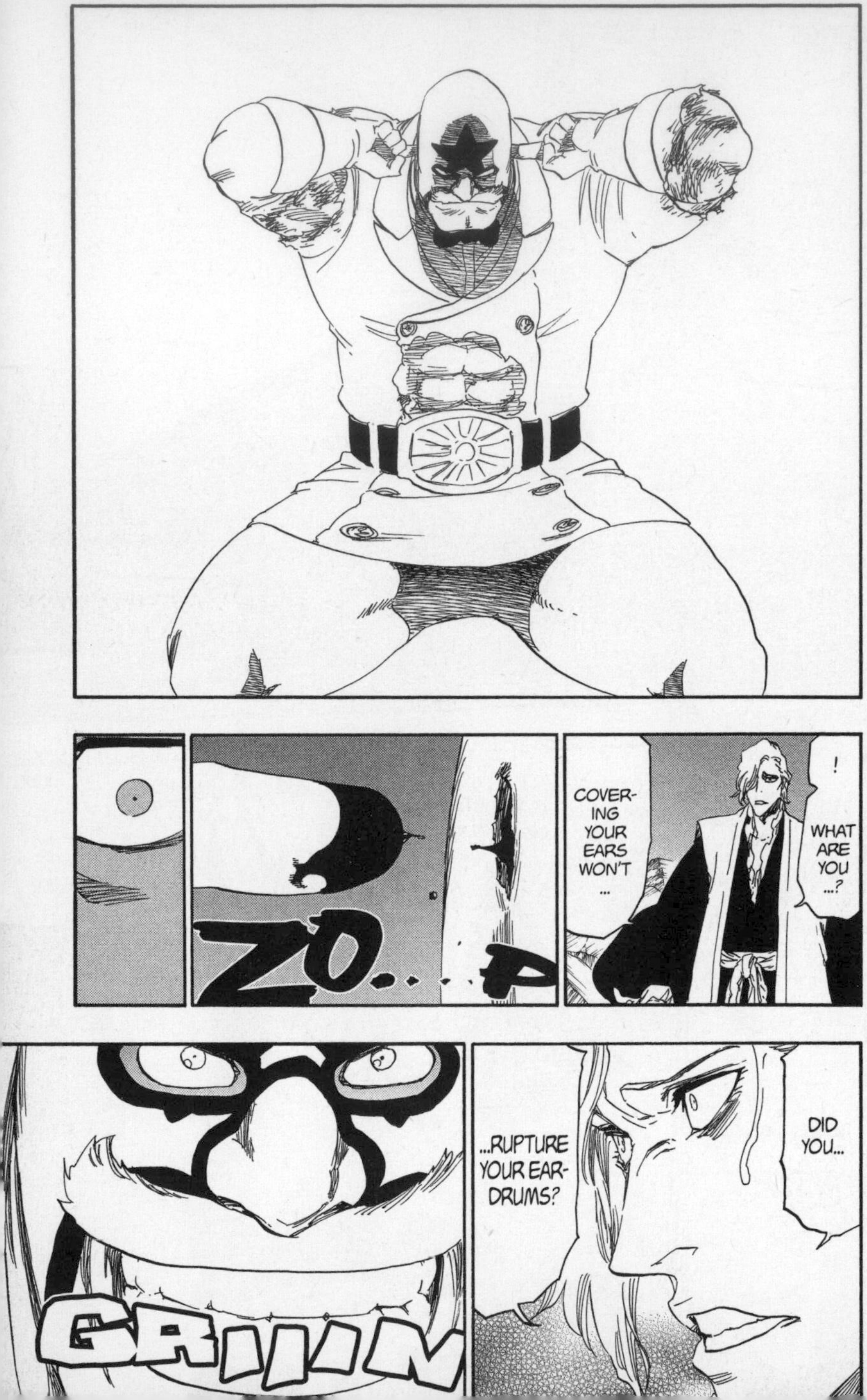
!
WHAT ARE YOU ...?
COVERING YOUR EARS WON'T ...
ZO...P
DID YOU...
...RUPTURE YOUR EAR-DRUMS?
GRIIIN

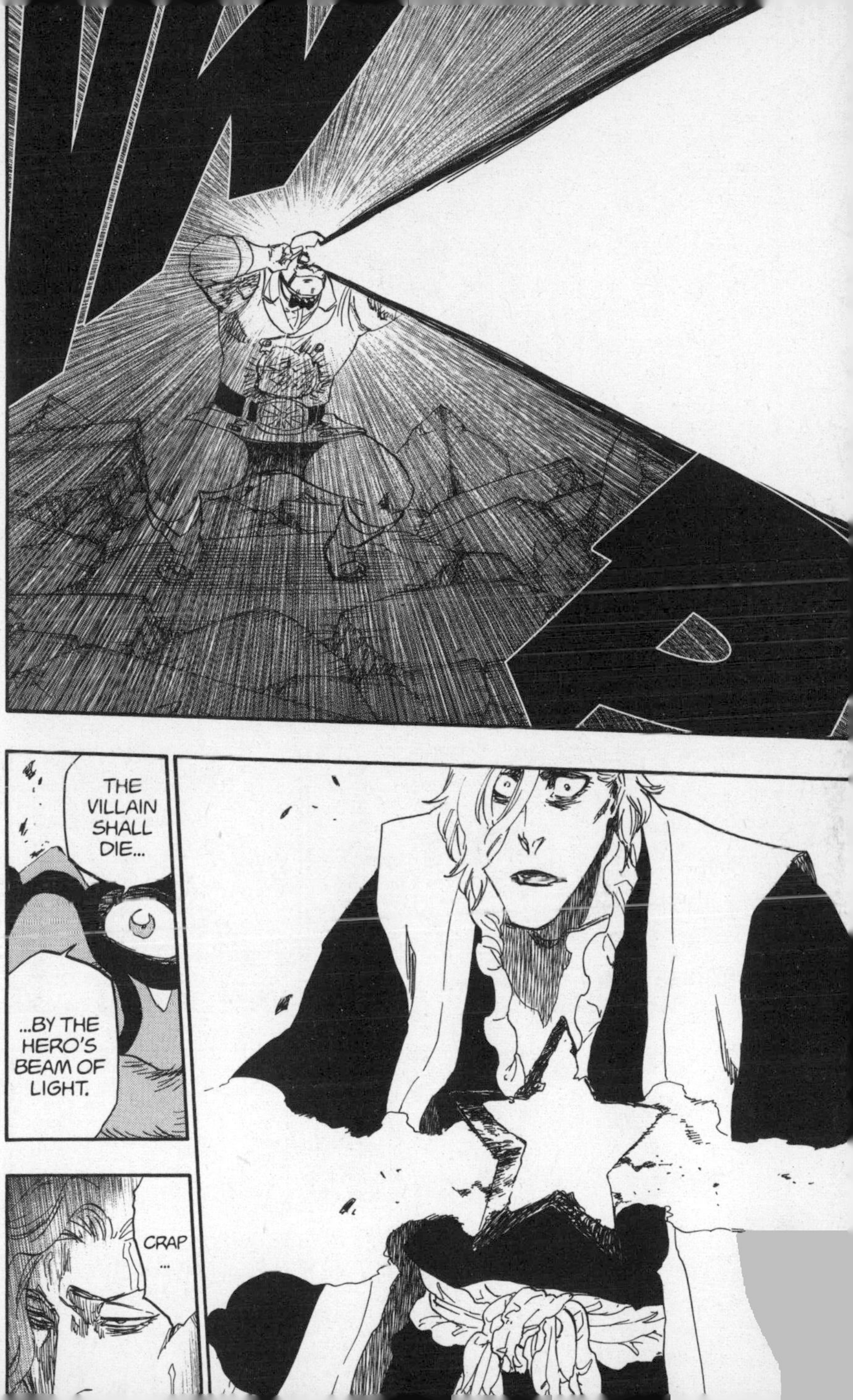
THE VILLAIN SHALL DIE...
...BY THE HERO'S BEAM OF LIGHT.
CRAP
...

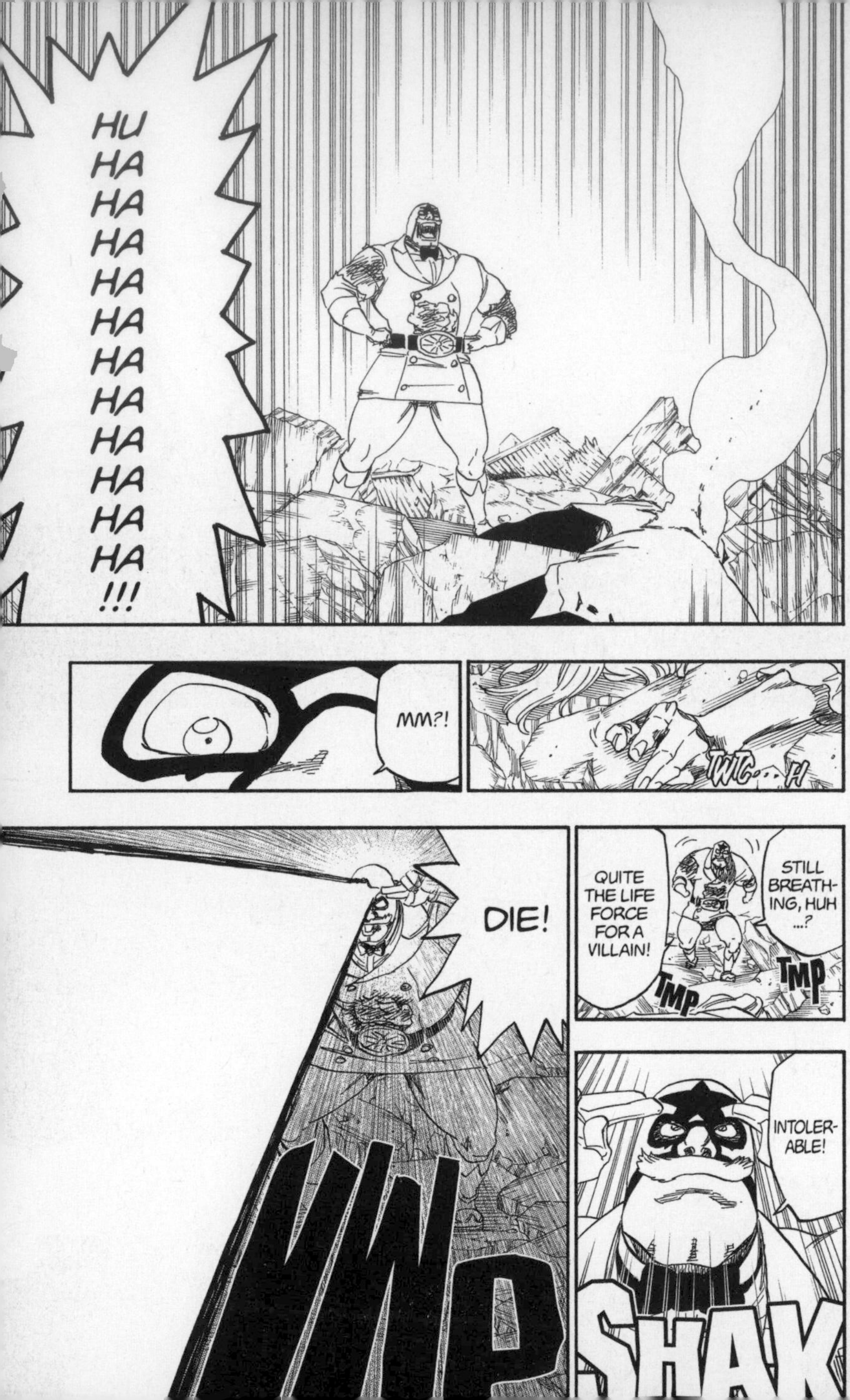
HU HA HA HA HA HA HA HA HA HA HA HA !!!
TWTC...H
MM?!
STILL BREATH-ING, HUH ...?
QUITE THE LIFE FORCE FOR A VILLAIN!
TMP
TMP
INTOLER-ABLE!
SHAK
DIE!

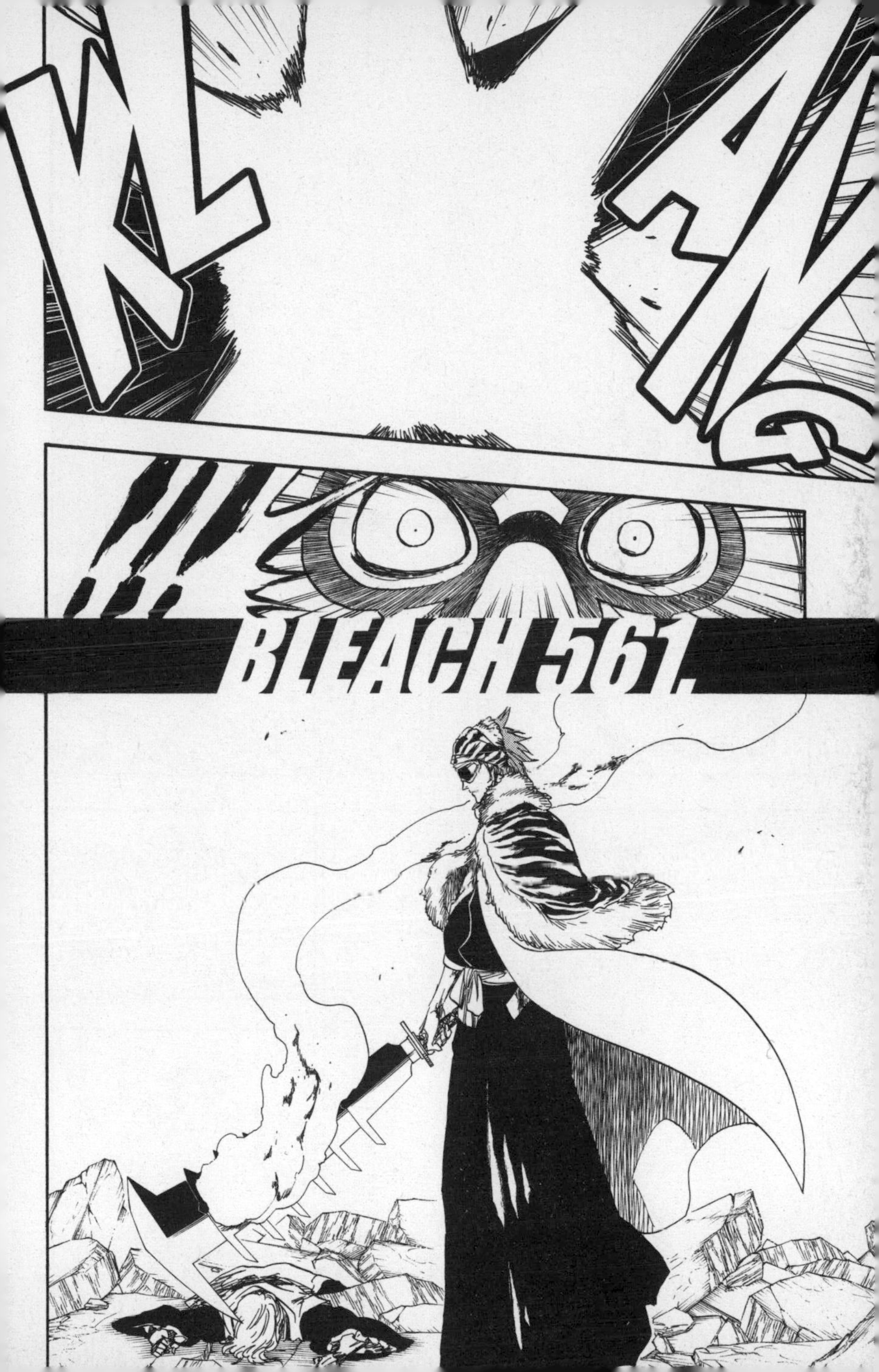
KLANG
!!
BLEACH 561.

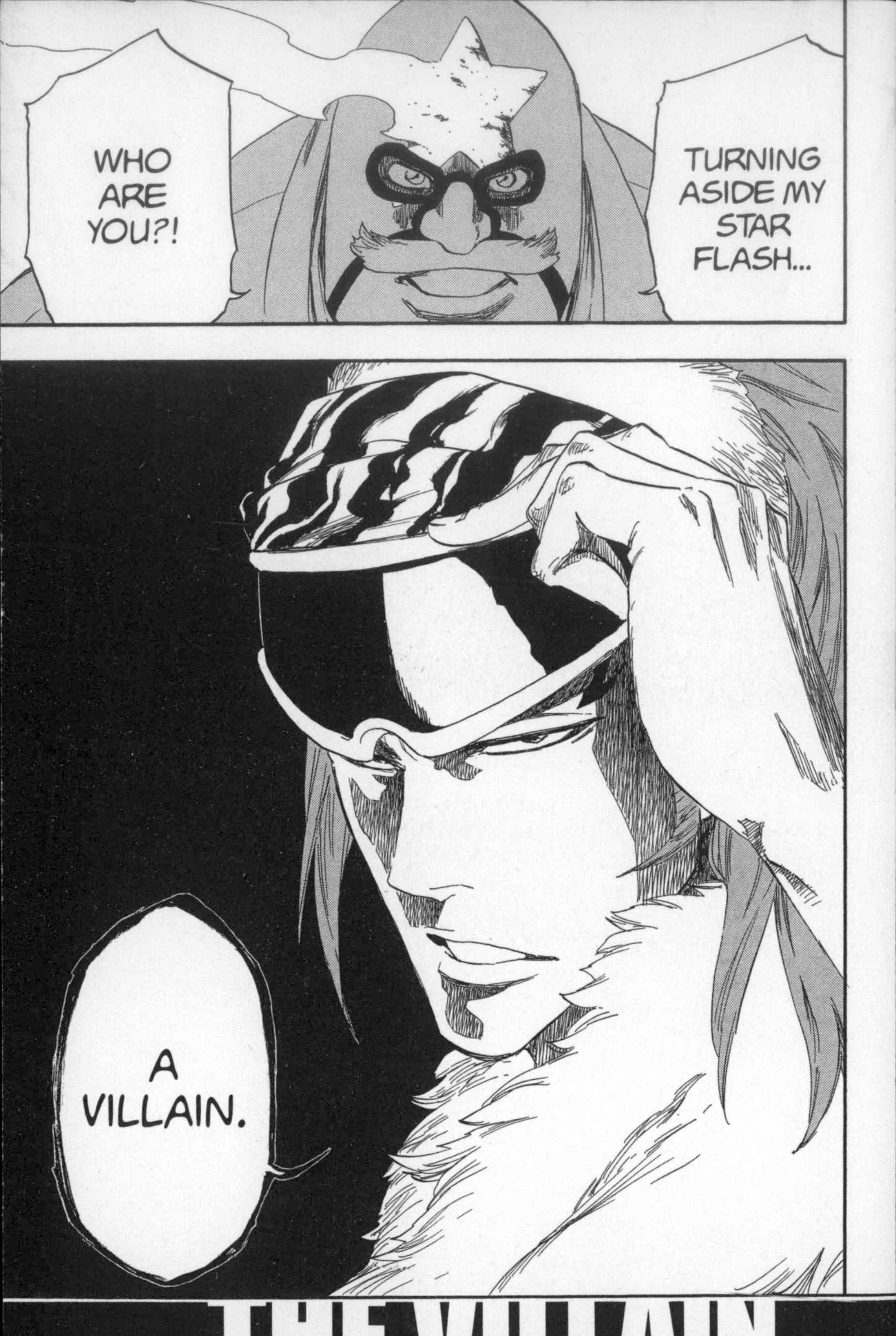
TURNING ASIDE MY STAR FLASH...
WHO ARE YOU?!
A VILLAIN.

THE VILLAIN

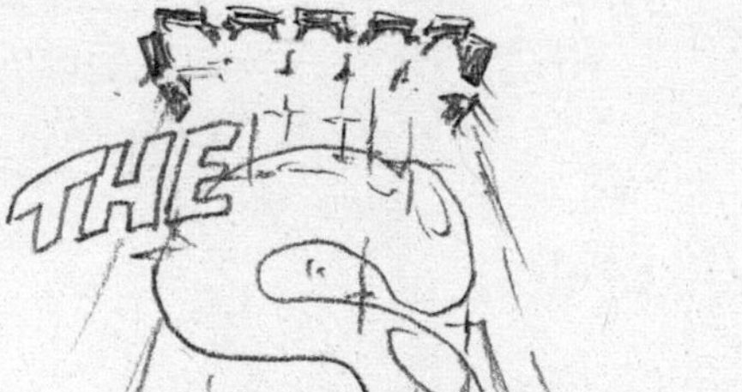
THE
S
UPERSTAR

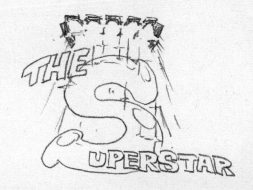

562. THE VILLAIN 2

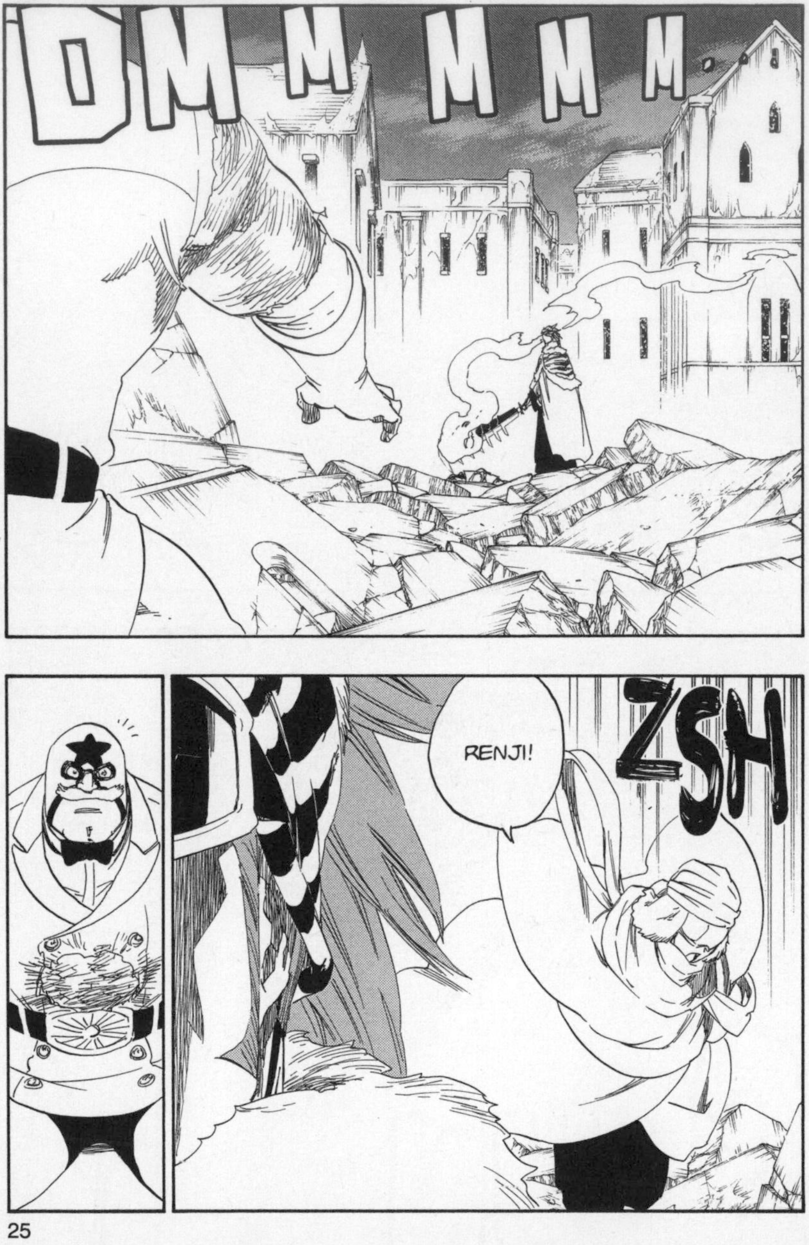
DMMMMM
RENJI!
ZSH

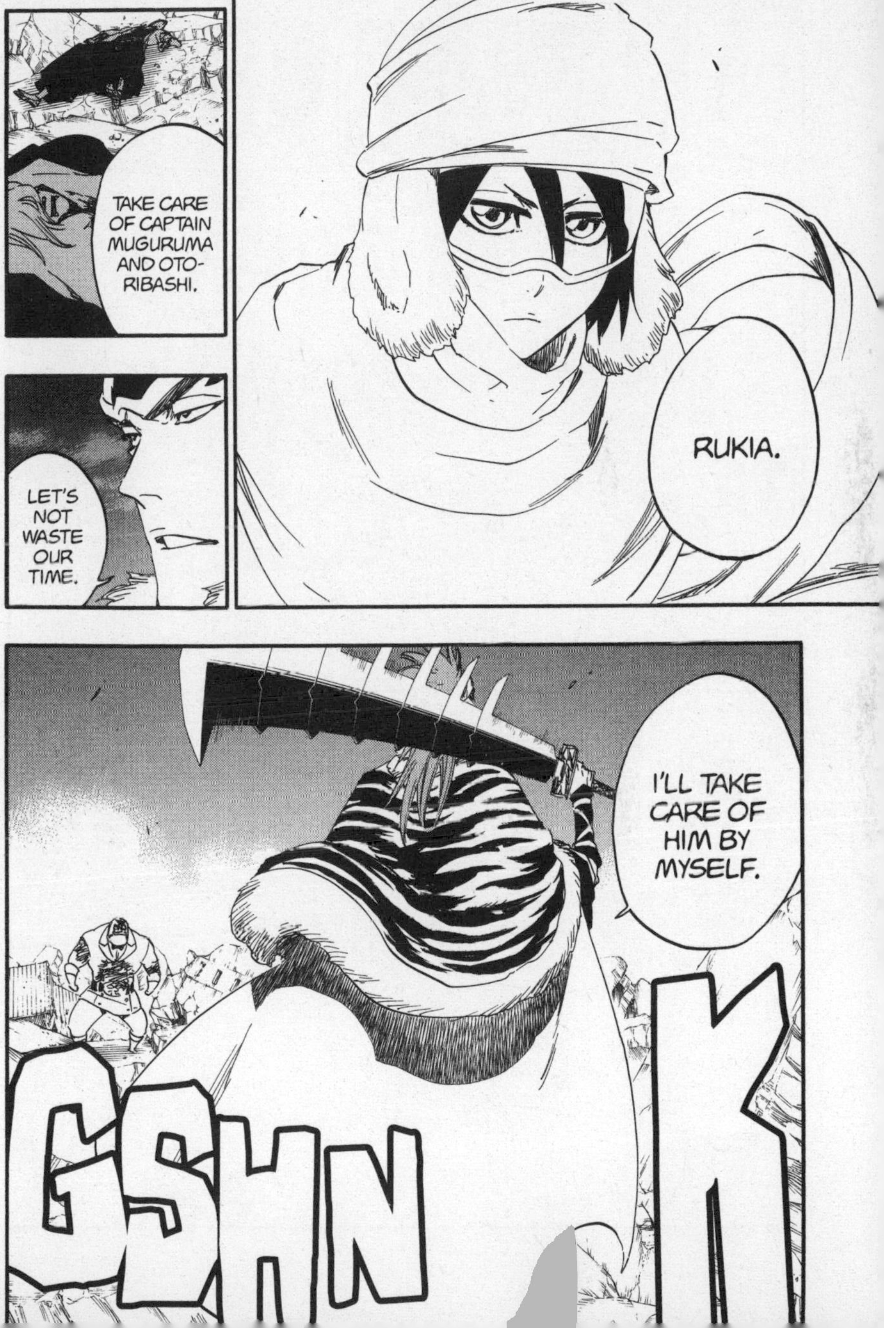
RUKIA.
TAKE CARE OF CAPTAIN MUGURUMA AND OTO-RIBASHI.
LET'S NOT WASTE OUR TIME.
I'LL TAKE CARE OF HIM BY MYSELF.
GSHNK

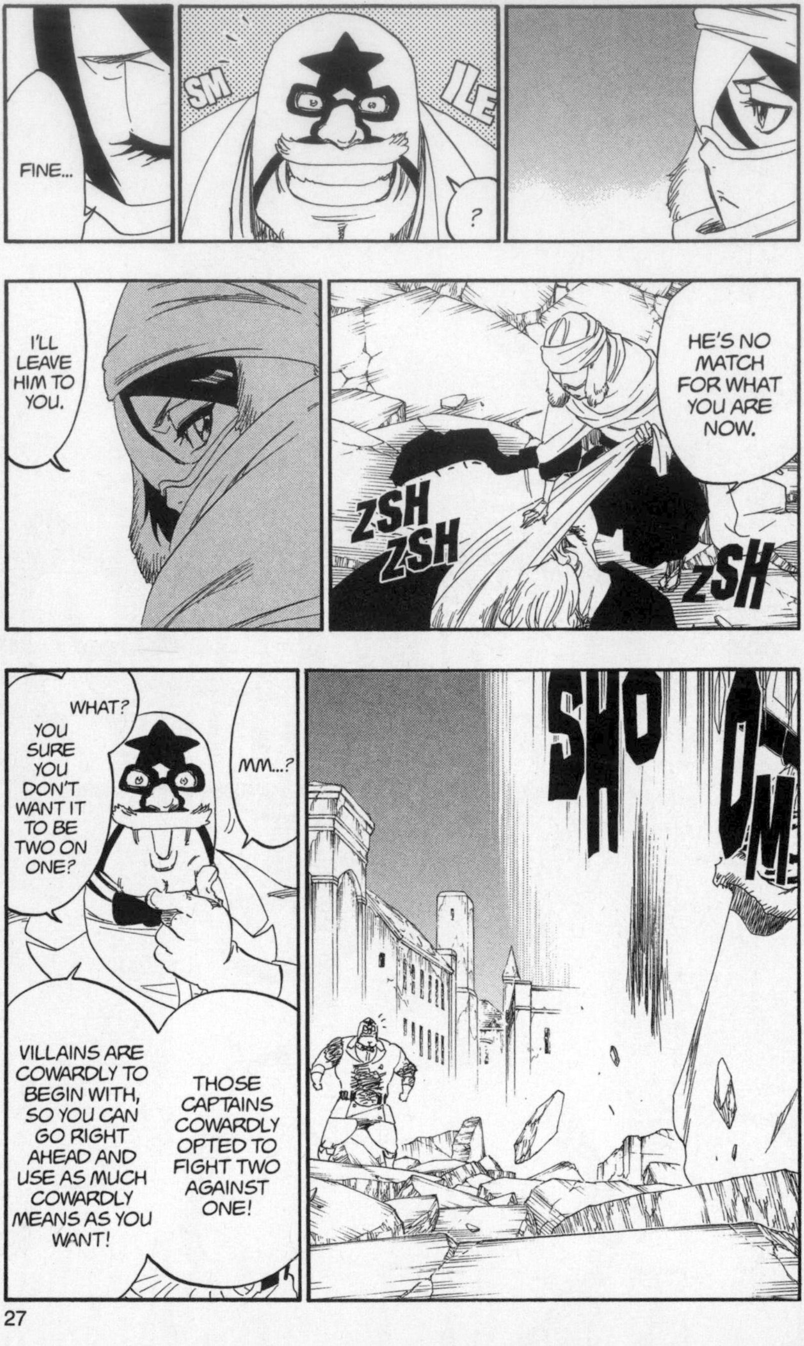
SM
ILE
?
FINE...
HE'S NO MATCH FOR WHAT YOU ARE NOW.
ZSH
ZSH
ZSH
I'LL LEAVE HIM TO YOU.
SHOOM
MM...?
WHAT? YOU SURE YOU DON'T WANT IT TO BE TWO ON ONE?
THOSE CAPTAINS COWARDLY OPTED TO FIGHT TWO AGAINST ONE!
VILLAINS ARE COWARDLY TO BEGIN WITH, SO YOU CAN GO RIGHT AHEAD AND USE AS MUCH COWARDLY MEANS AS YOU WANT!

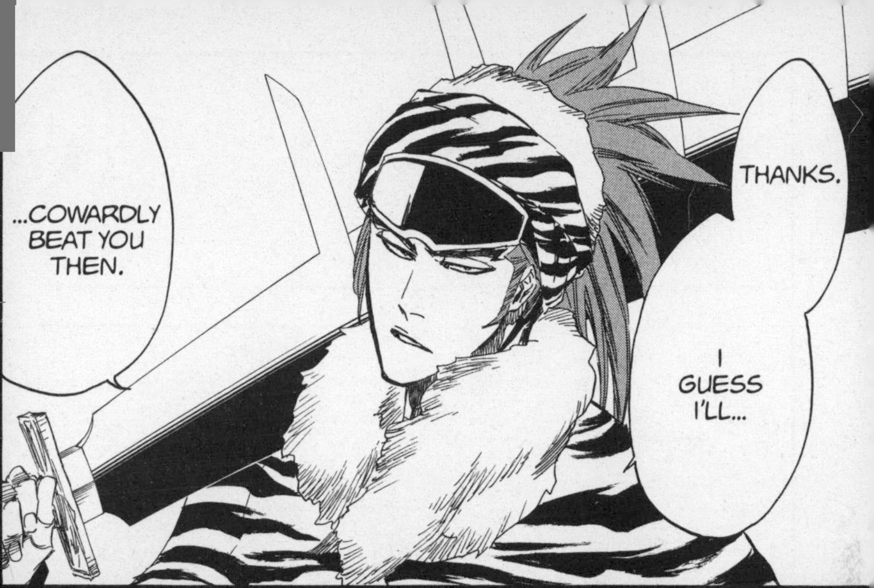
THANKS.
I GUESS I'LL...
...COWARDLY BEAT YOU THEN.

BLEACH 562. THE VILLAIN 2

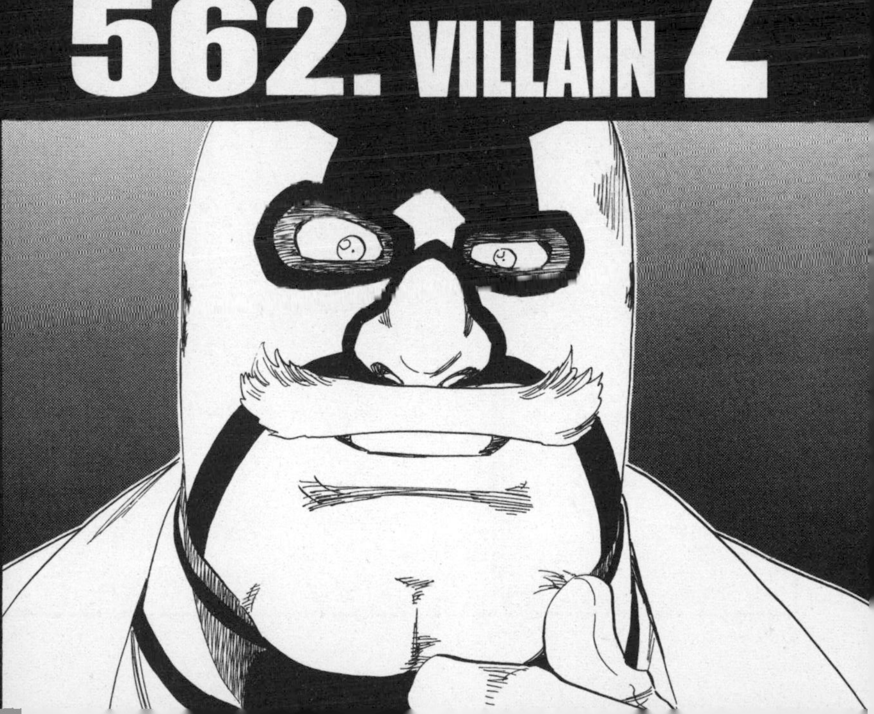

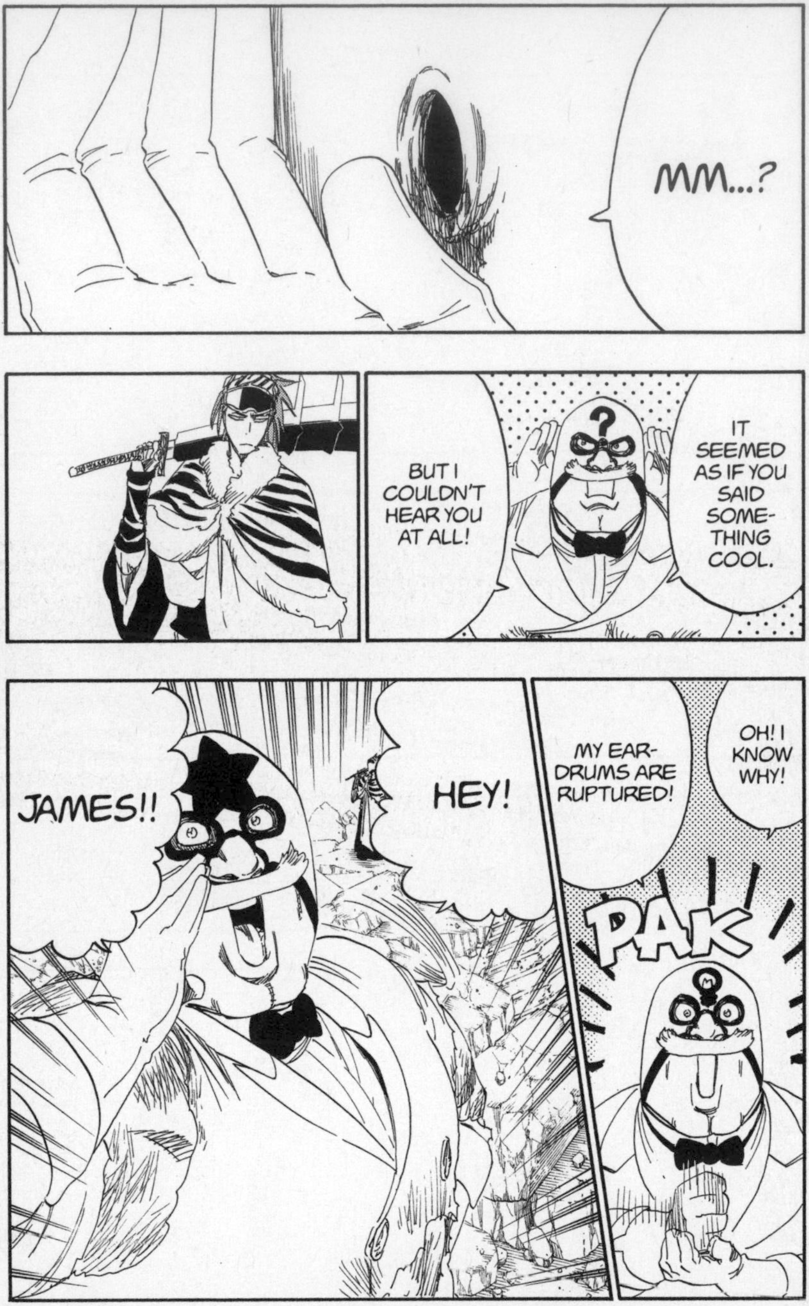
MM...?
IT SEEMED AS IF YOU SAID SOME-THING COOL.
BUT I COULDN'T HEAR YOU AT ALL!
OH! I KNOW WHY!
MY EAR-DRUMS ARE RUPTURED!
PAK
HEY!
JAMES!!

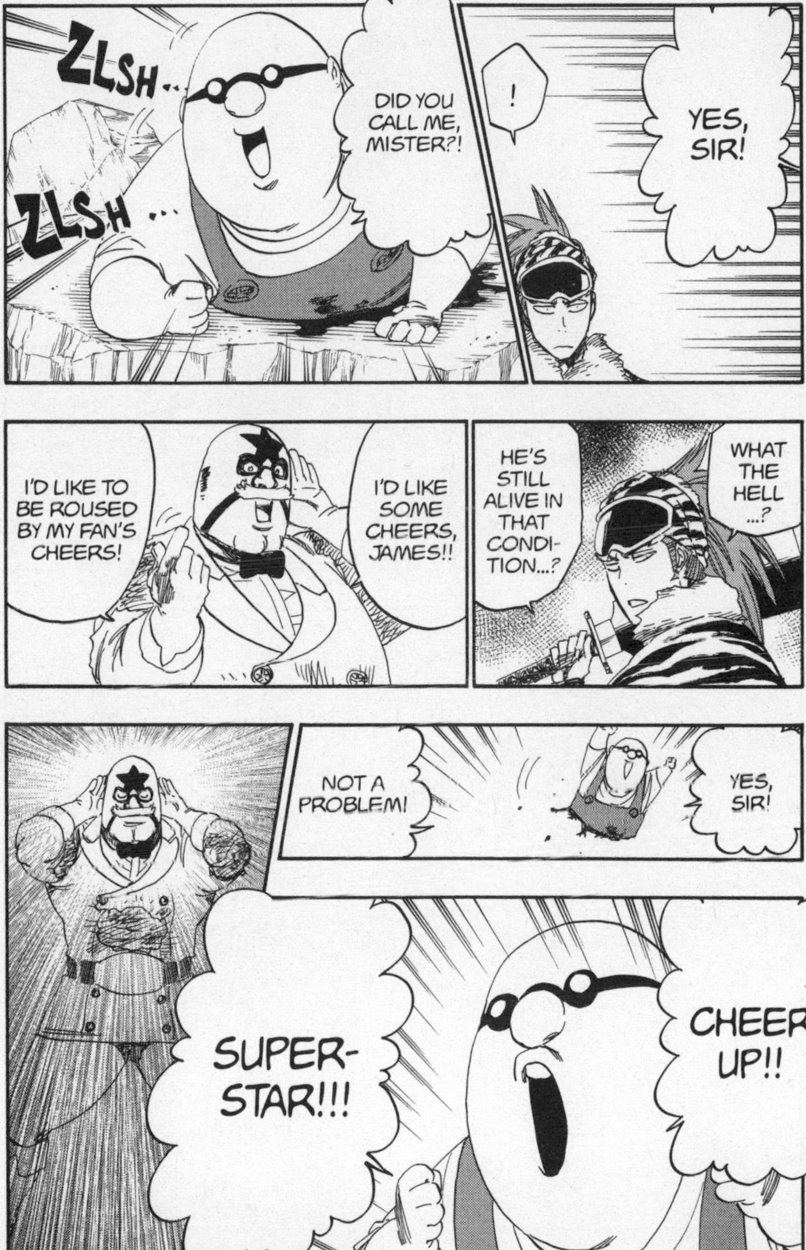
YES, SIR!
!
DID YOU CALL ME, MISTER?!
ZLSH...
ZLSH...
WHAT THE HELL ...?
HE'S STILL ALIVE IN THAT CONDI-TION...?
I'D LIKE SOME CHEERS, JAMES!!
I'D LIKE TO BE ROUSED BY MY FAN'S CHEERS!
YES, SIR!
NOT A PROBLEM!
CHEER UP!!
SUPER-STAR!!!

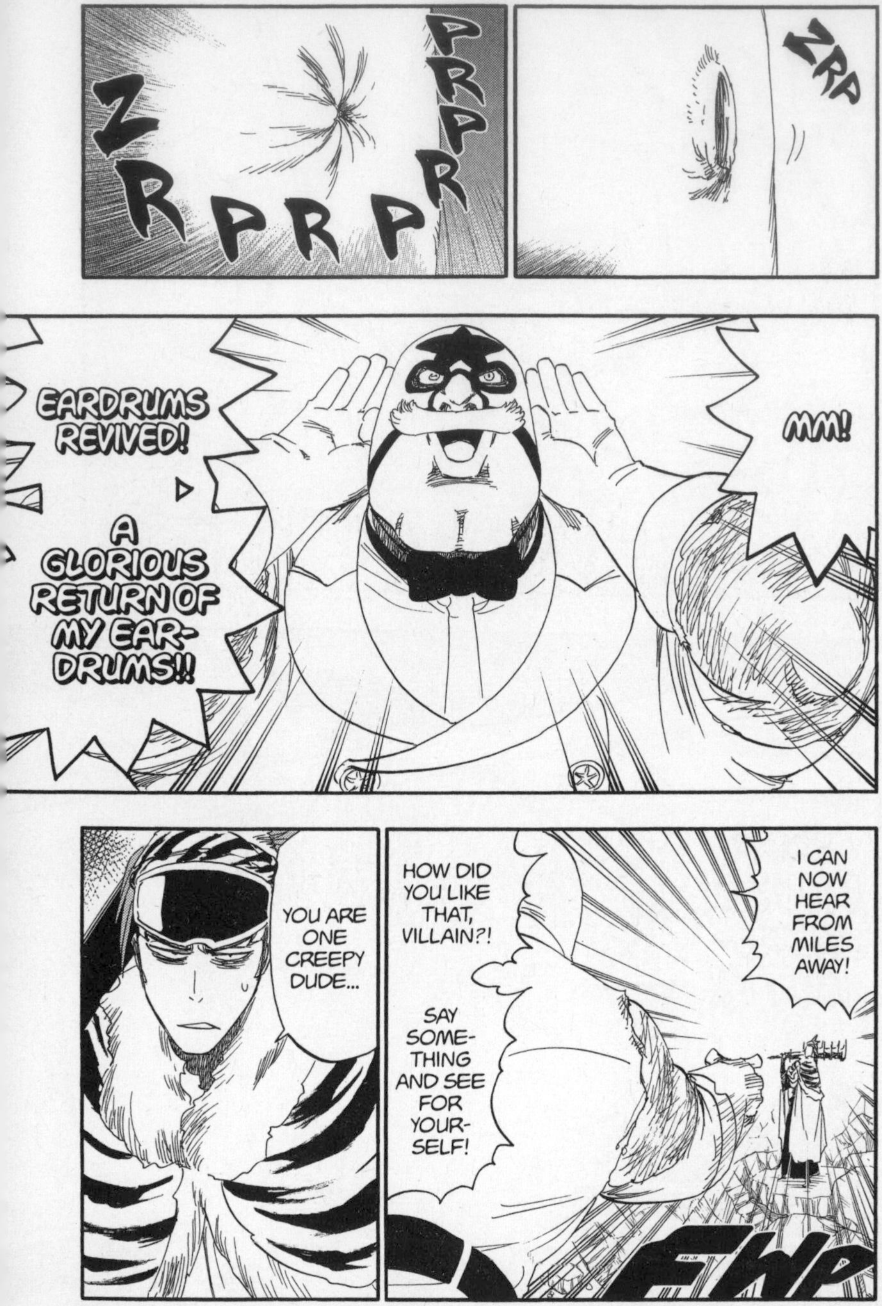
ZRP
ZRPRPRPRPRP
MM!
EARDRUMS REVIVED!
A GLORIOUS RETURN OF MY EAR-DRUMS!!
I CAN NOW HEAR FROM MILES AWAY!
HOW DID YOU LIKE THAT, VILLAIN?!
SAY SOME-THING AND SEE FOR YOUR-SELF!
FWP
YOU ARE ONE CREEPY DUDE...

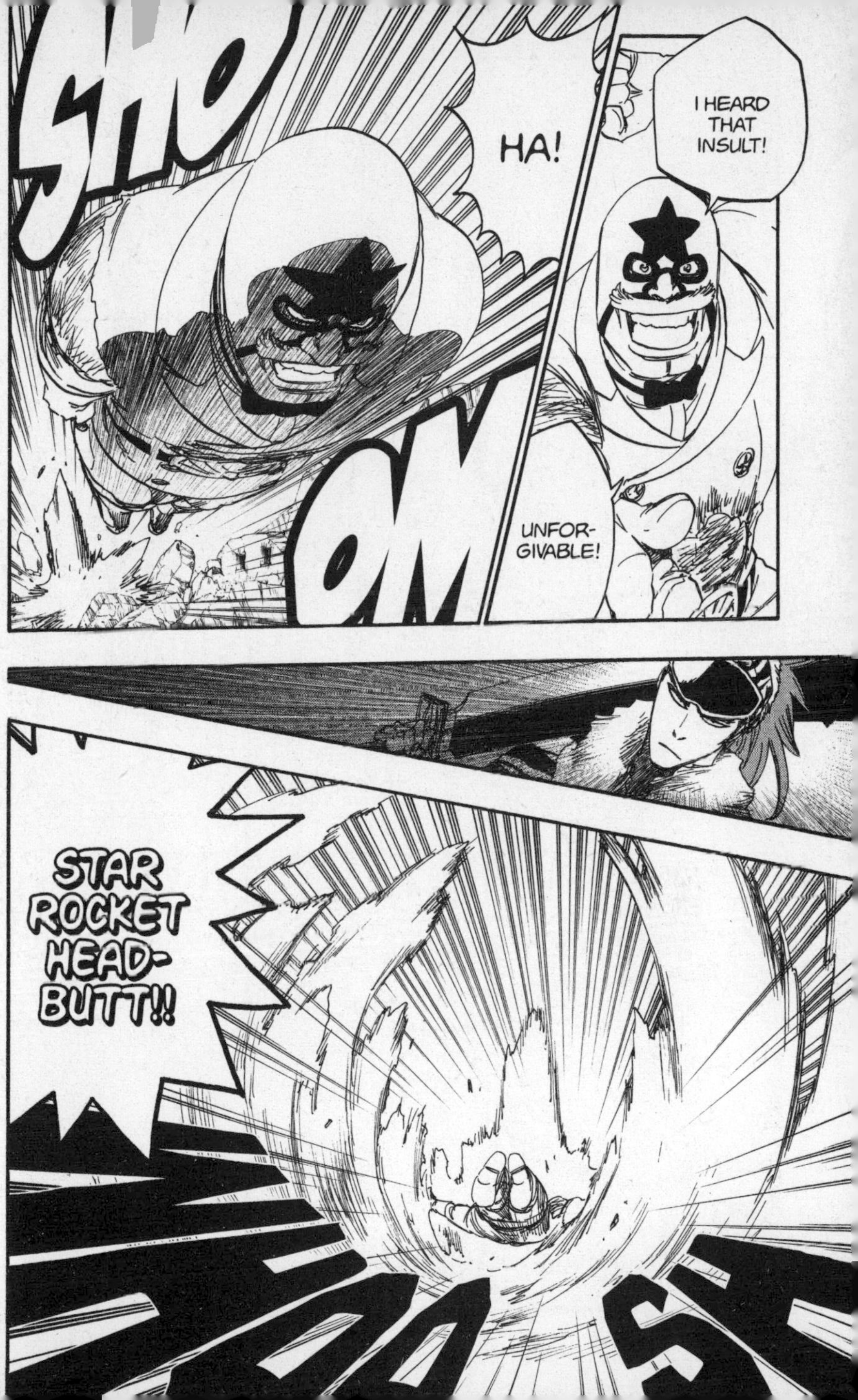
I HEARD THAT INSULT!
UNFORGIVABLE!
SHO
HA!
OM
STAR ROCKET HEAD-BUTT!!

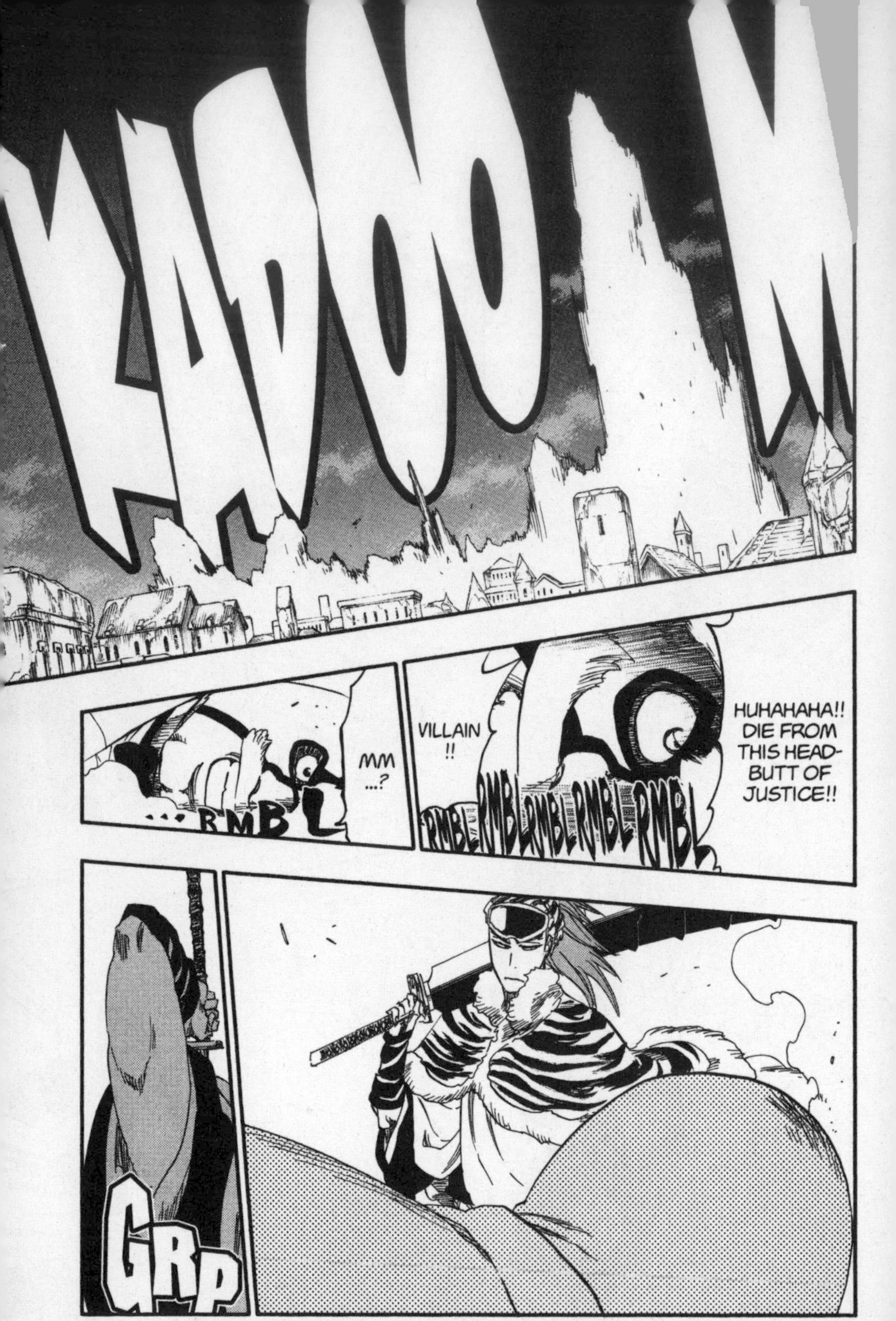
HUHAHAHA!! DIE FROM THIS HEAD-BUTT OF JUSTICE!!
VILLAIN !!
RMBL RMBL RMBL RMBL RMBL
MM ...?
... RMBL
GRP

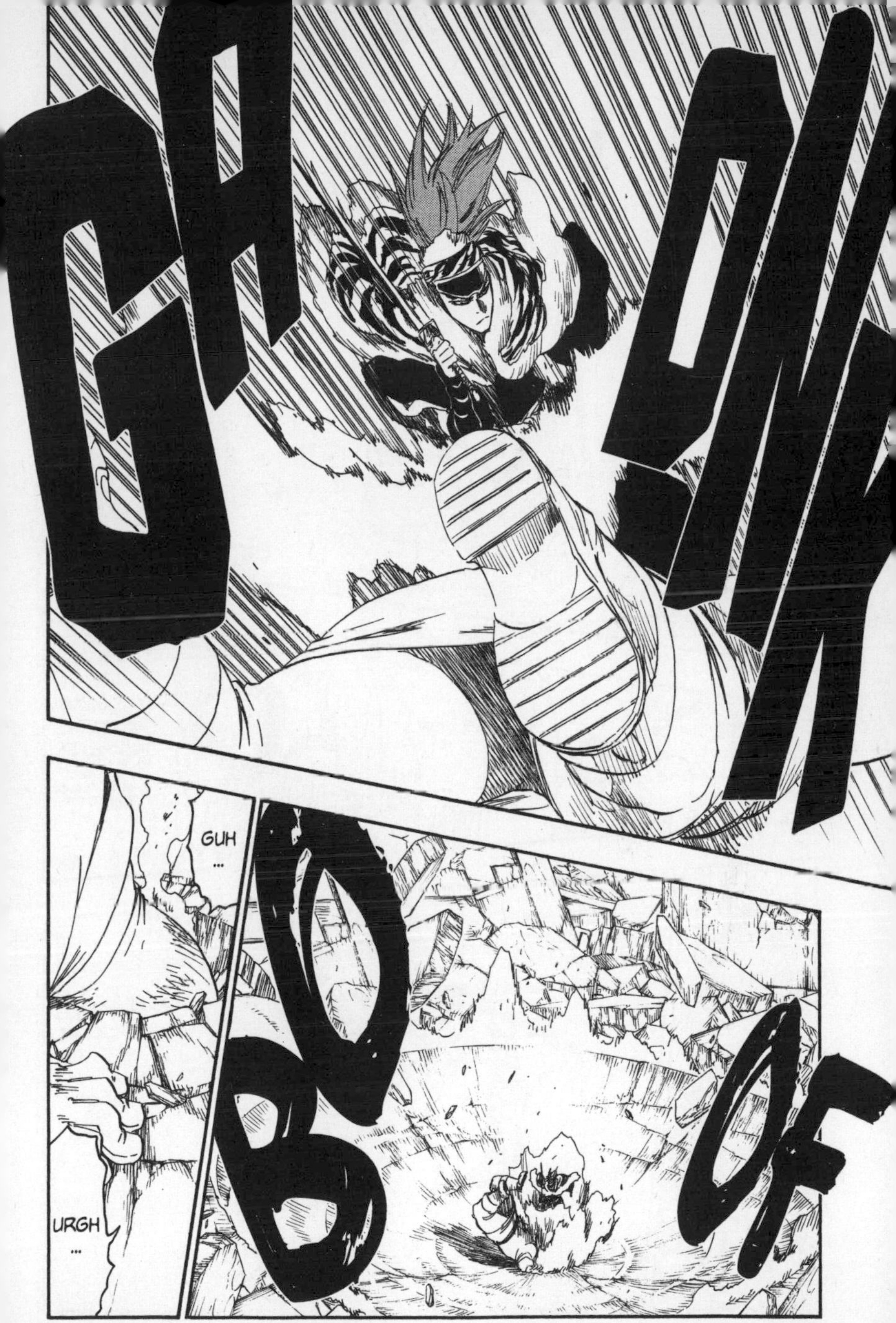
GUH …
URGH …

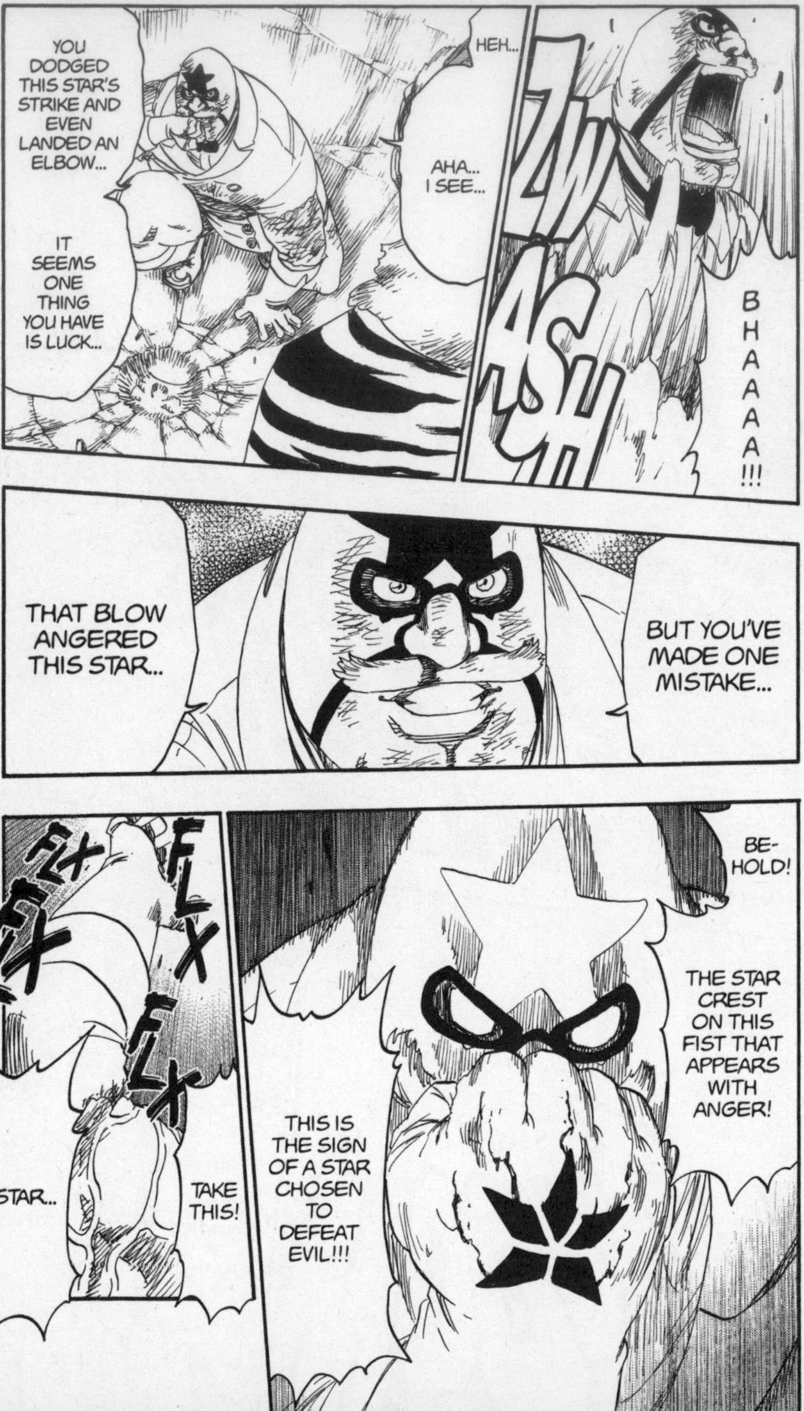
BHAAAAA!!!
HEH...
YOU DODGED THIS STAR'S STRIKE AND EVEN LANDED AN ELBOW...
AHA... I SEE...
IT SEEMS ONE THING YOU HAVE IS LUCK...
BUT YOU'VE MADE ONE MISTAKE...
THAT BLOW ANGERED THIS STAR...
BE-HOLD!
THE STAR CREST ON THIS FIST THAT APPEARS WITH ANGER!
THIS IS THE SIGN OF A STAR CHOSEN TO DEFEAT EVIL!!!
FLX
FLX
FLX
FLX
TAKE THIS!
STAR...

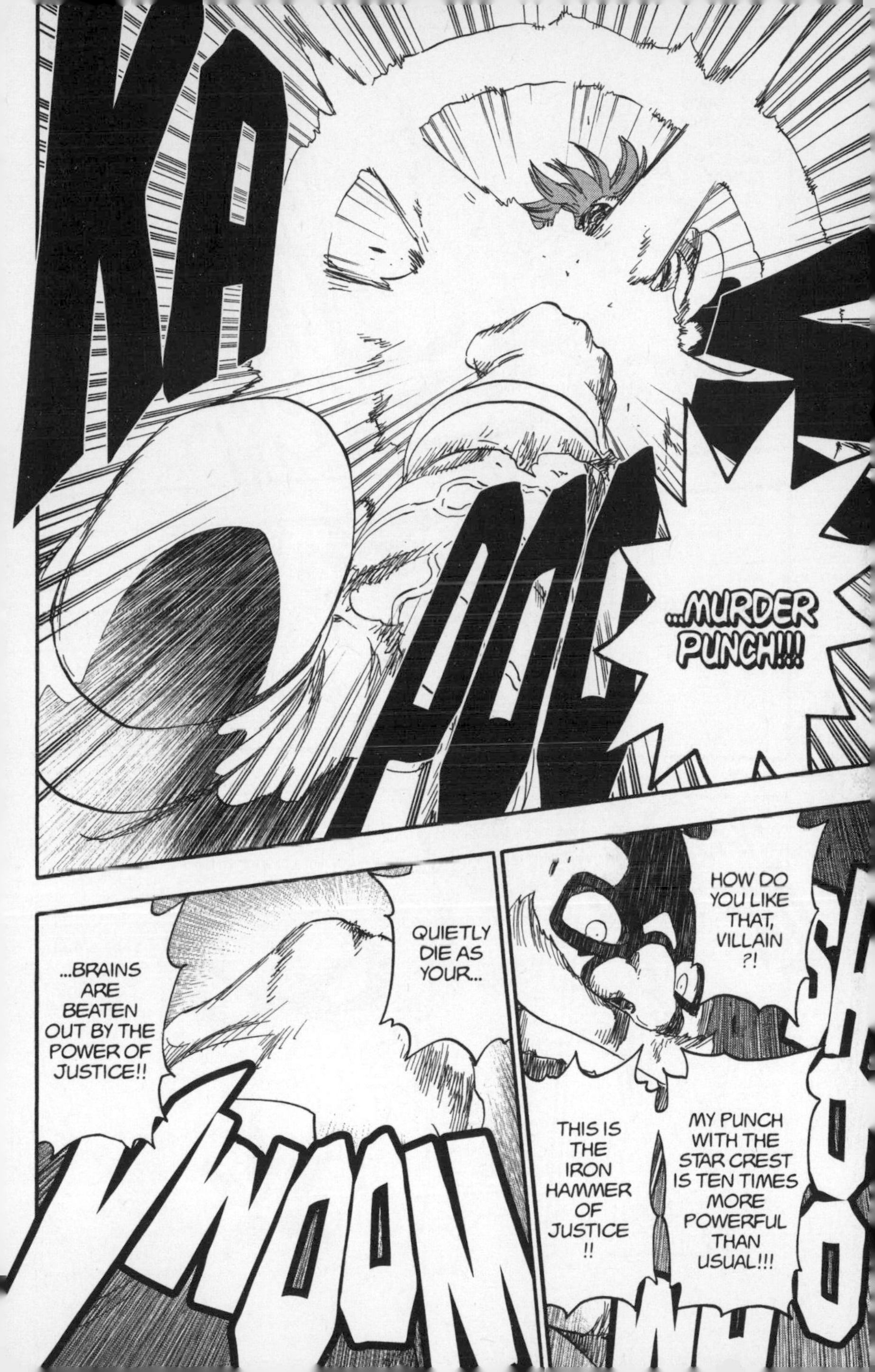
KA
...MURDER PUNCH!!!
HOW DO YOU LIKE THAT, VILLAIN?!
MY PUNCH WITH THE STAR CREST IS TEN TIMES MORE POWERFUL THAN USUAL!!!
THIS IS THE IRON HAMMER OF JUSTICE!!
QUIETLY DIE AS YOUR...
...BRAINS ARE BEATEN OUT BY THE POWER OF JUSTICE!!

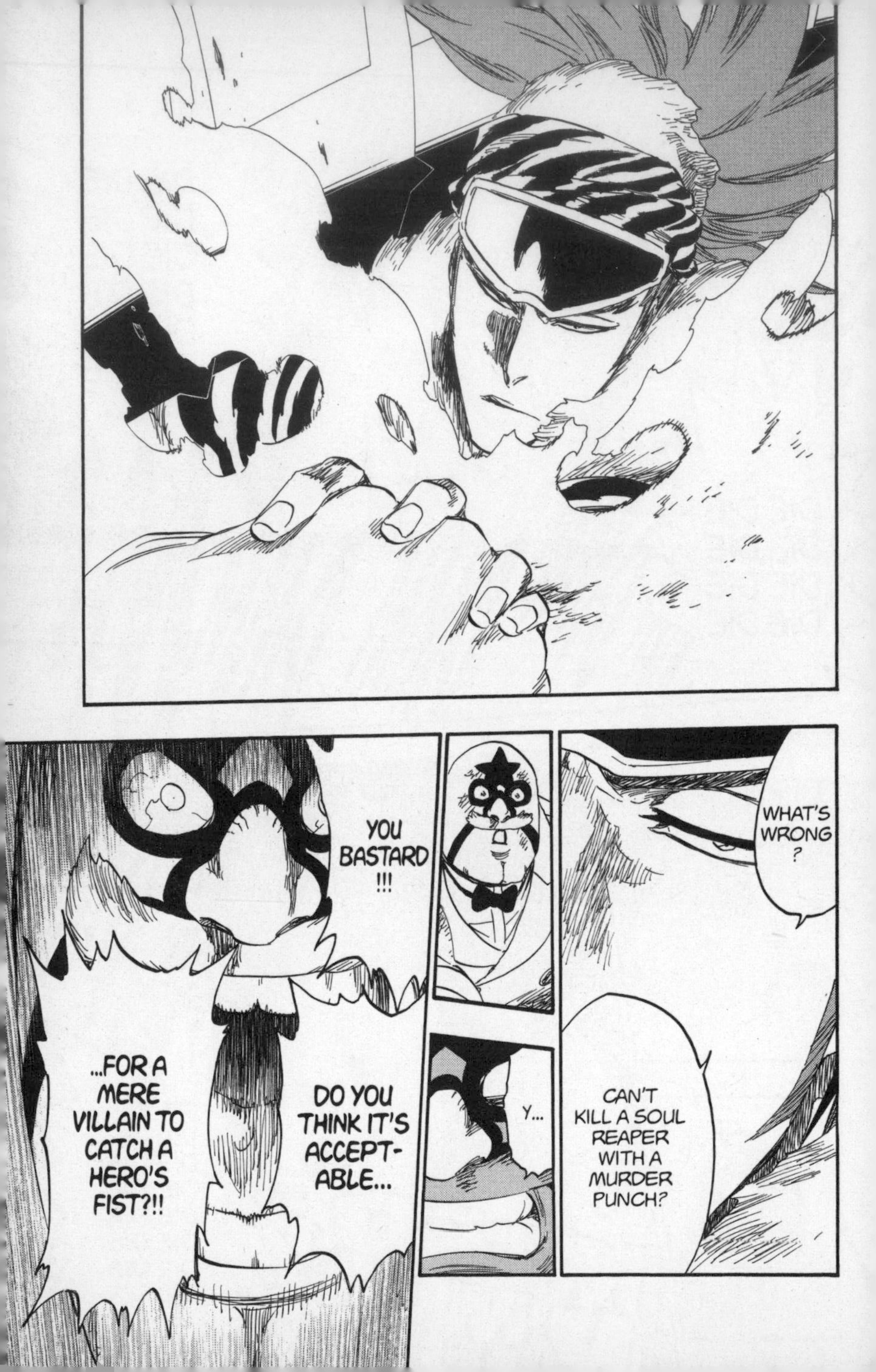
WHAT'S WRONG?
CAN'T KILL A SOUL REAPER WITH A MURDER PUNCH?
Y...
YOU BASTARD!!!
DO YOU THINK IT'S ACCEPTABLE...
...FOR A MERE VILLAIN TO CATCH A HERO'S FIST?!!

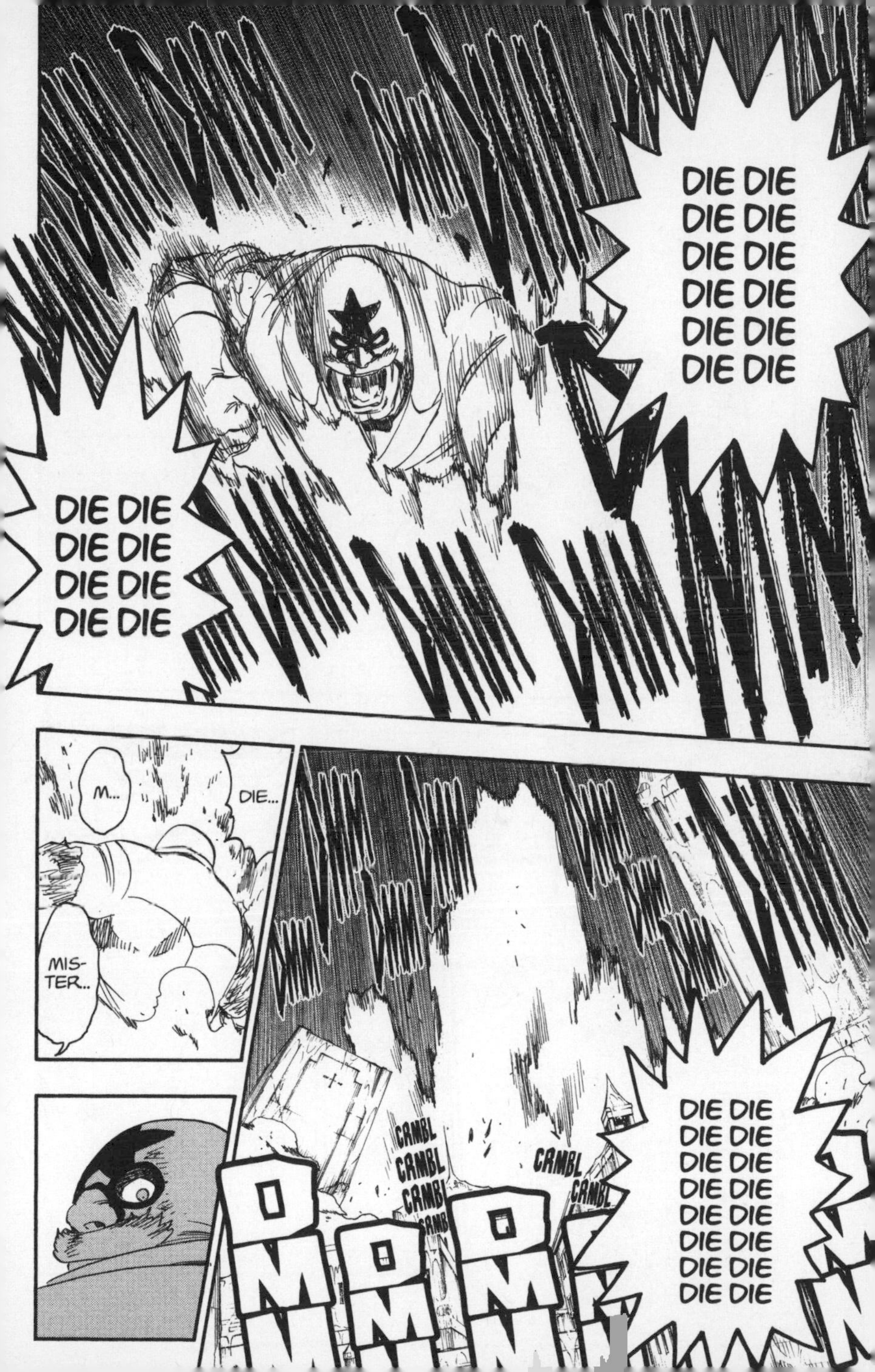
DIE DIE
DIE DIE
DIE DIE
DIE DIE
DIE DIE
DIE DIE
DIE DIE
DIE DIE
DIE DIE
DIE DIE
DIE DIE
DIE DIE
DIE DIE
DIE DIE
DIE DIE
DIE DIE
DIE DIE
DIE DIE
CRMBL
CRMBL
CRMBL
CRMBL
CRMBL
CRMBL
DIE...
M...
MIS-
TER..

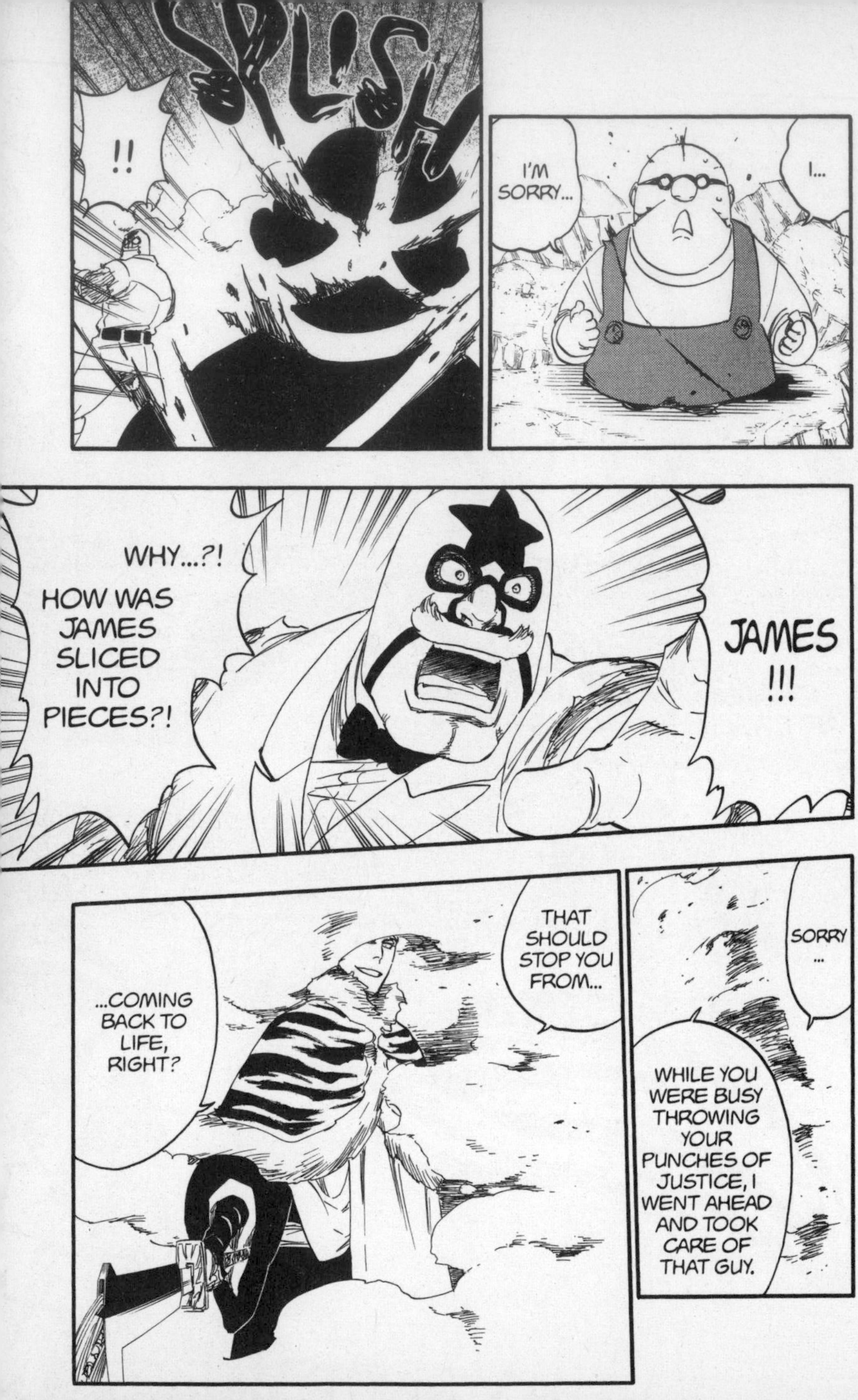
I...
I'M SORRY...
SPLISH
!!
JAMES !!!
WHY...?!
HOW WAS JAMES SLICED INTO PIECES?!
SORRY ...
WHILE YOU WERE BUSY THROWING YOUR PUNCHES OF JUSTICE, I WENT AHEAD AND TOOK CARE OF THAT GUY.
THAT SHOULD STOP YOU FROM...
...COMING BACK TO LIFE, RIGHT?

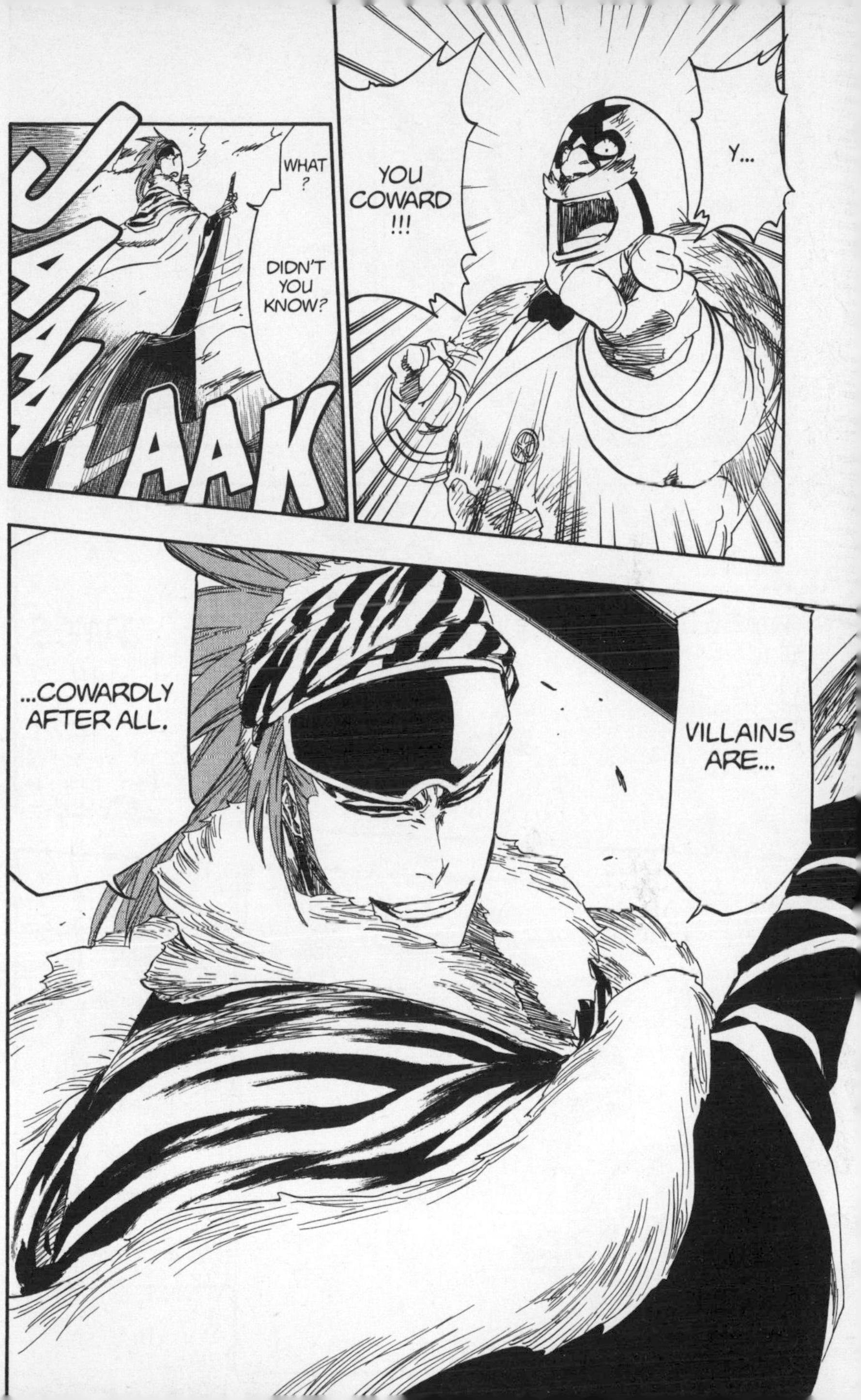
Y...
YOU COWARD!!!
WHAT?
DIDN'T YOU KNOW?
JAAAAAK
VILLAINS ARE...
...COWARDLY AFTER ALL.

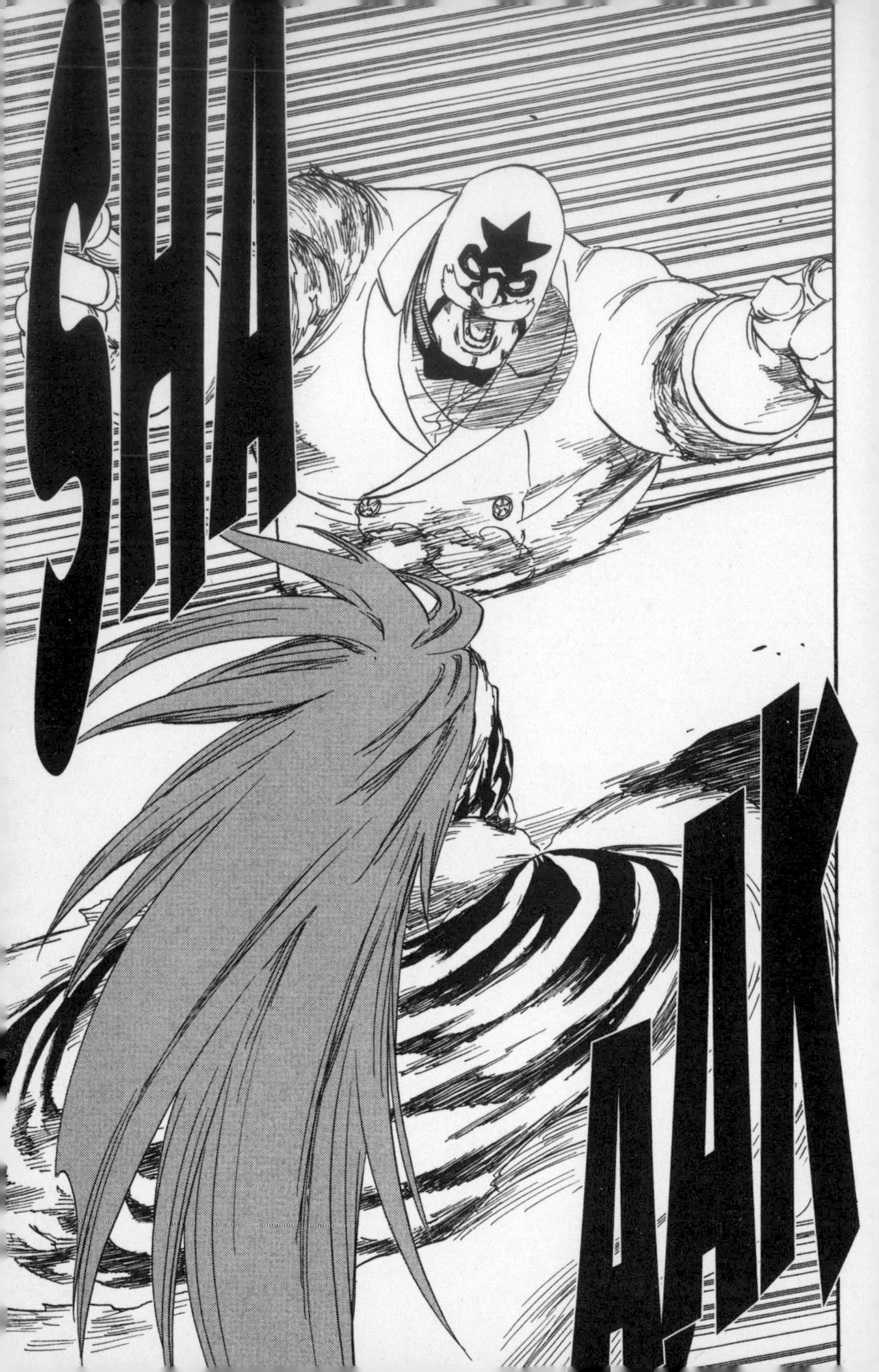
SHA
AAK

YOU THINK THE TIGER PRINT IS LAME?
DON'T SAY THAT, RENJI ACTUALLY LIKES IT.
?

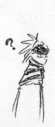

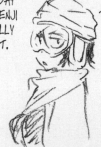

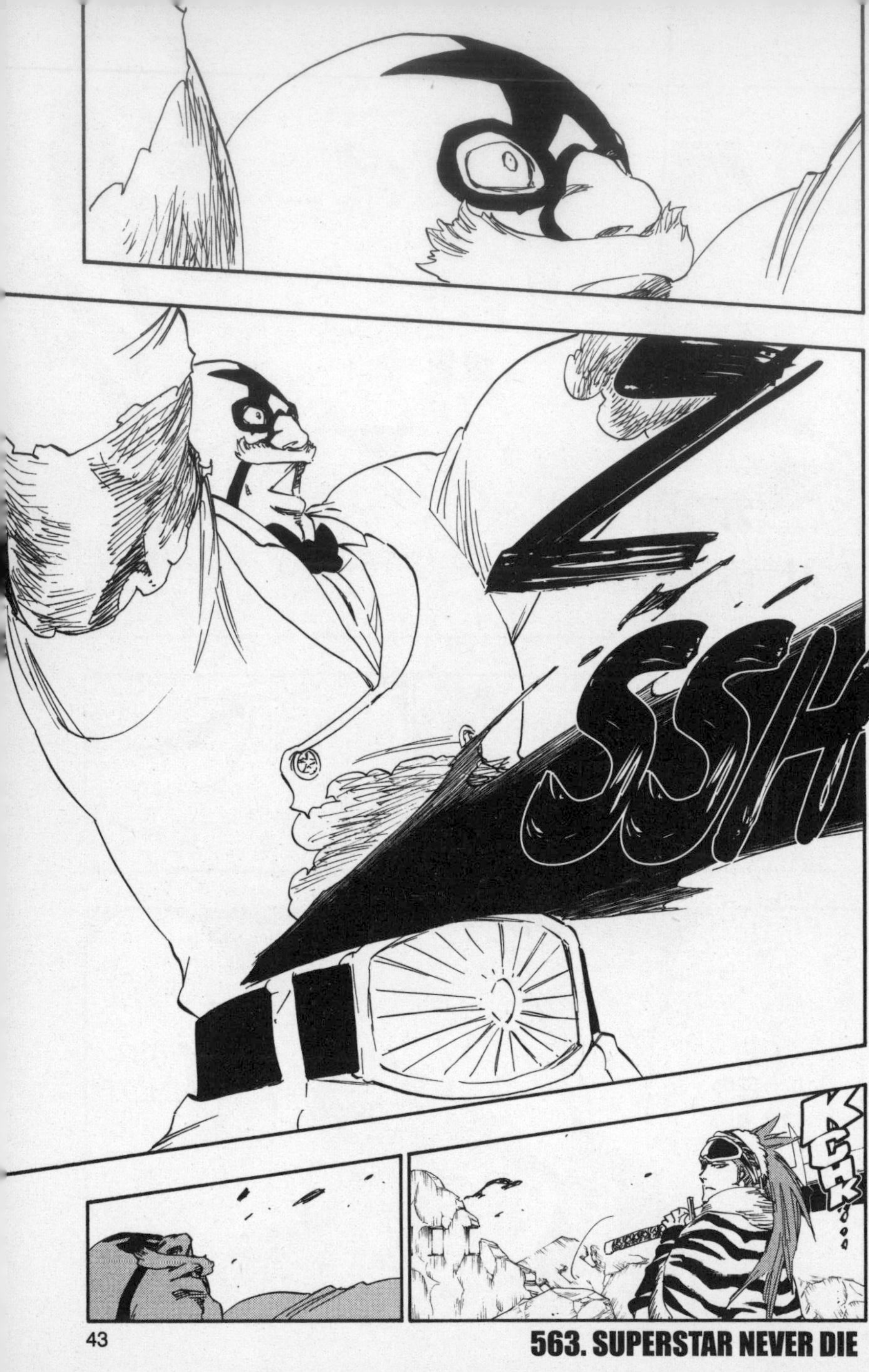
ZSSH
KCHAK...

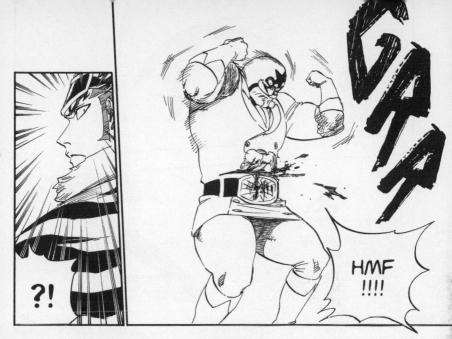

GAAA

HMF
!!!!

?!

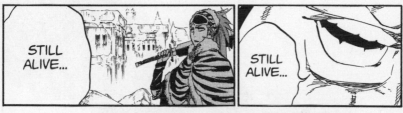

STILL
ALIVE...

STILL
ALIVE...

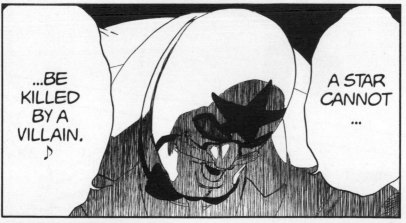

...BE
KILLED
BY A
VILLAIN. ♪

A STAR
CANNOT
...

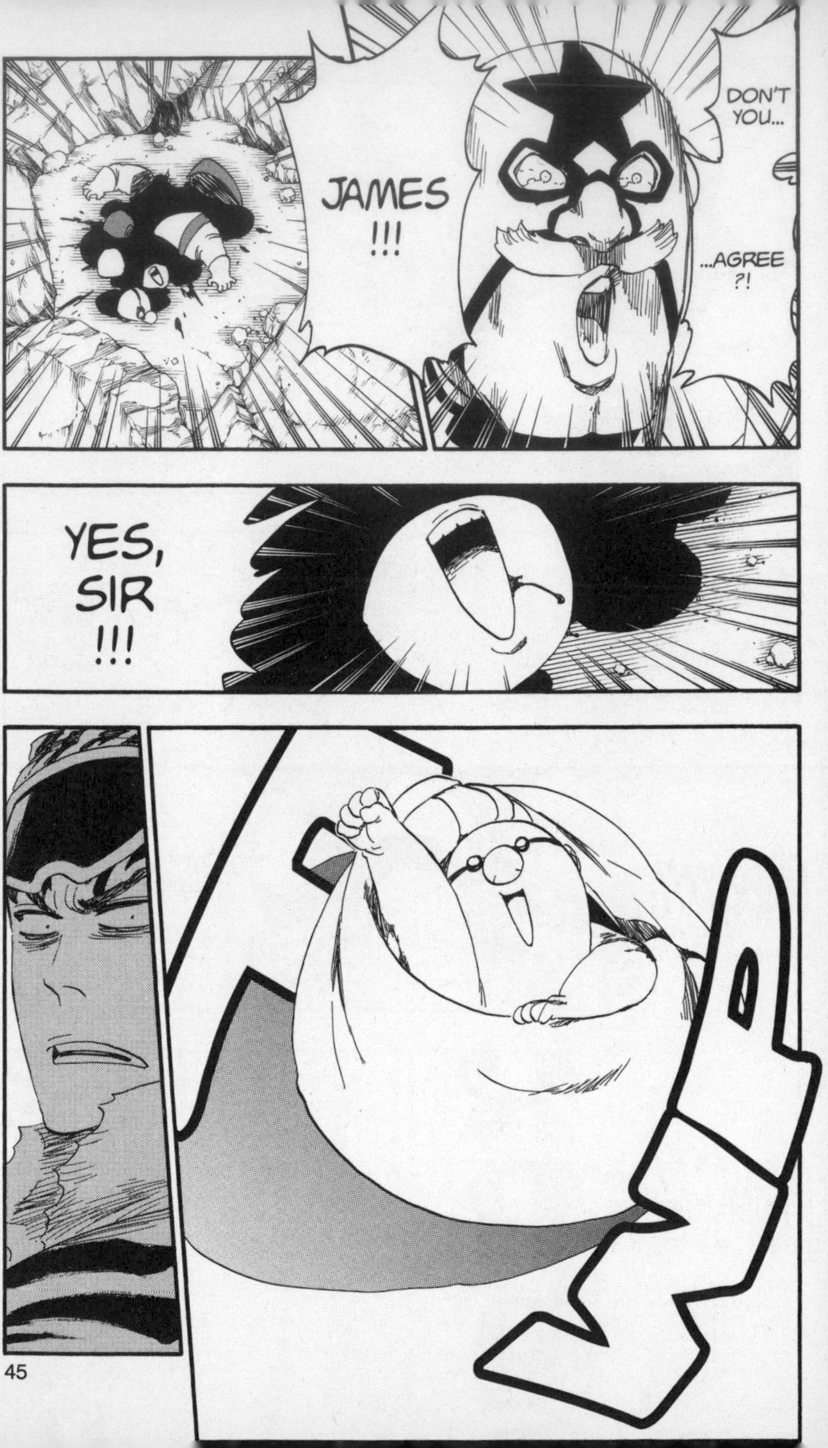
DON'T YOU...
...AGREE ?!
JAMES !!!
YES, SIR !!!

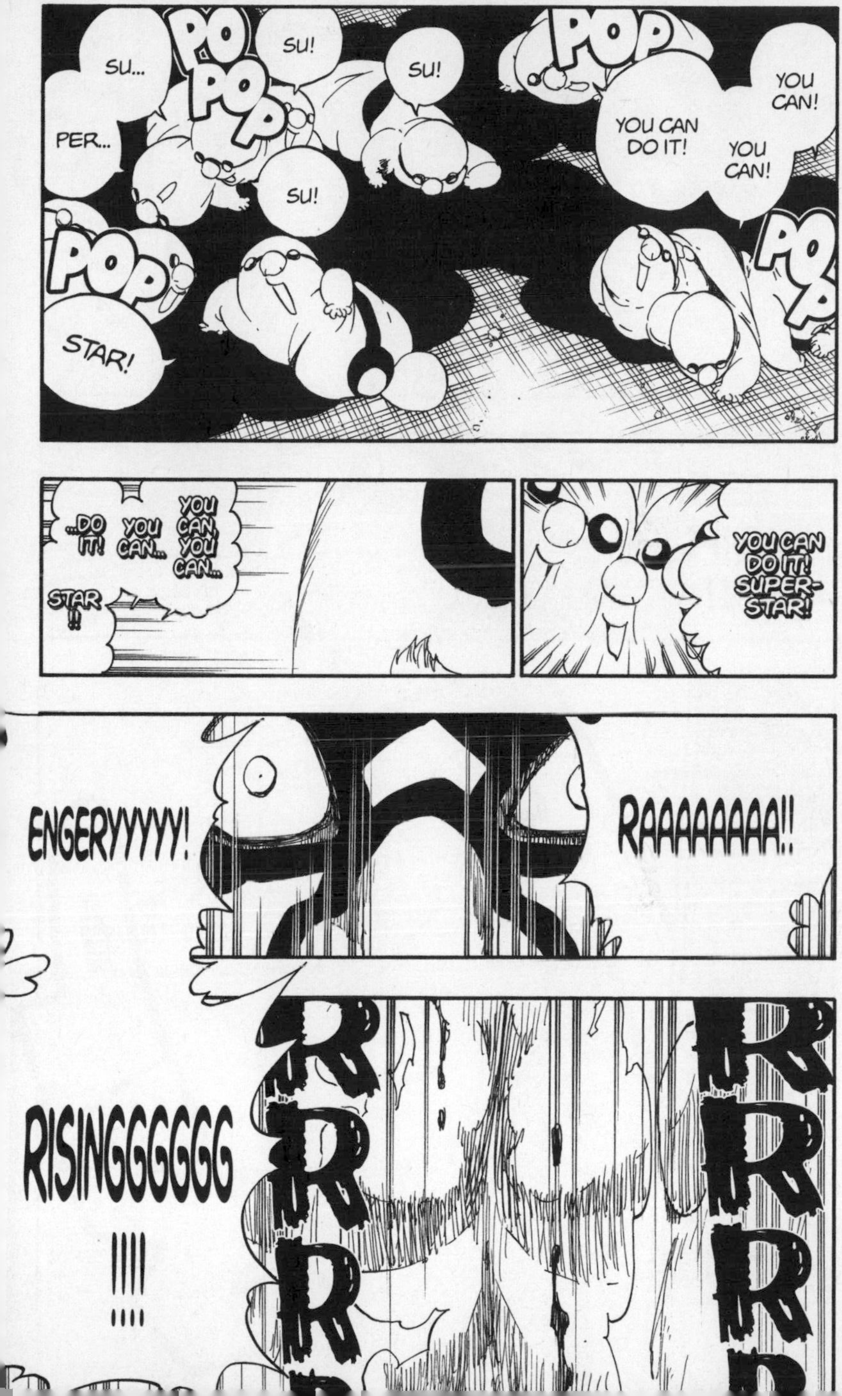
POP
YOU CAN!
YOU CAN!
YOU CAN DO IT!
POP P
SU!
SU!
POP POP
SU...
PER...
SU!
POP
STAR!
YOU CAN DO IT! SUPER-STAR!
YOU CAN, YOU CAN...
YOU CAN...
...DO IT!
STAR!!
RAAAAAAA!!
ENGERYYYYY!
RRRR
RRRR
RISINGGGGGG !!!!

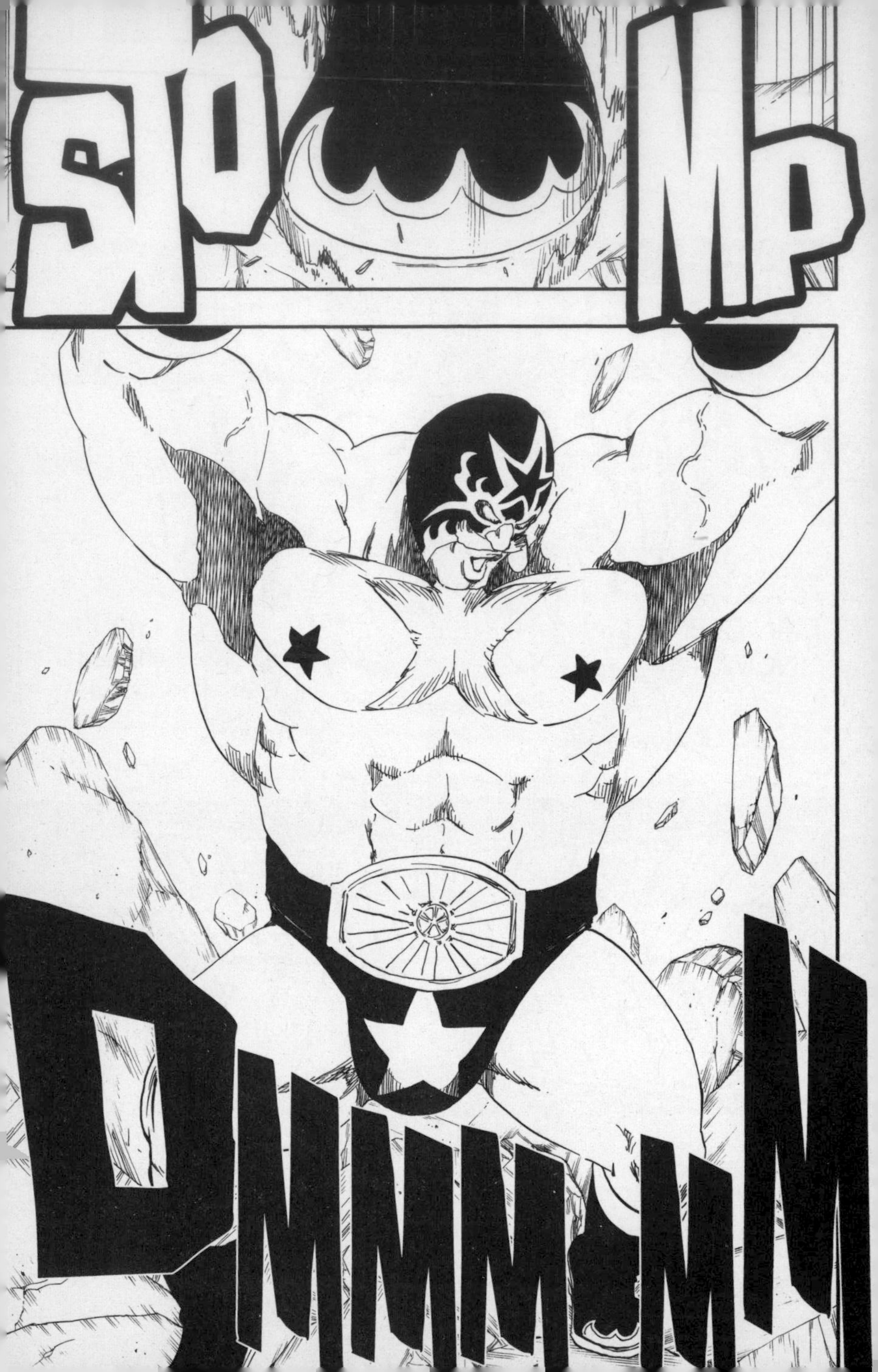
STOMP

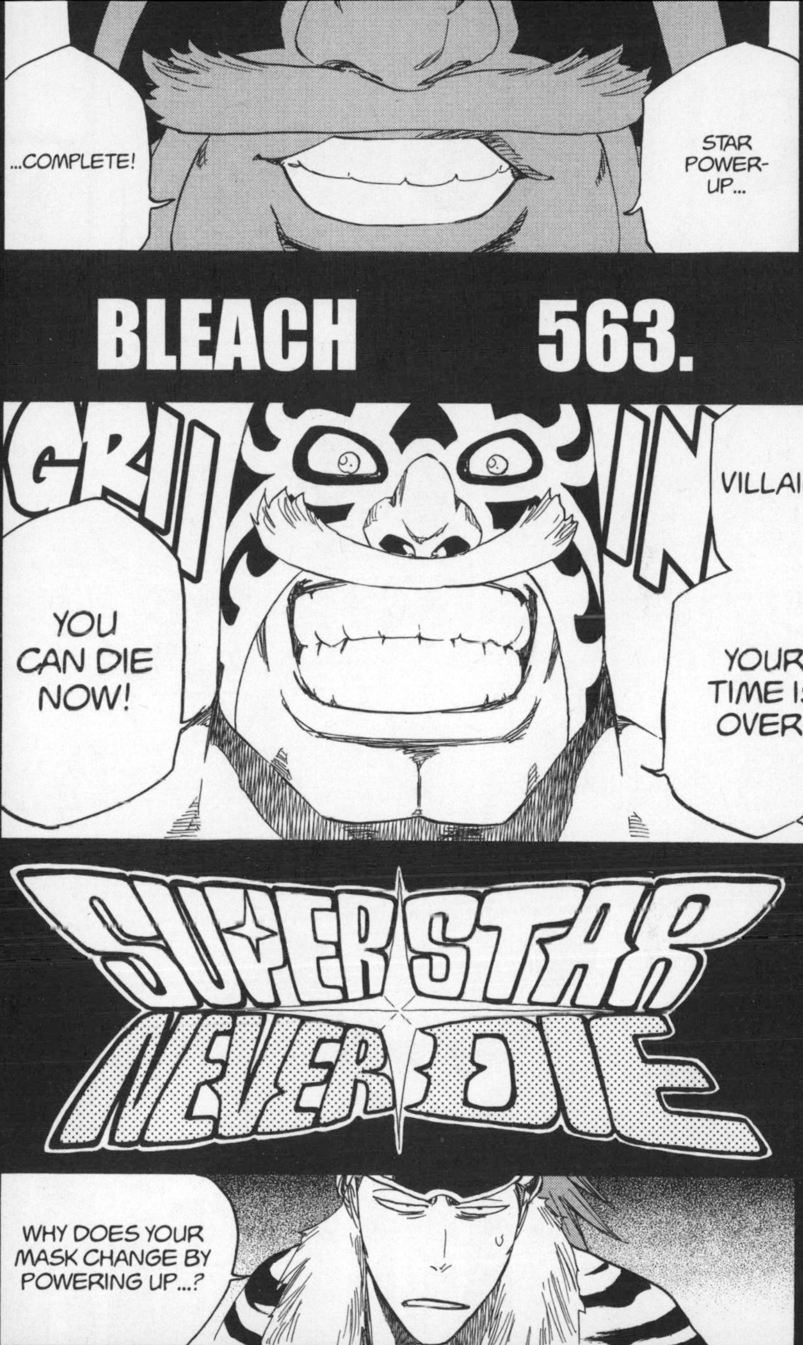
STAR POWER-UP...
...COMPLETE!
BLEACH 563.
GRIIIN
VILLAIN.
YOUR TIME IS OVER!
YOU CAN DIE NOW!
SUPER STAR NEVER DIE
WHY DOES YOUR MASK CHANGE BY POWERING UP...?

READ THIS WAY

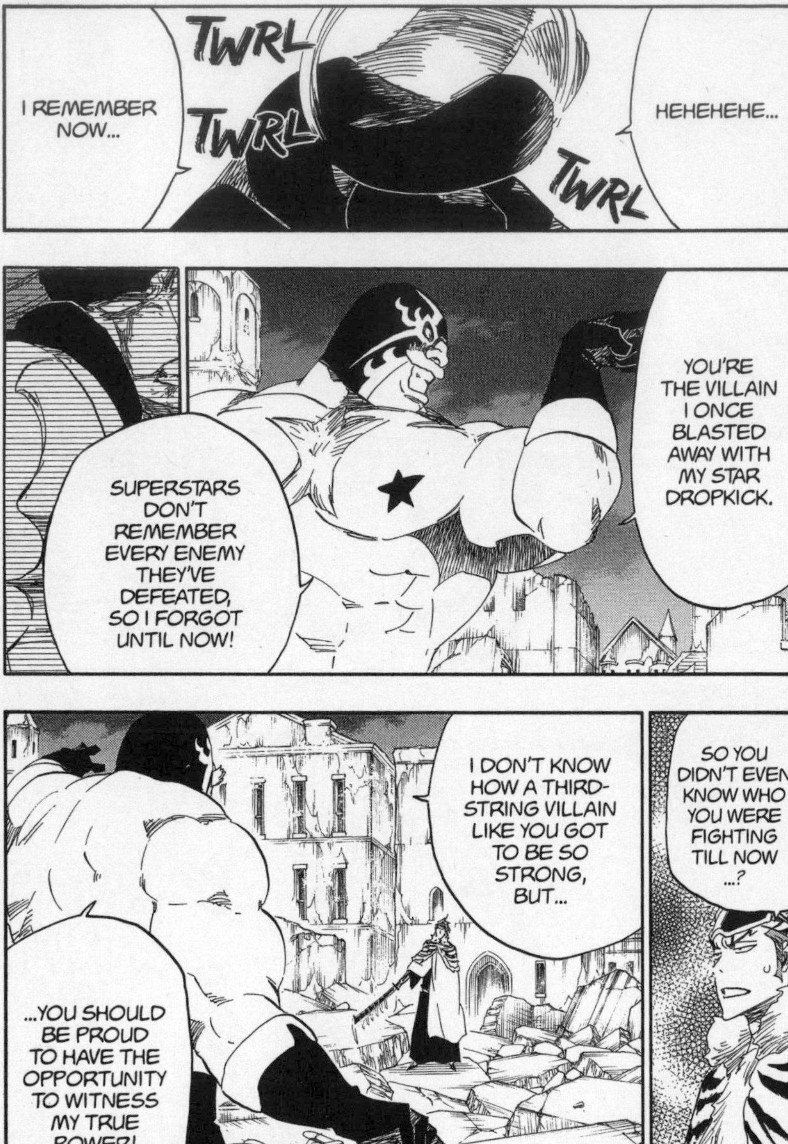
HEHEHEHE...
TWRL
TWRL
TWRL
I REMEMBER NOW...
YOU'RE THE VILLAIN I ONCE BLASTED AWAY WITH MY STAR DROPKICK.
SUPERSTARS DON'T REMEMBER EVERY ENEMY THEY'VE DEFEATED, SO I FORGOT UNTIL NOW!
SO YOU DIDN'T EVEN KNOW WHO YOU WERE FIGHTING TILL NOW ...?
I DON'T KNOW HOW A THIRD-STRING VILLAIN LIKE YOU GOT TO BE SO STRONG, BUT...
...YOU SHOULD BE PROUD TO HAVE THE OPPORTUNITY TO WITNESS MY TRUE POWER!

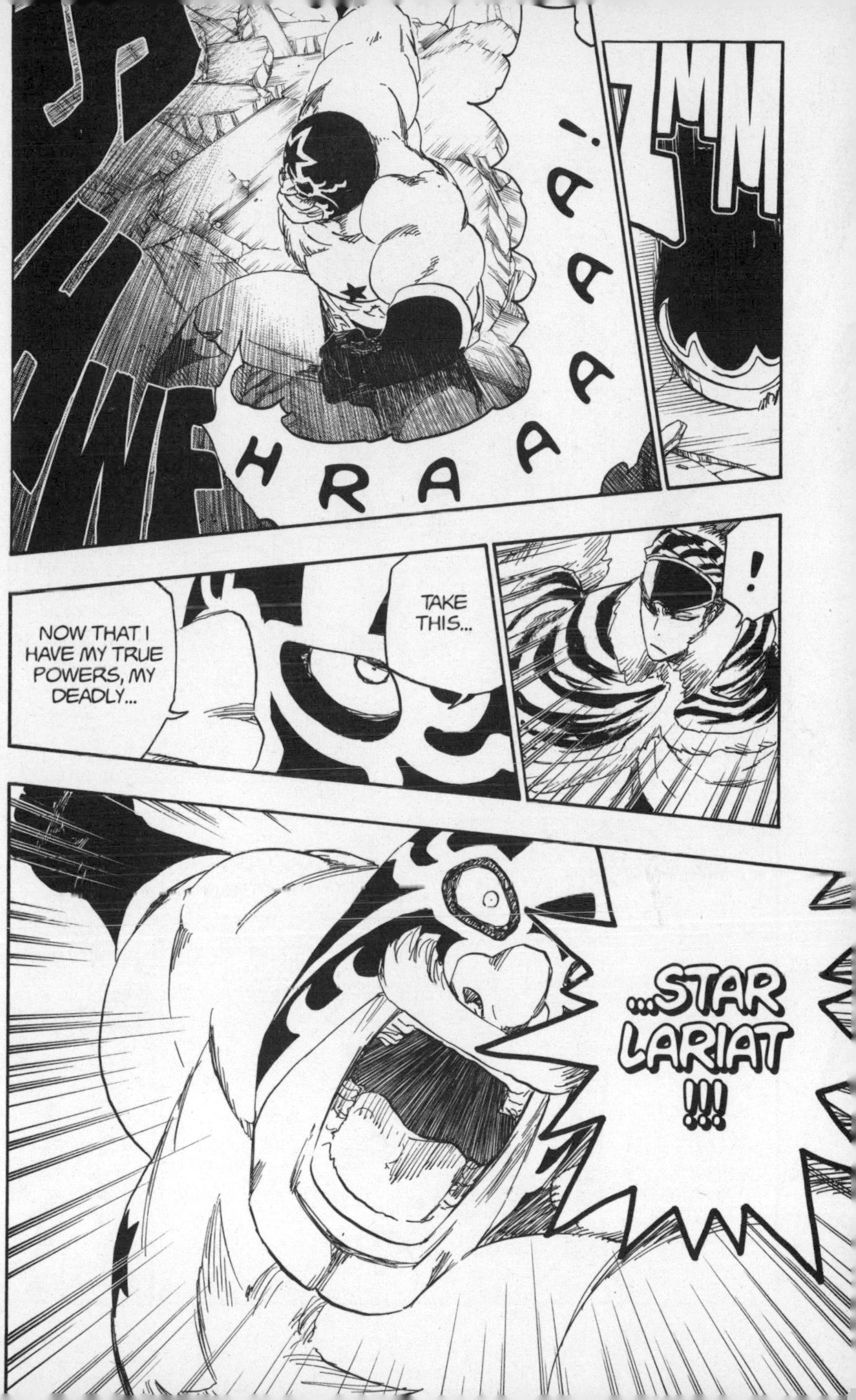
ZMM
HRAAAAA!
!
TAKE THIS...
NOW THAT I HAVE MY TRUE POWERS, MY DEADLY...
...STAR LARIAT !!!

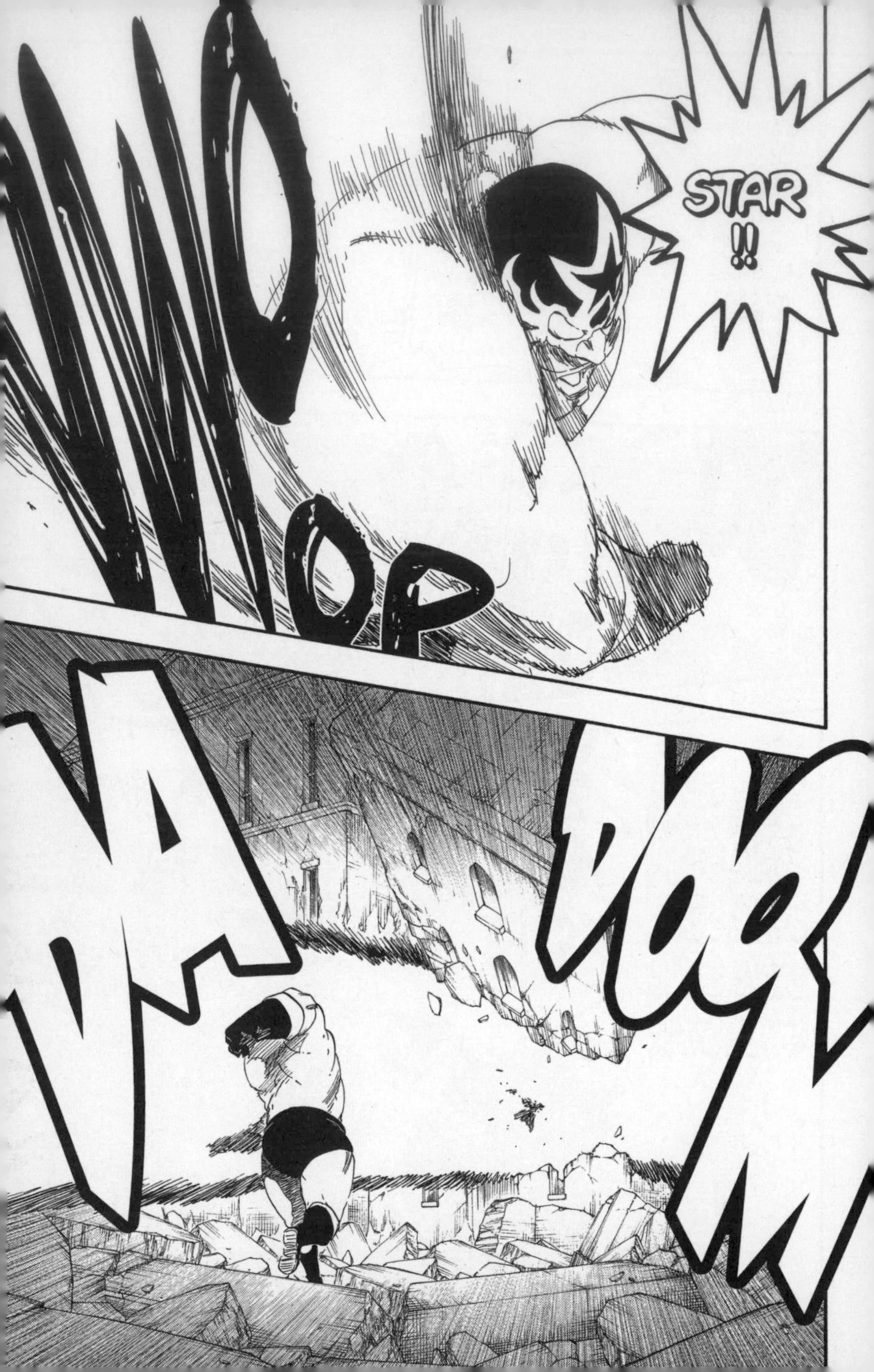
STAR !!

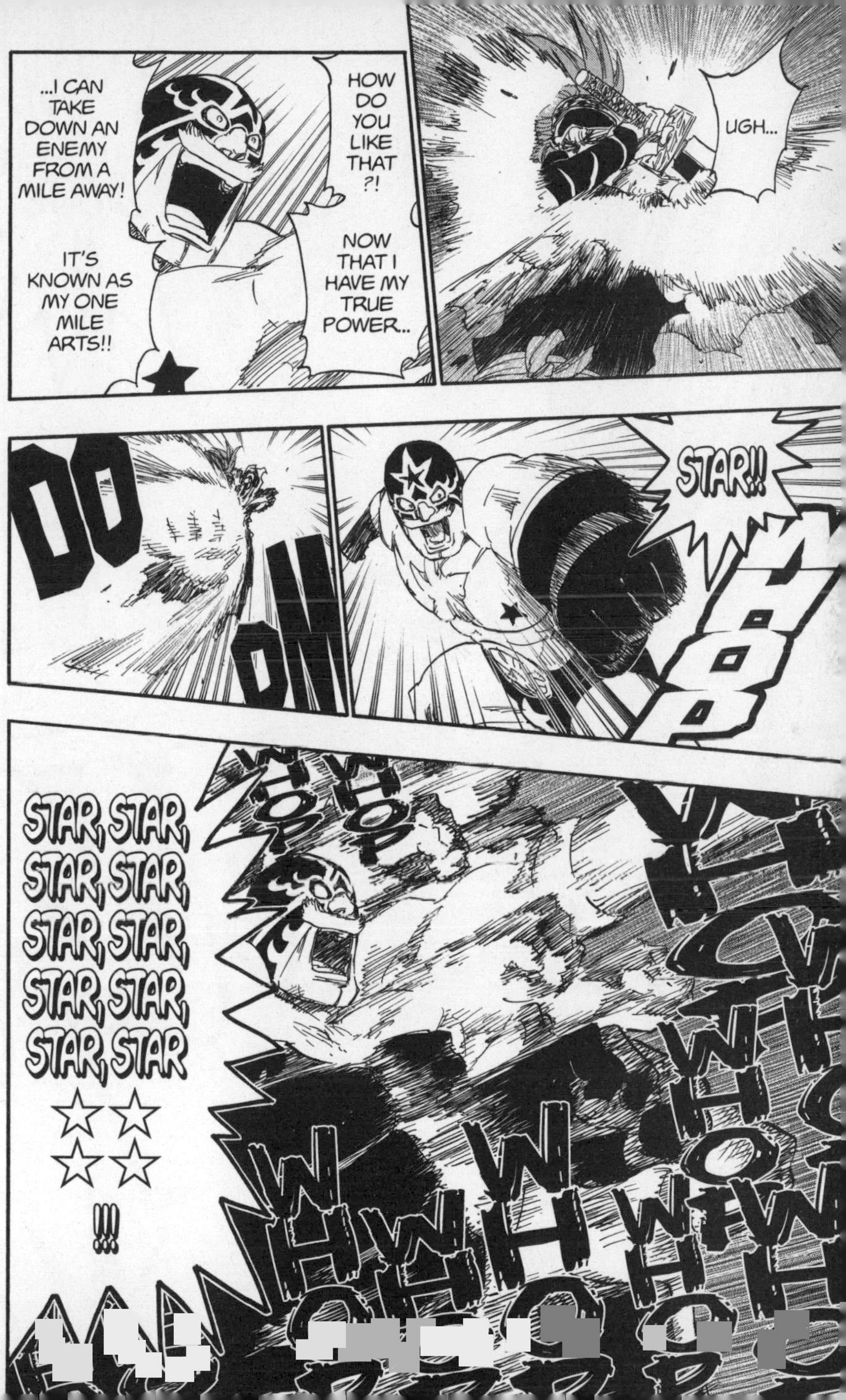
UGH...
HOW DO YOU LIKE THAT?!
NOW THAT I HAVE MY TRUE POWER...
...I CAN TAKE DOWN AN ENEMY FROM A MILE AWAY!
IT'S KNOWN AS MY ONE MILE ARTS!!
STAR!!
DOOM
STAR, STAR, STAR, STAR, STAR, STAR, STAR, STAR, STAR, STAR ☆☆☆☆!!!

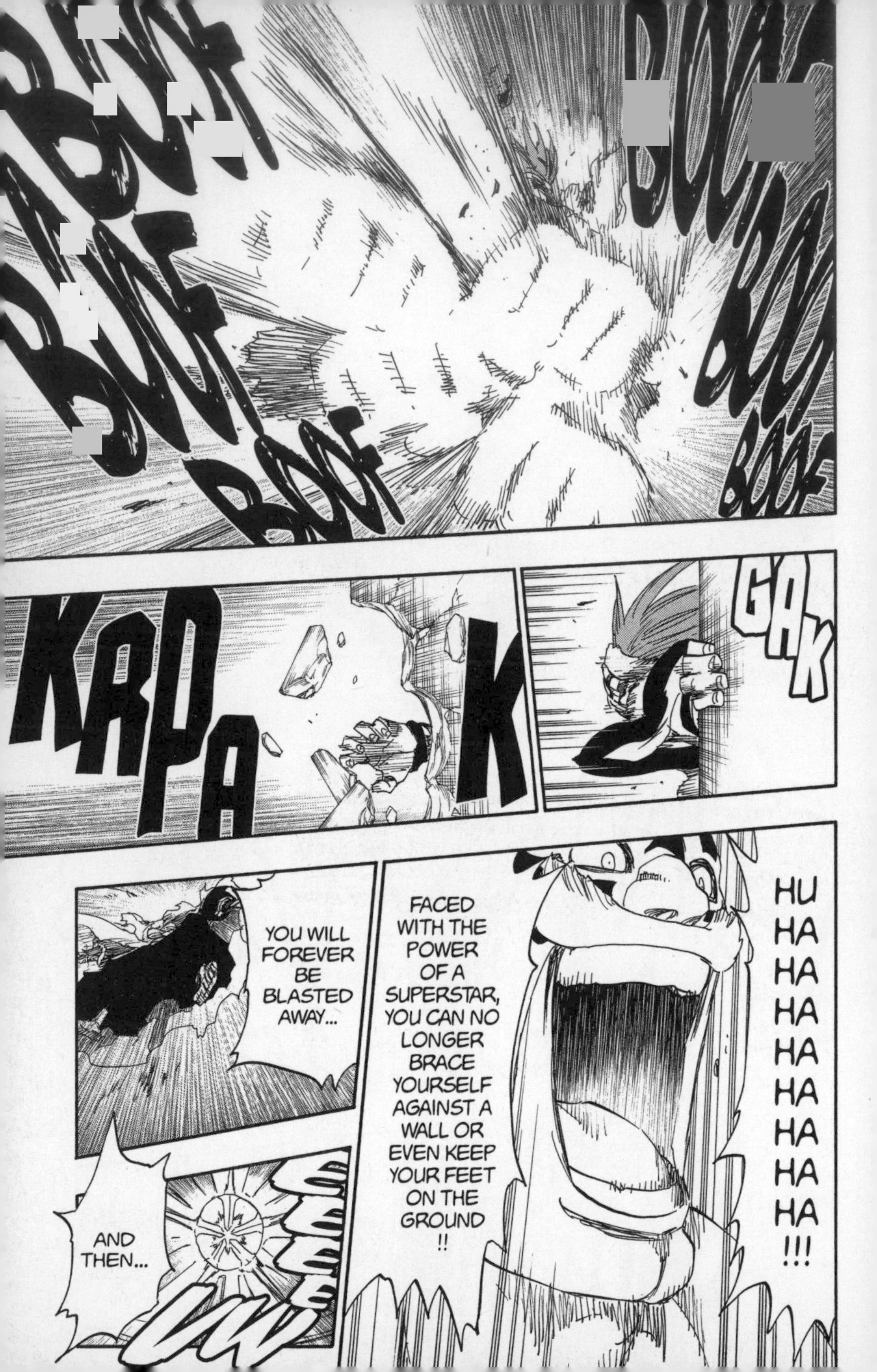
GAK
KRPAK
HU HA HA HA HA HA HA HA HA HA!!!
FACED WITH THE POWER OF A SUPERSTAR, YOU CAN NO LONGER BRACE YOURSELF AGAINST A WALL OR EVEN KEEP YOUR FEET ON THE GROUND!!
YOU WILL FOREVER BE BLASTED AWAY...
AND THEN...

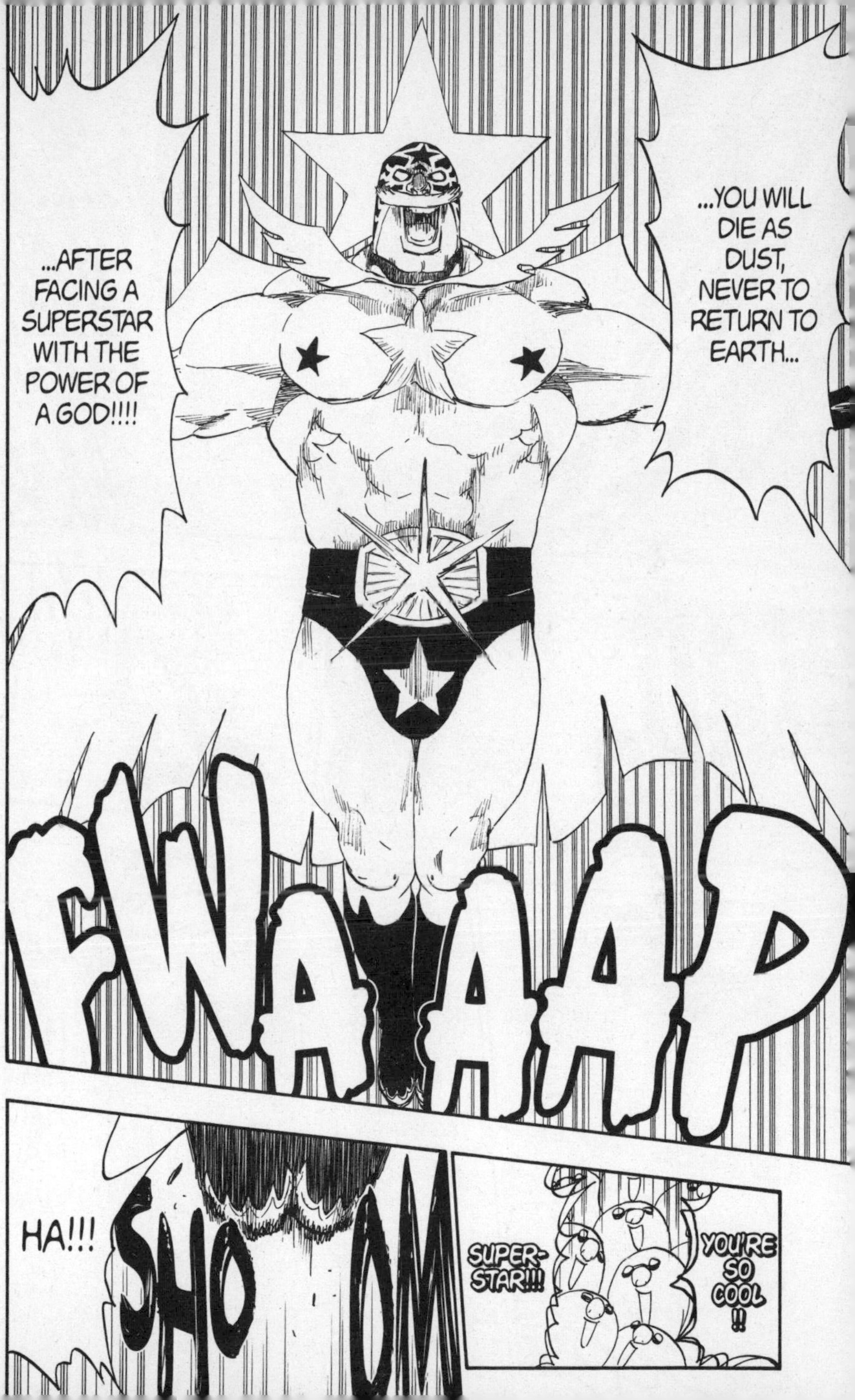
...YOU WILL DIE AS DUST, NEVER TO RETURN TO EARTH...
...AFTER FACING A SUPERSTAR WITH THE POWER OF A GOD!!!!
FWAAAP
YOU'RE SO COOL!!
SUPER-STAR!!!
SHOOM
HA!!!

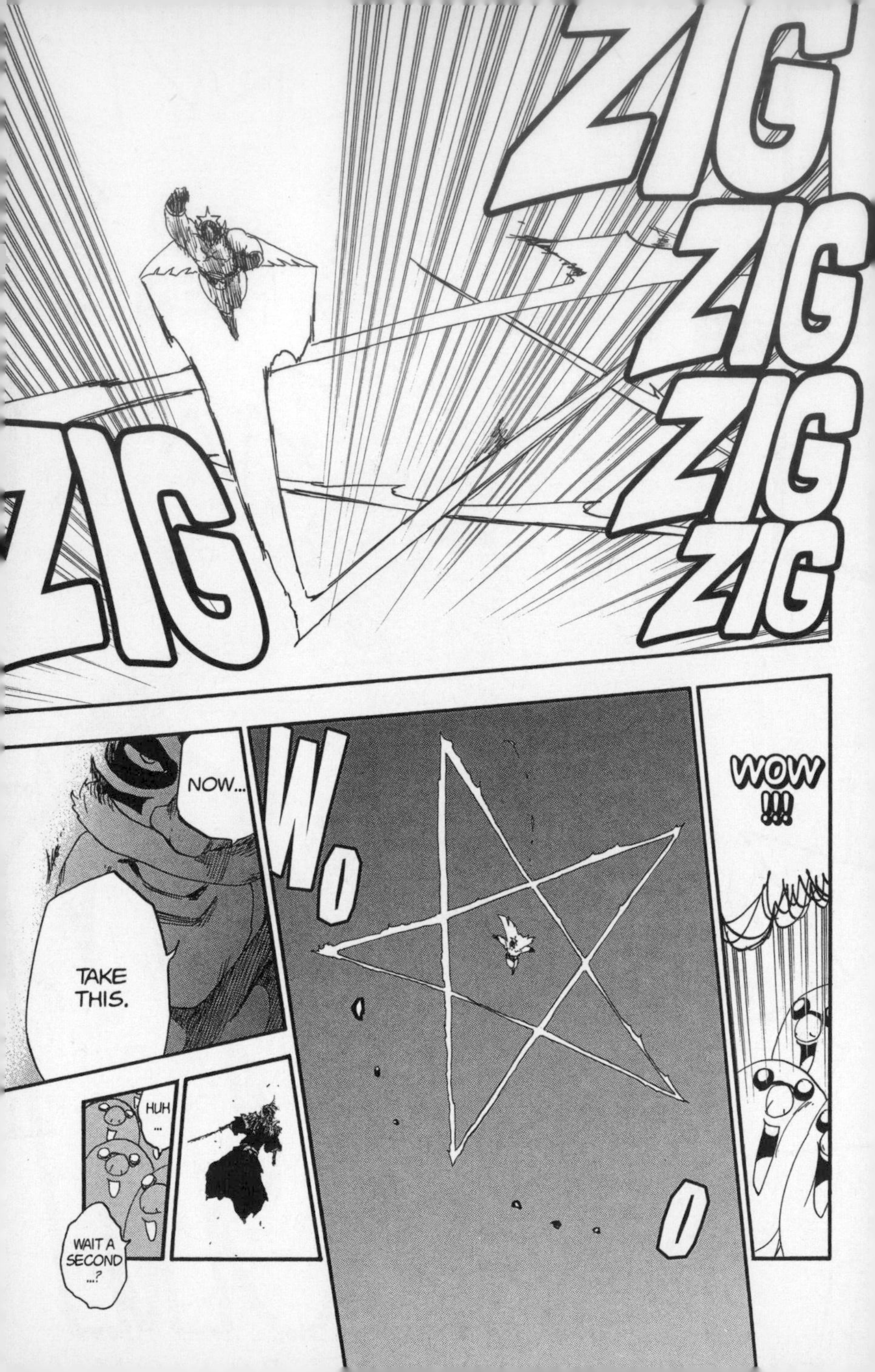
ZIG
ZIG
ZIG
ZIG
ZIG
WOW !!!
WOO
NOW...
TAKE THIS.
HUH ...
WAIT A SECOND ...?

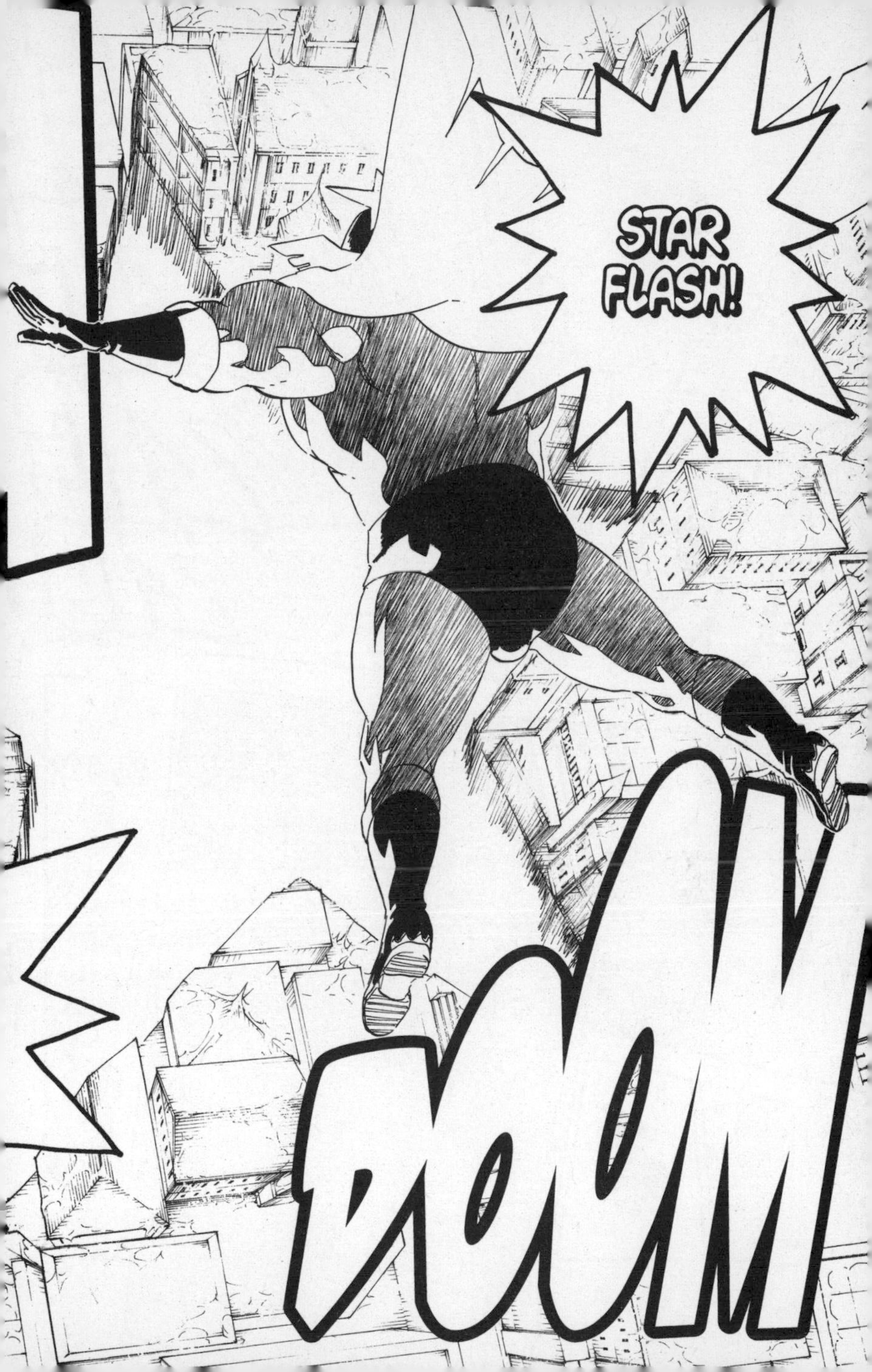
STAR FLASH!
DOOM

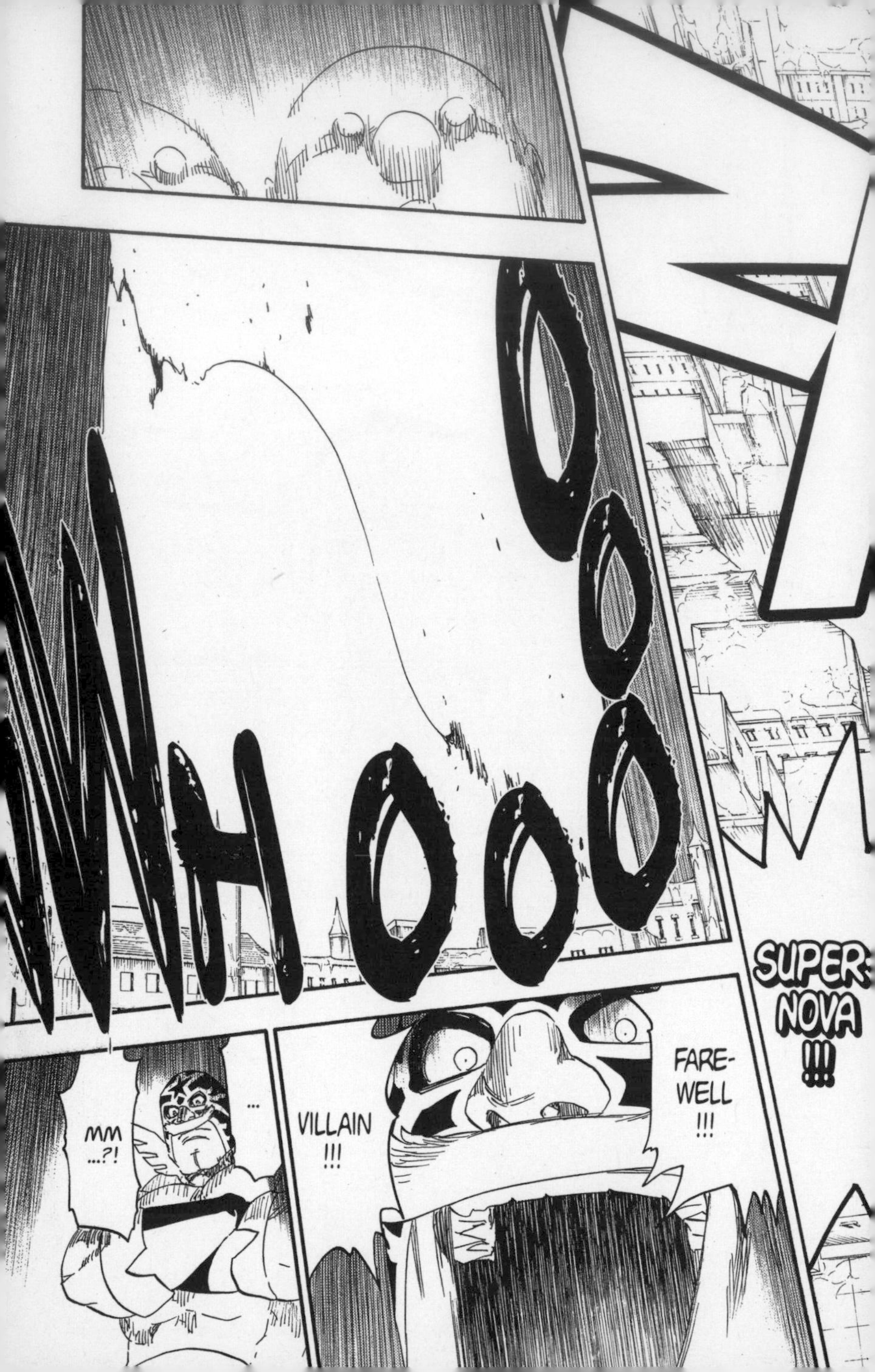
SUPER-NOVA!!!
WHOOOOOM
FARE-WELL!!!
VILLAIN!!!
...
MM ...?!

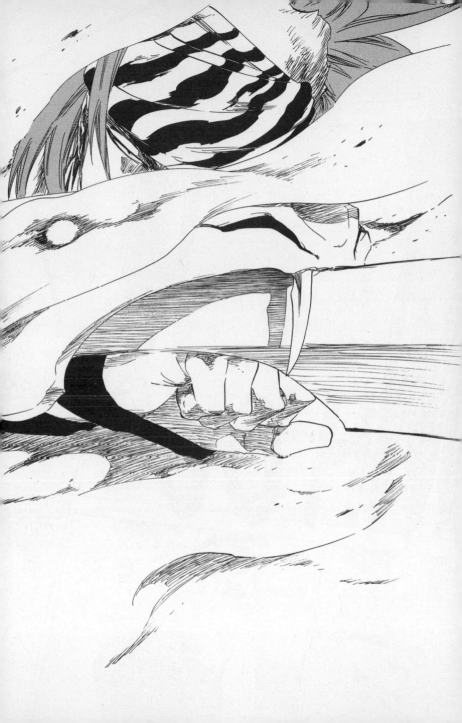

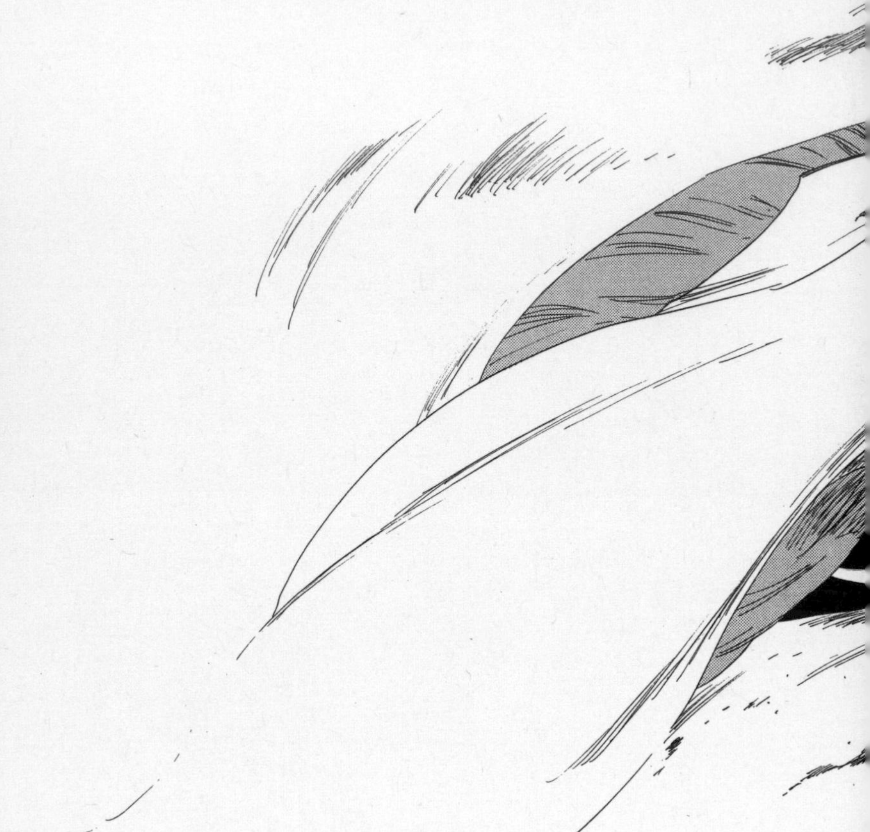

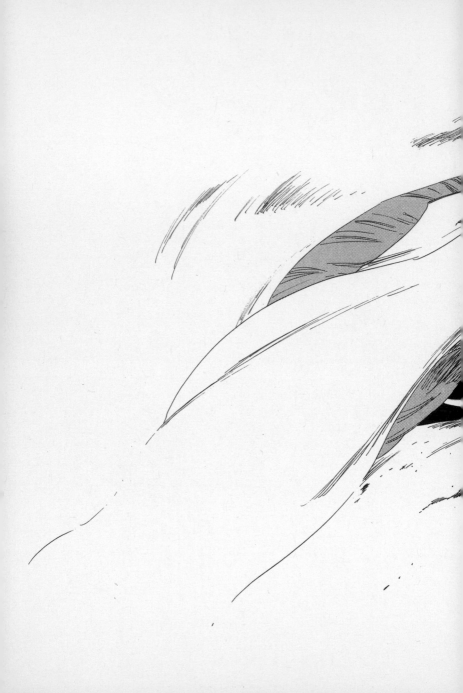

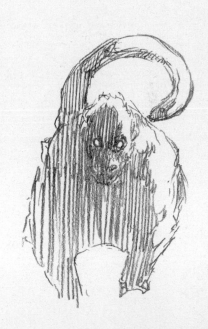

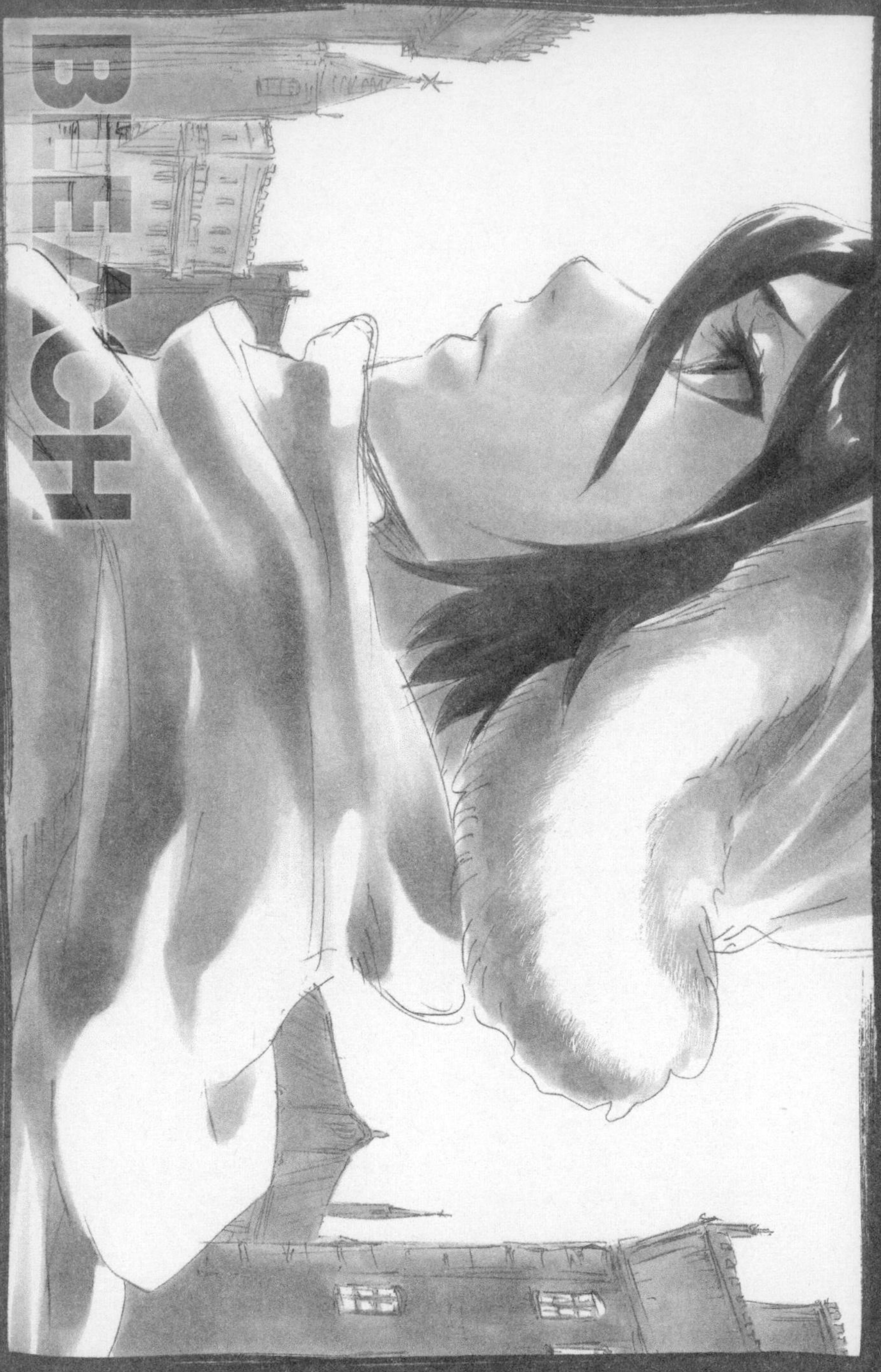
BLEACH

BLEACH
ブリーチ

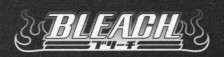

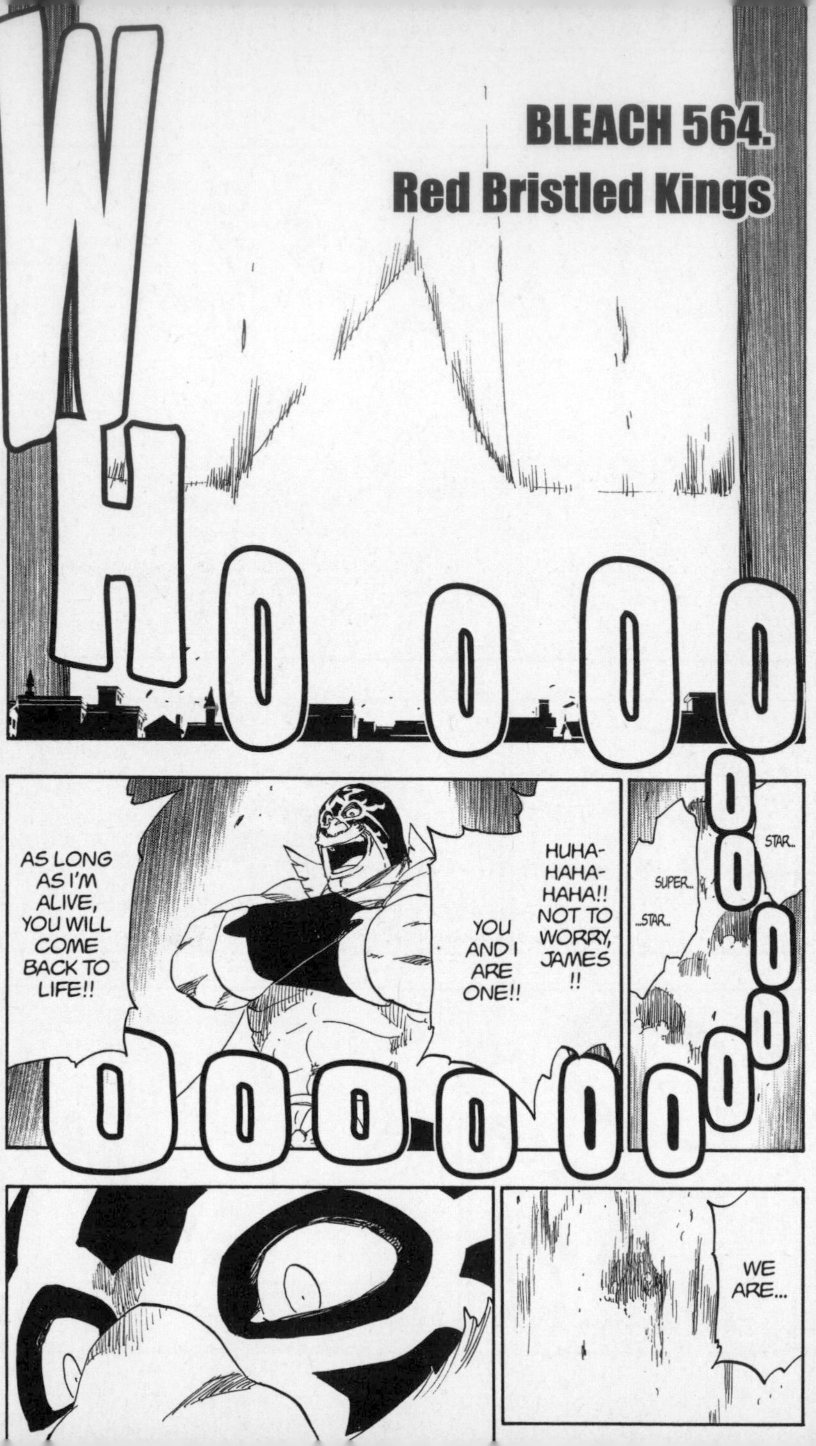
BLEACH 564.
Red Bristled Kings
WHOOOOOOOOOOOOOOOOOO
STAR..
SUPER..
...STAR..
HUHAHAHAHAHA!! NOT TO WORRY, JAMES!!
YOU AND I ARE ONE!!
AS LONG AS I'M ALIVE, YOU WILL COME BACK TO LIFE!!
WE ARE...

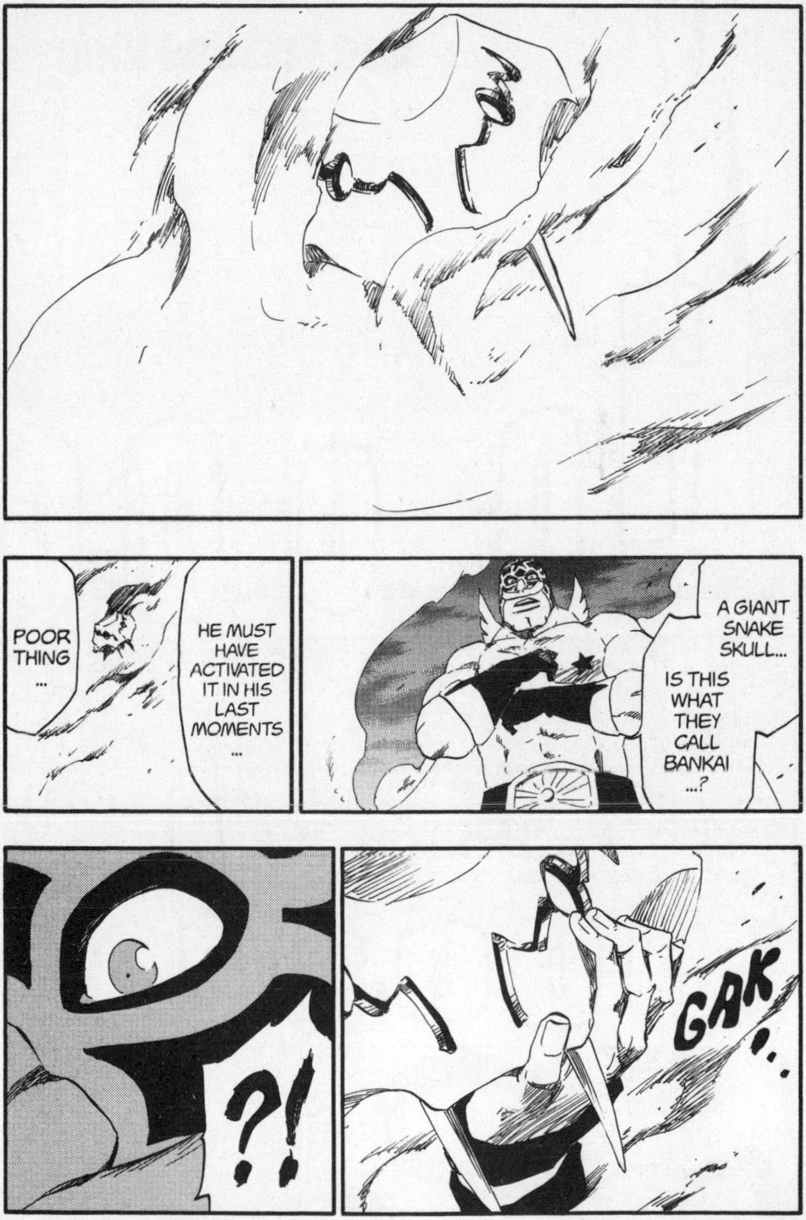
A GIANT SNAKE SKULL...
IS THIS WHAT THEY CALL BANKAI ...?
HE MUST HAVE ACTIVATED IT IN HIS LAST MOMENTS ...
POOR THING ...
GAK ..
?!

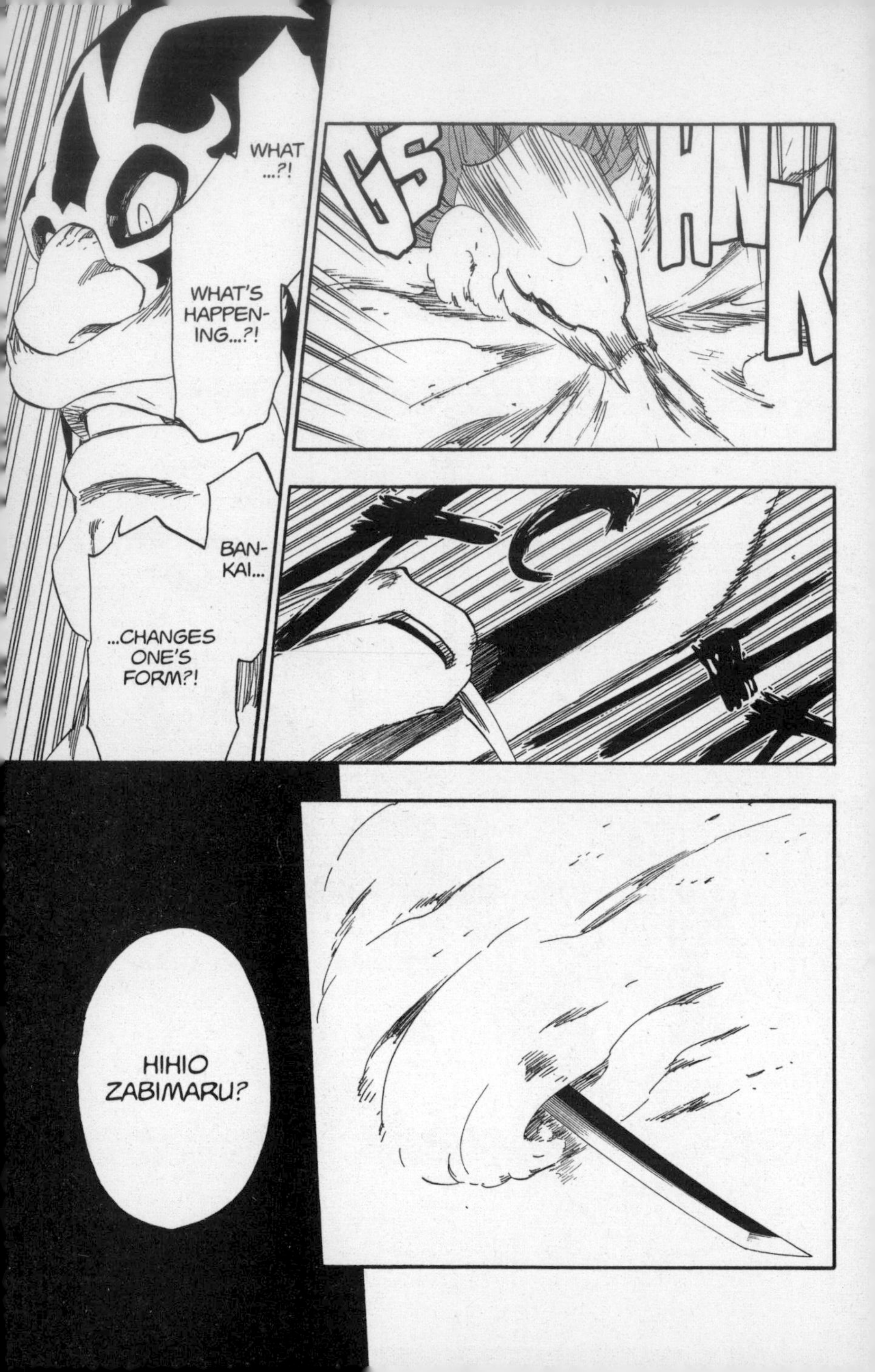
GS
HNK
WHAT ...?!
WHAT'S HAPPENING...?!
BANKAI...
...CHANGES ONE'S FORM?!
HIHIO ZABIMARU?

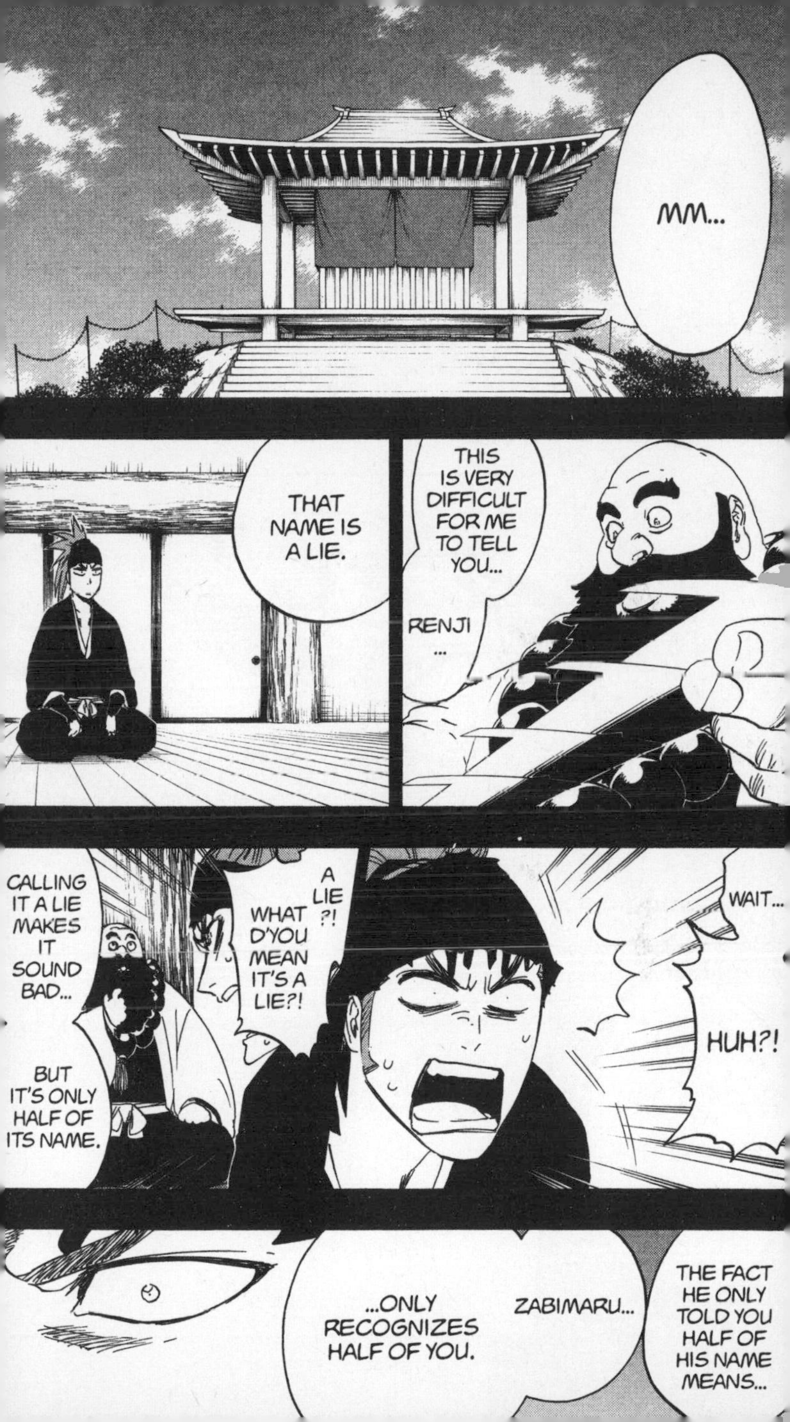
MM...
THIS IS VERY DIFFICULT FOR ME TO TELL YOU...
RENJI...
THAT NAME IS A LIE.
WAIT...
HUH?!
A LIE?!
WHAT D'YOU MEAN IT'S A LIE?!
CALLING IT A LIE MAKES IT SOUND BAD...
BUT IT'S ONLY HALF OF ITS NAME.
THE FACT HE ONLY TOLD YOU HALF OF HIS NAME MEANS...
ZABIMARU...
...ONLY RECOGNIZES HALF OF YOU.

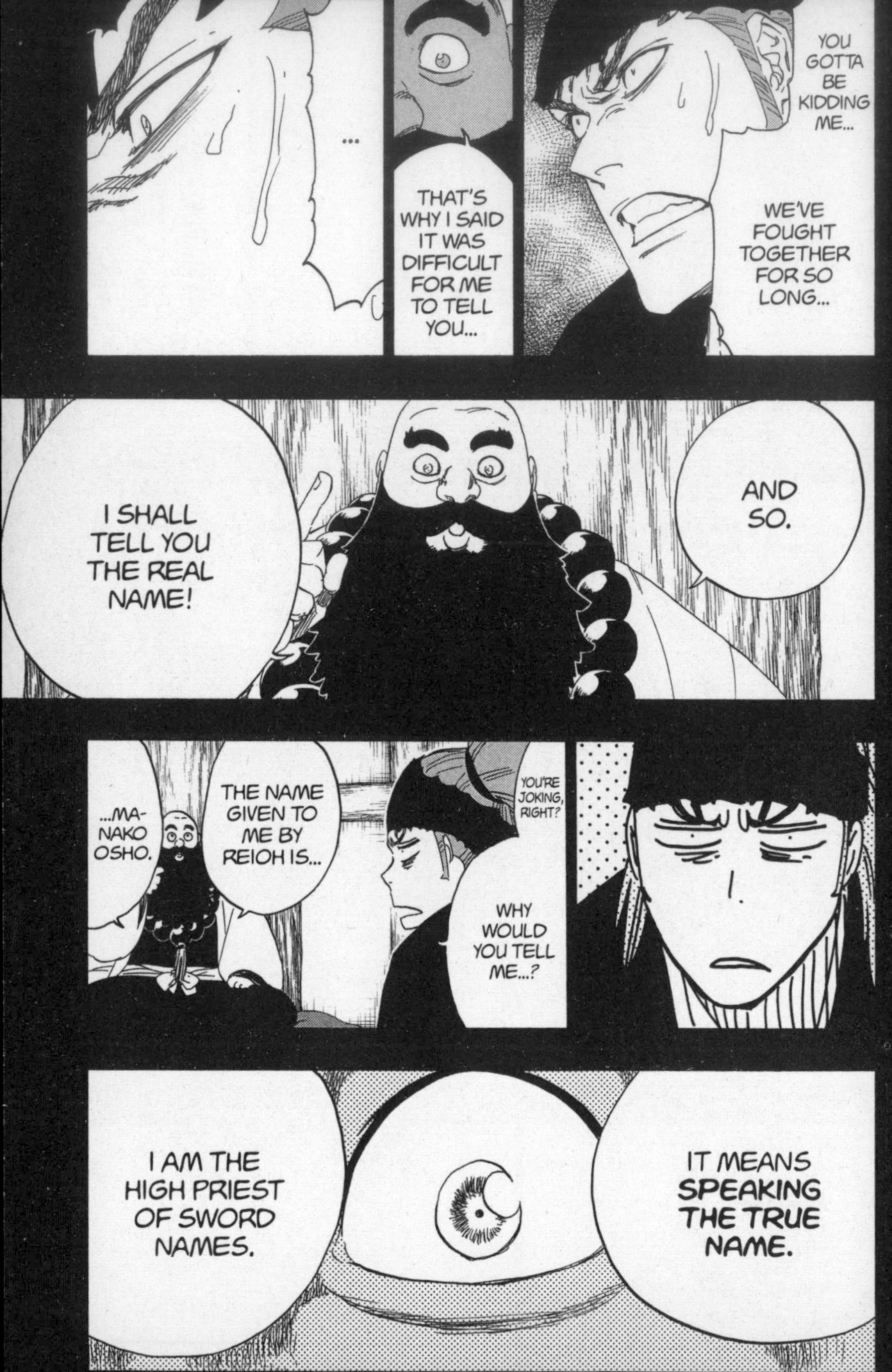
YOU GOTTA BE KIDDING ME...
WE'VE FOUGHT TOGETHER FOR SO LONG...
THAT'S WHY I SAID IT WAS DIFFICULT FOR ME TO TELL YOU...
...
AND SO.
I SHALL TELL YOU THE REAL NAME!
YOU'RE JOKING, RIGHT?
WHY WOULD YOU TELL ME...?
THE NAME GIVEN TO ME BY REIOH IS...
...MA-NAKO OSHO.
IT MEANS SPEAKING THE TRUE NAME.
I AM THE HIGH PRIEST OF SWORD NAMES.

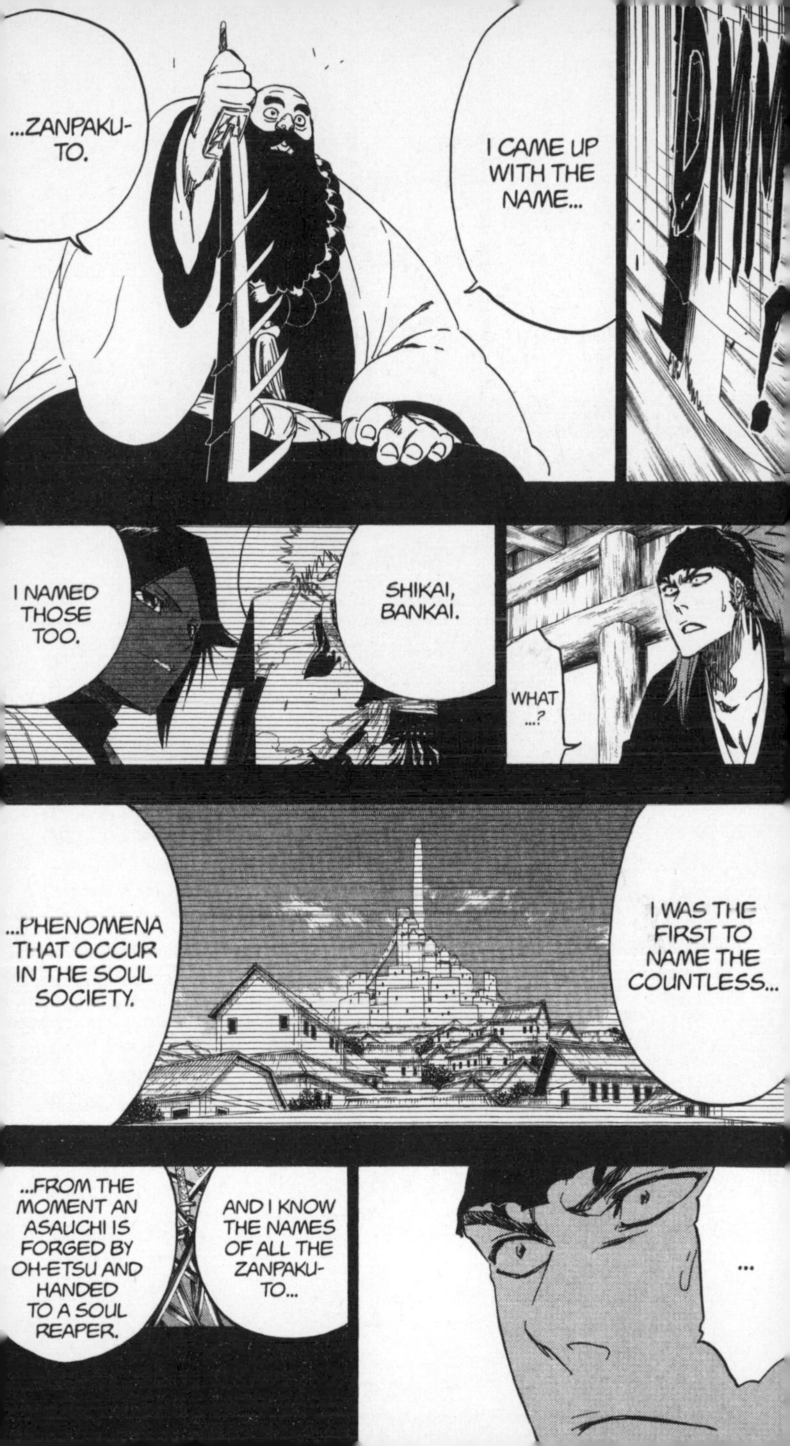
DMM!
I CAME UP WITH THE NAME...
...ZANPAKU-TO.
WHAT ...?
SHIKAI, BANKAI.
I NAMED THOSE TOO.
I WAS THE FIRST TO NAME THE COUNTLESS...
...PHENOMENA THAT OCCUR IN THE SOUL SOCIETY.
...
AND I KNOW THE NAMES OF ALL THE ZANPAKU-TO...
...FROM THE MOMENT AN ASAUCHI IS FORGED BY OH-ETSU AND HANDED TO A SOUL REAPER.

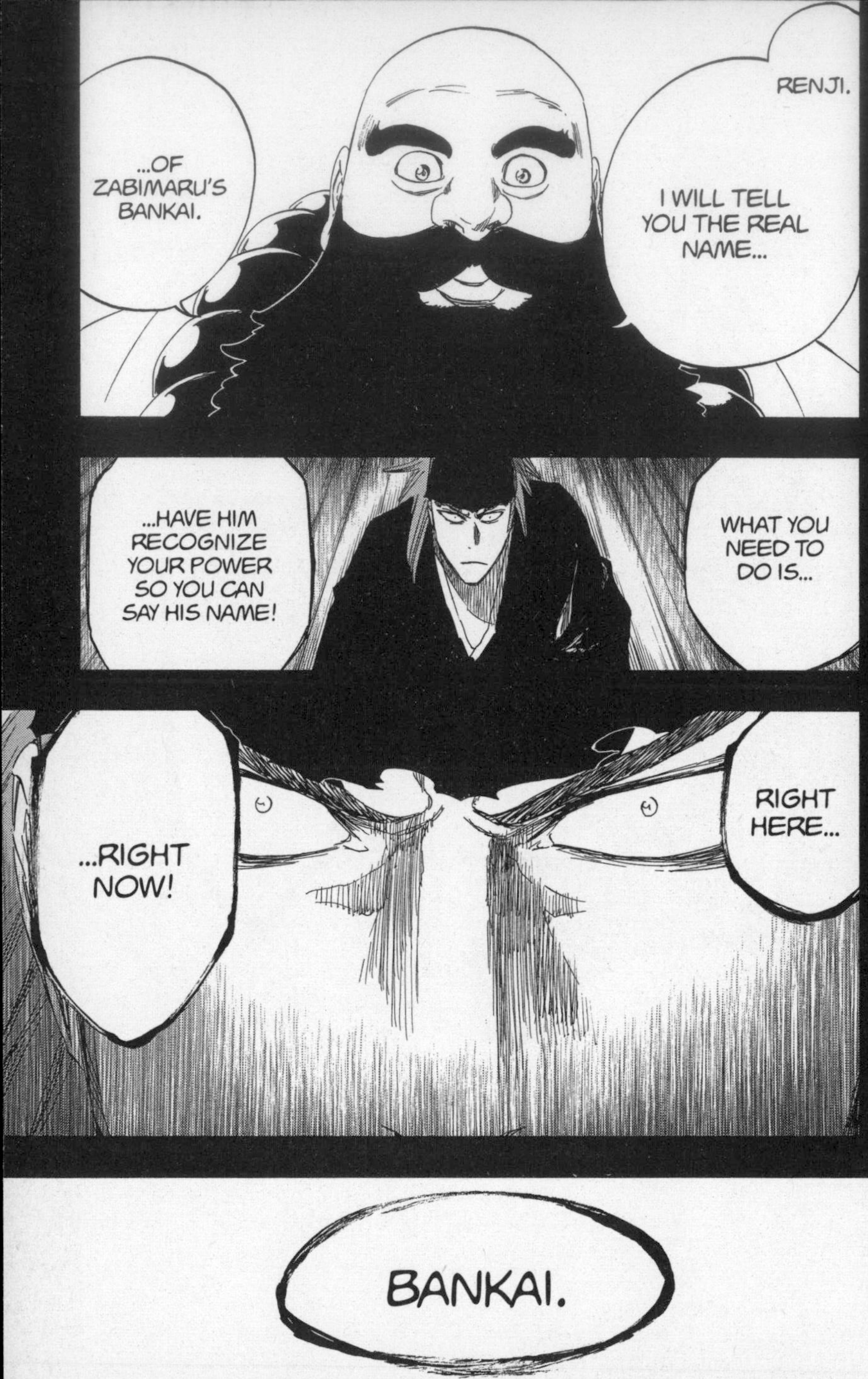
RENJI.
I WILL TELL YOU THE REAL NAME...
...OF ZABIMARU'S BANKAI.
WHAT YOU NEED TO DO IS...
...HAVE HIM RECOGNIZE YOUR POWER SO YOU CAN SAY HIS NAME!
RIGHT HERE...
...RIGHT NOW!
BANKAI.

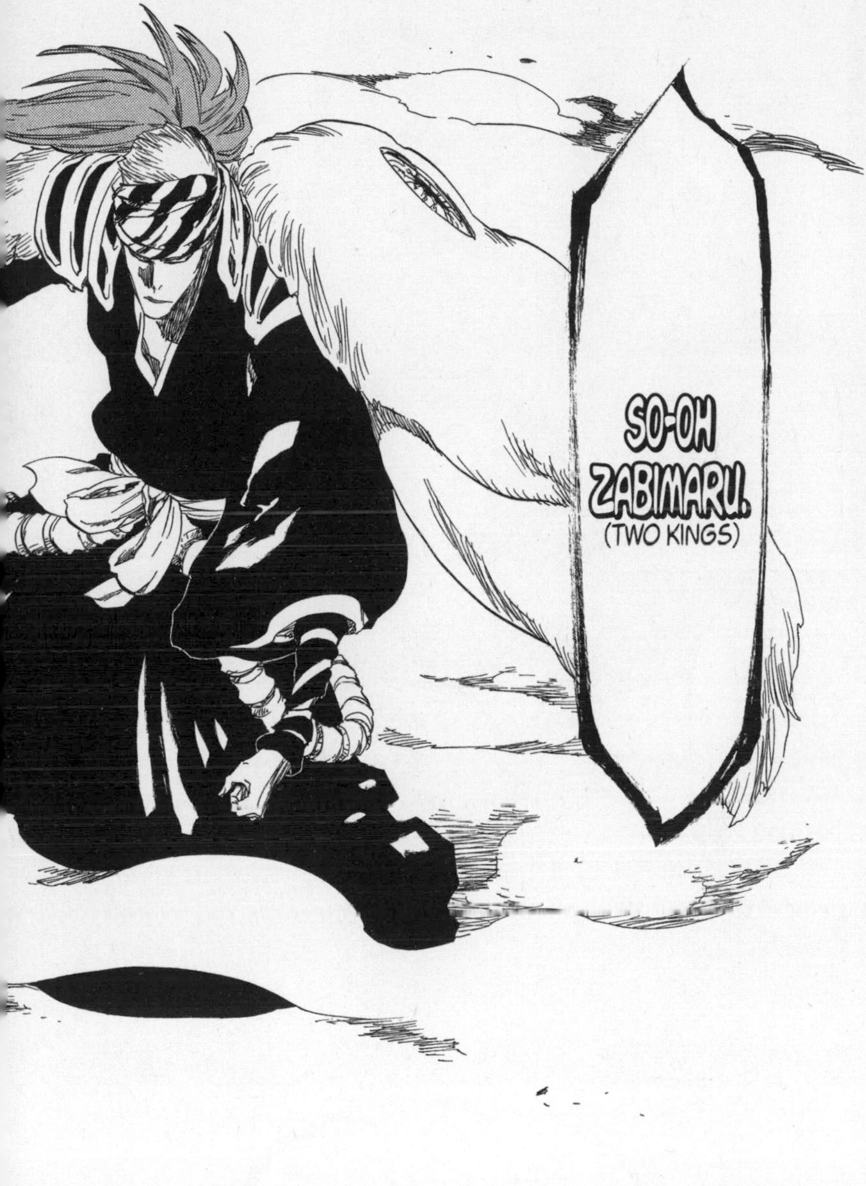
SO-OH ZABIMARU.
(TWO KINGS)

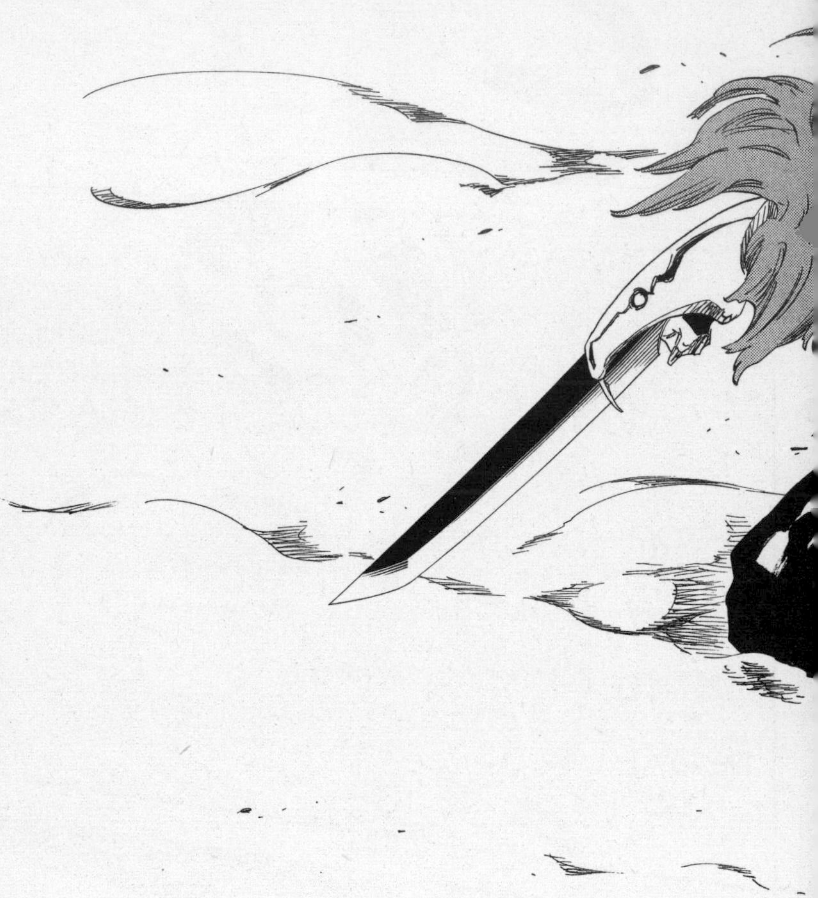

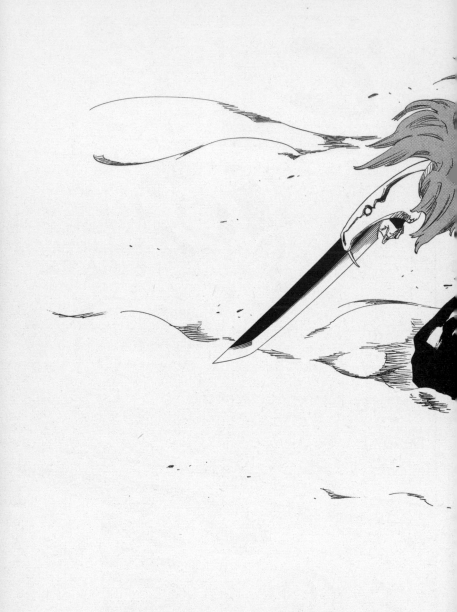

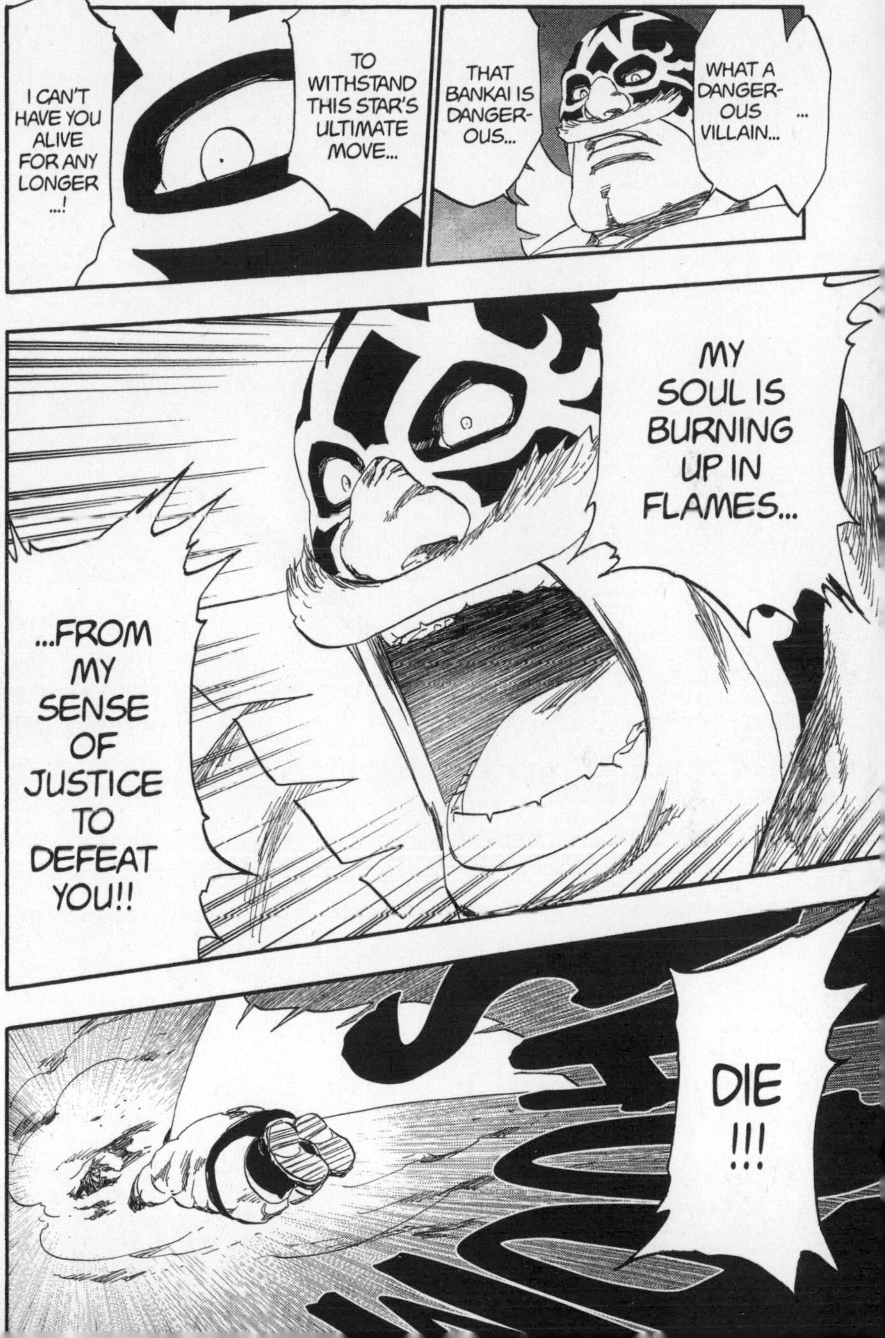
...
WHAT A DANGEROUS VILLAIN...
THAT BANKAI IS DANGEROUS...
TO WITHSTAND THIS STAR'S ULTIMATE MOVE...
I CAN'T HAVE YOU ALIVE FOR ANY LONGER...!
MY SOUL IS BURNING UP IN FLAMES...
...FROM MY SENSE OF JUSTICE TO DEFEAT YOU!!
DIE!!!

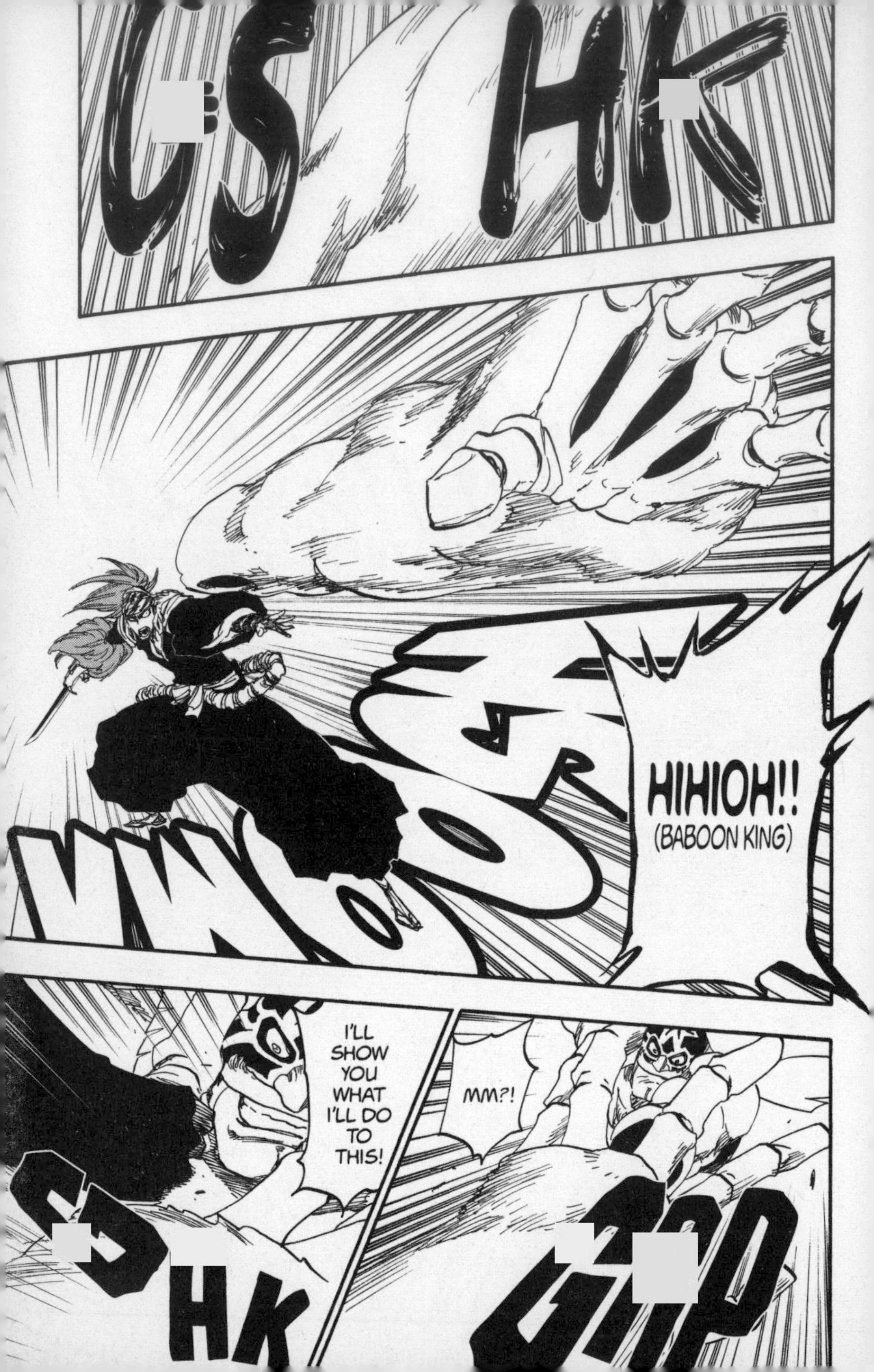
HIHIOH!!
(BABOON KING)
MM?!
I'LL SHOW YOU WHAT I'LL DO TO THIS!

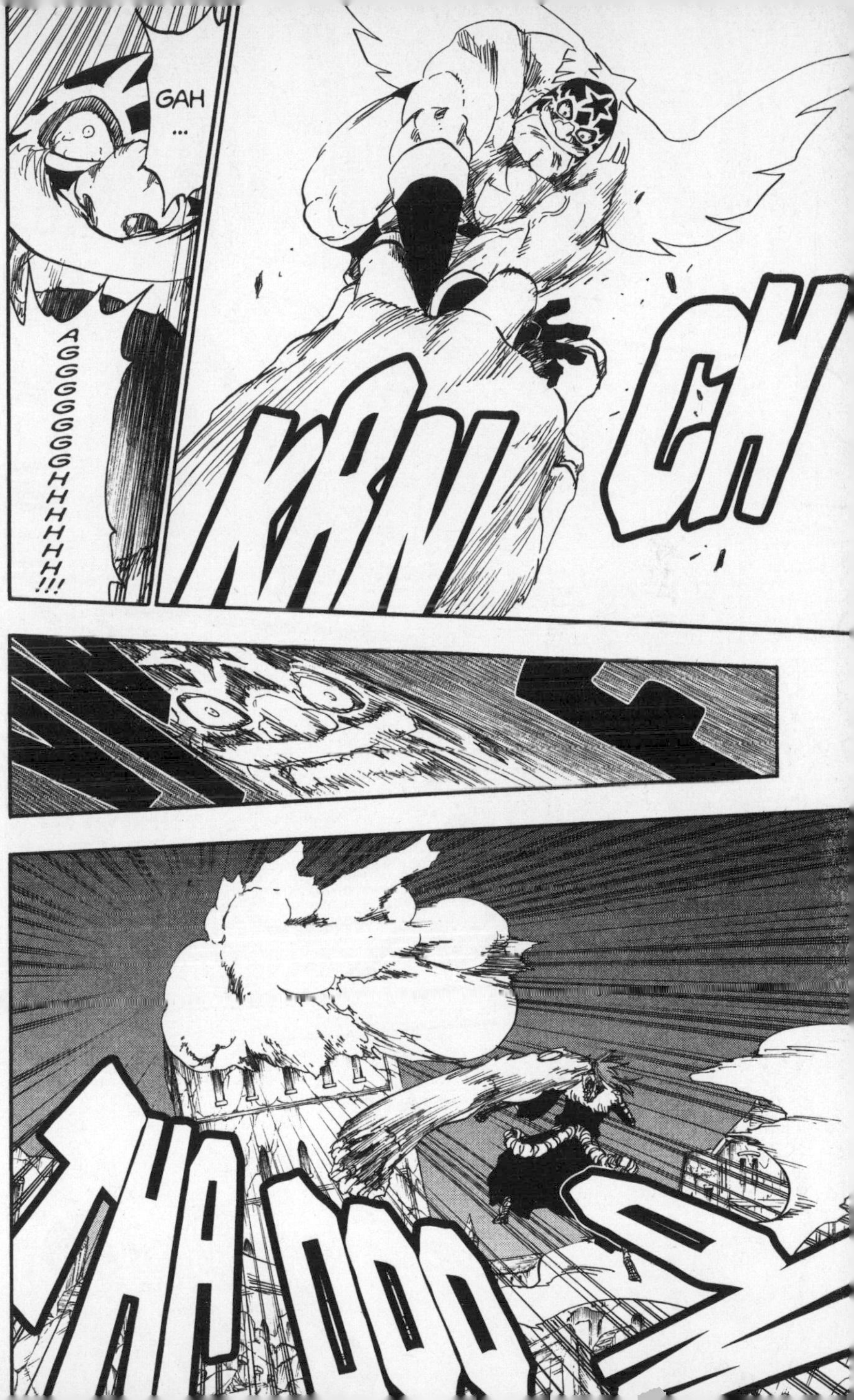
KRANCH
GAH ...
AGGGGGGGHHHHHH!!!

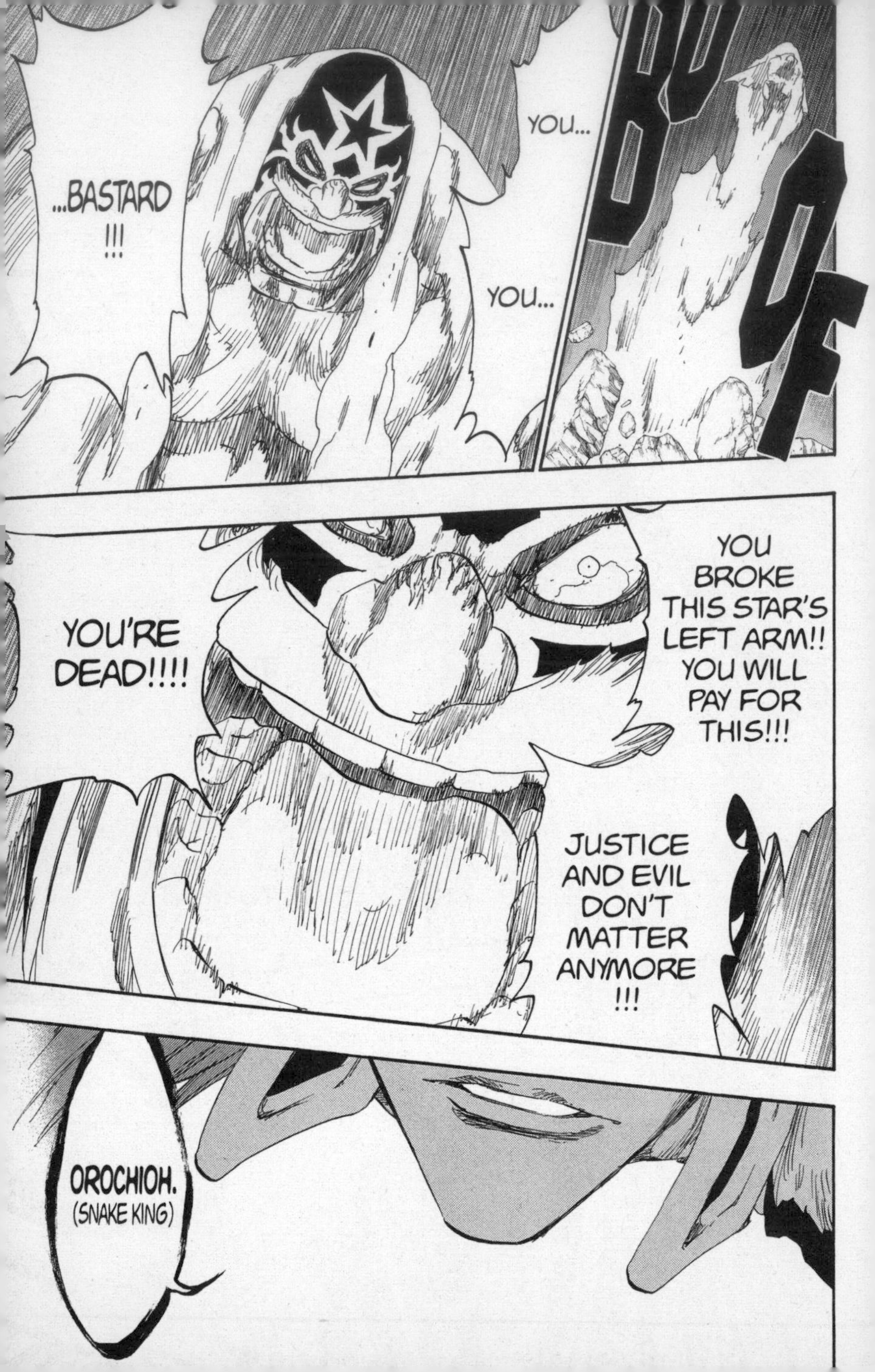
YOU...
YOU...
...BASTARD !!!
YOU BROKE THIS STAR'S LEFT ARM!! YOU WILL PAY FOR THIS!!!
YOU'RE DEAD!!!!
JUSTICE AND EVIL DON'T MATTER ANYMORE !!!
OROCHIOH. (SNAKE KING)

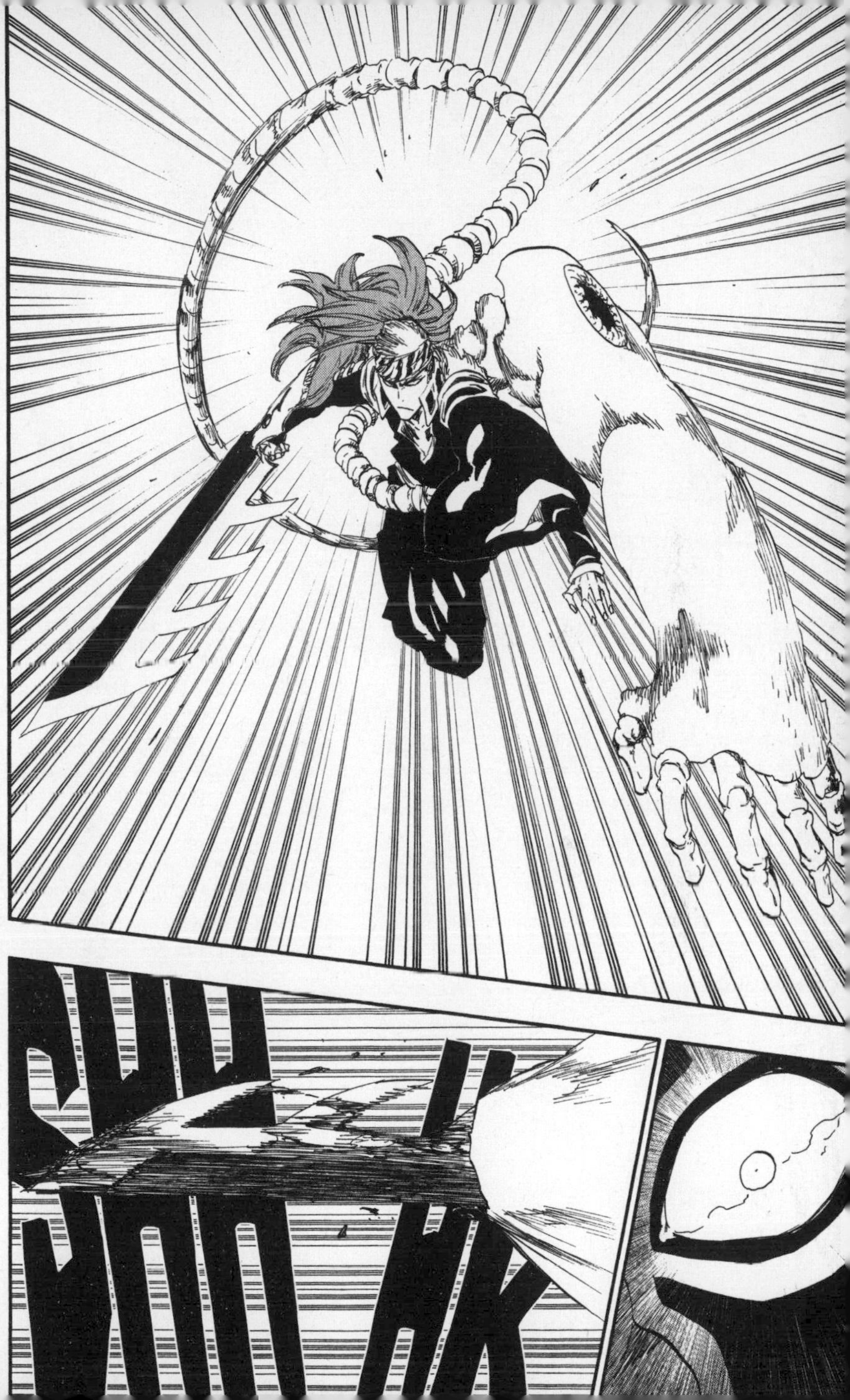
SHHAK

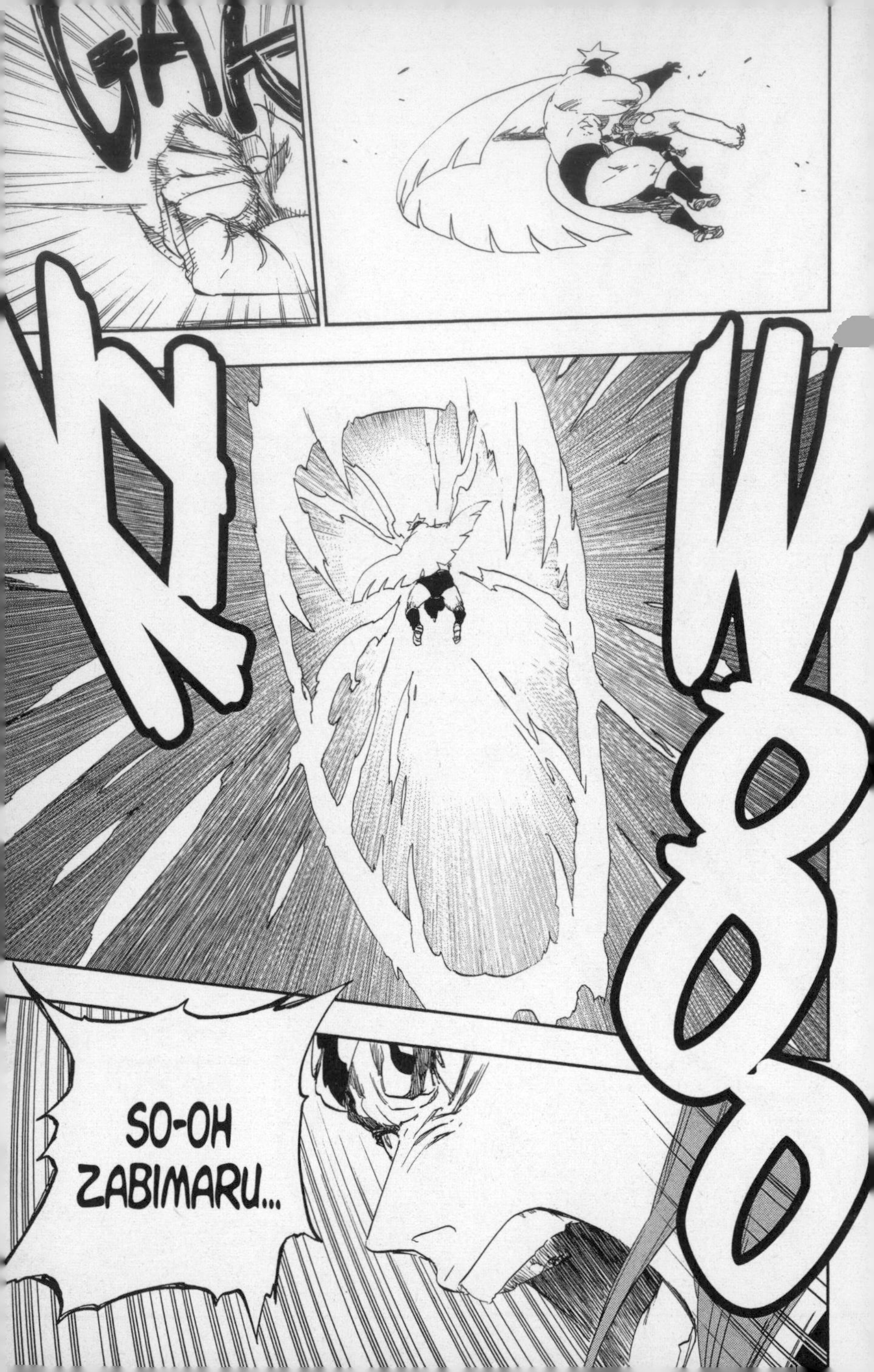
GAK
SO-OH
ZABIMARU...

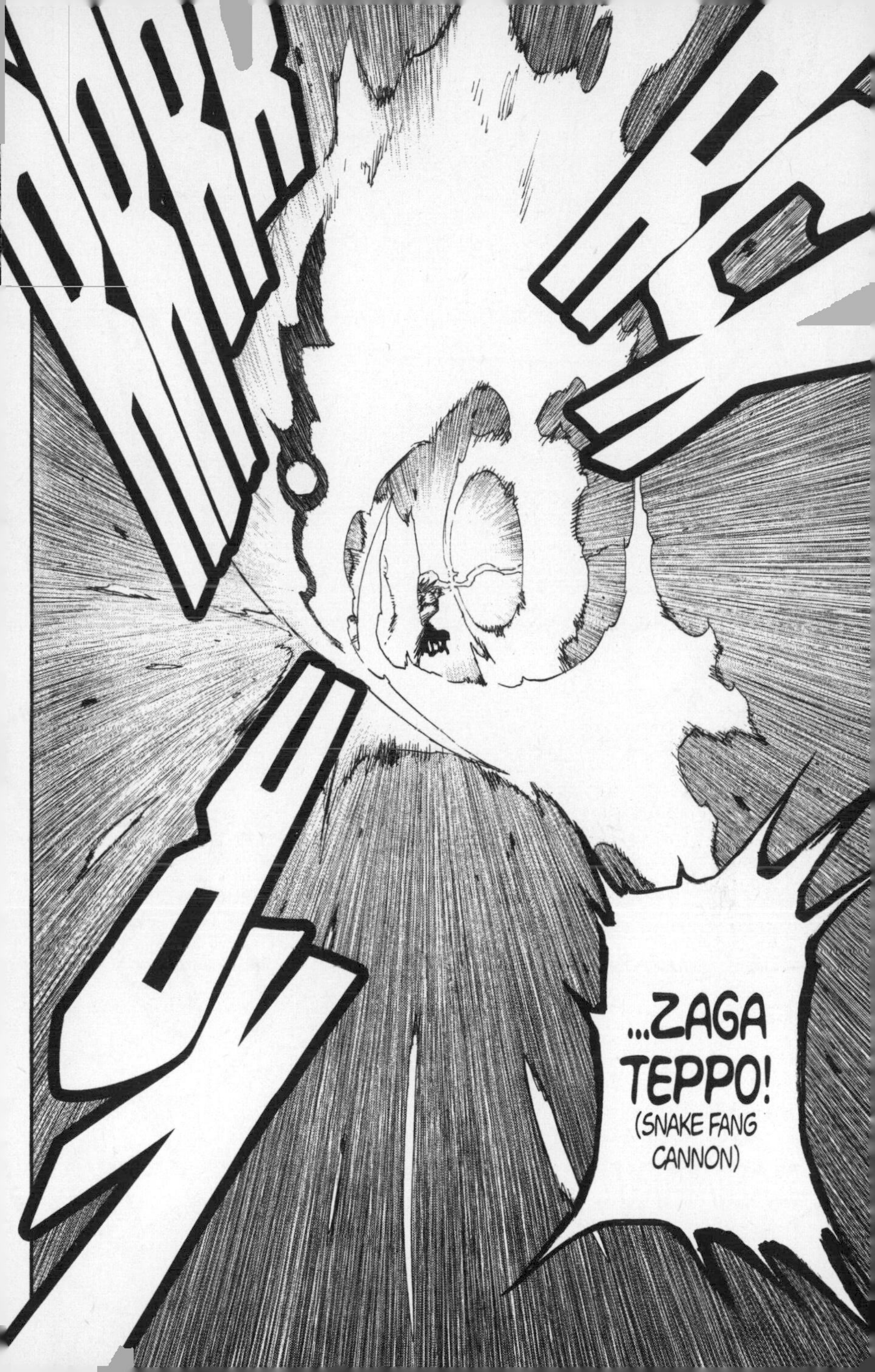
...ZAGA TEPPO!
(SNAKE FANG CANNON)

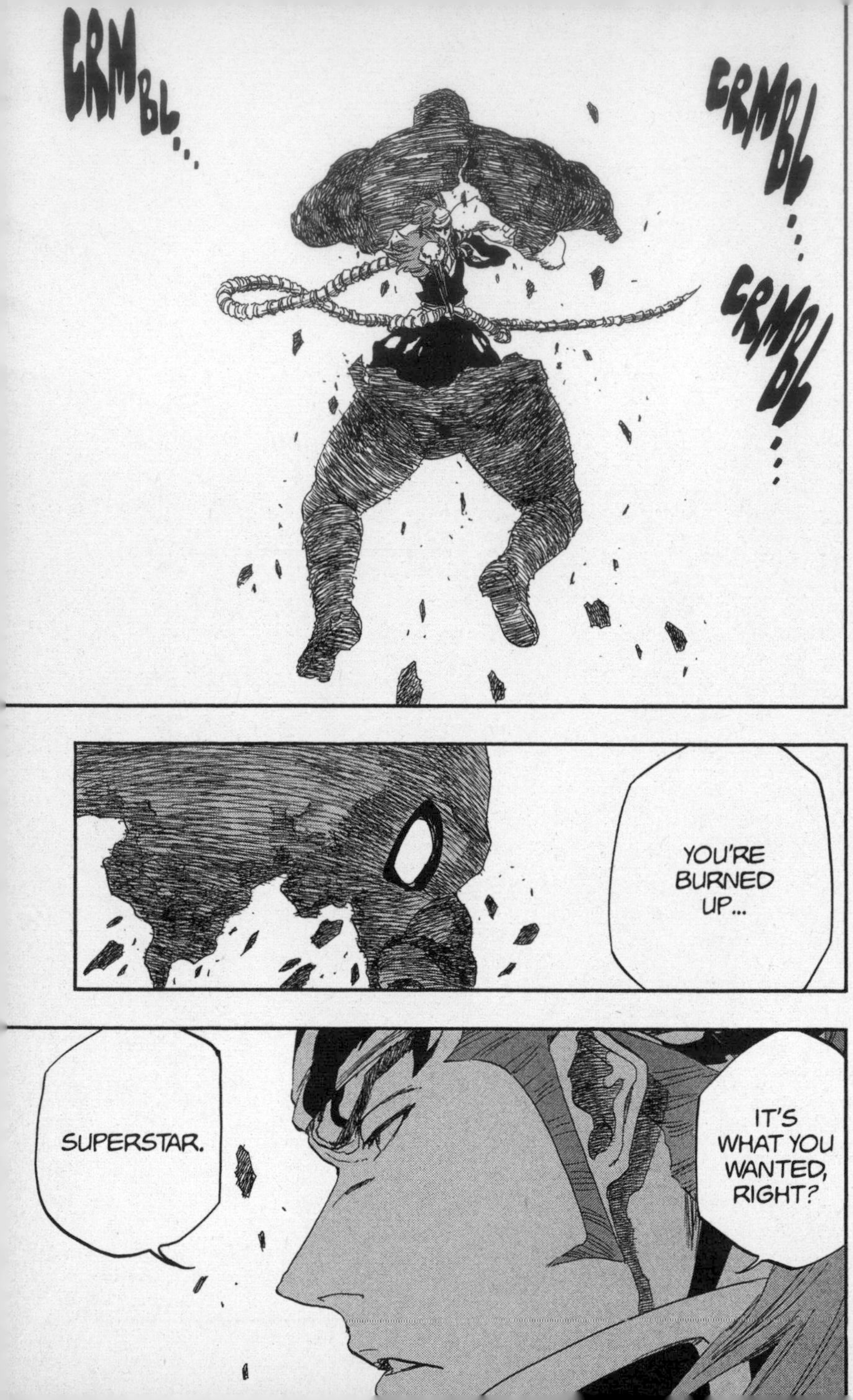
CRMBL...
CRMBL...
CRMBL...
YOU'RE BURNED UP...
IT'S WHAT YOU WANTED, RIGHT?
SUPERSTAR.

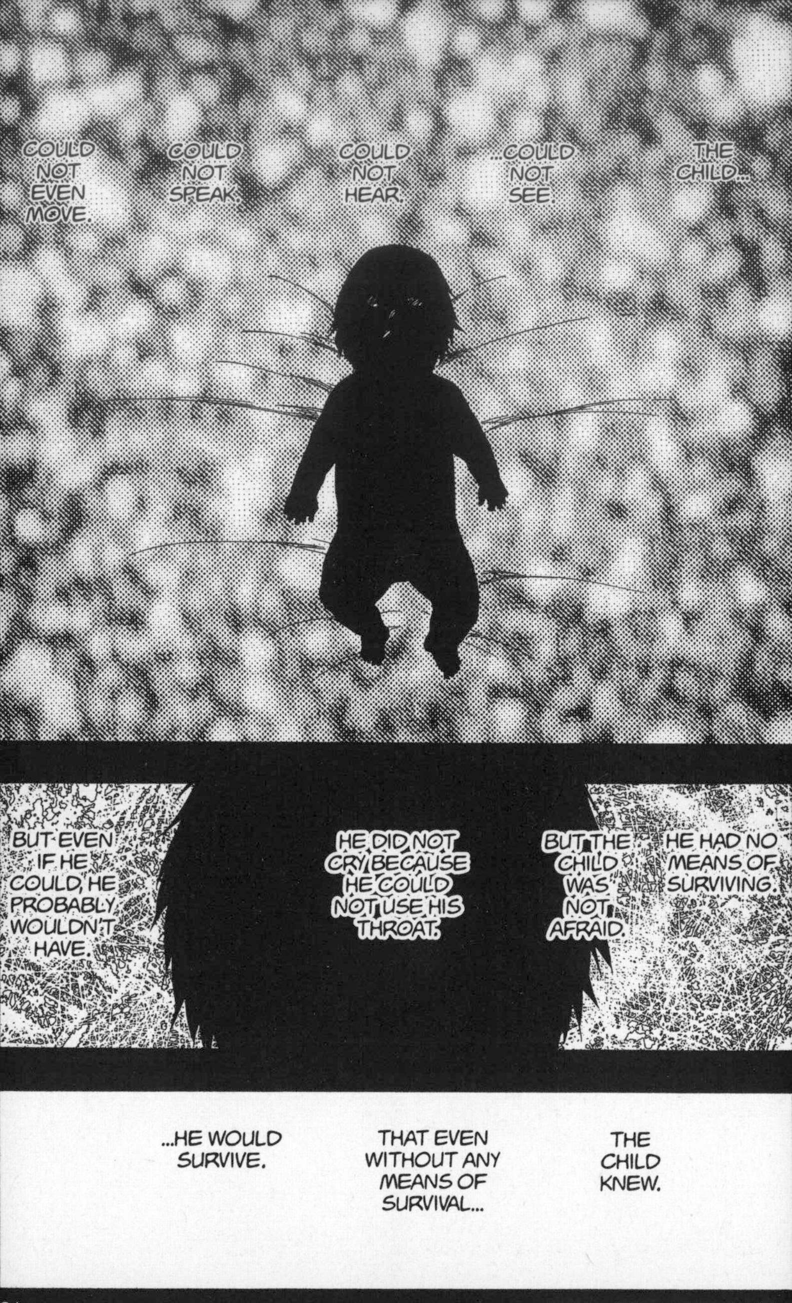
THE CHILD...
...COULD NOT SEE
COULD NOT HEAR.
COULD NOT SPEAK.
COULD NOT EVEN MOVE.
HE HAD NO MEANS OF SURVIVING.
BUT THE CHILD WAS NOT AFRAID.
HE DID NOT CRY BECAUSE HE COULD NOT USE HIS THROAT.
BUT EVEN IF HE COULD, HE PROBABLY WOULDN'T HAVE.
THE CHILD KNEW.
THAT EVEN WITHOUT ANY MEANS OF SURVIVAL...
...HE WOULD SURVIVE.

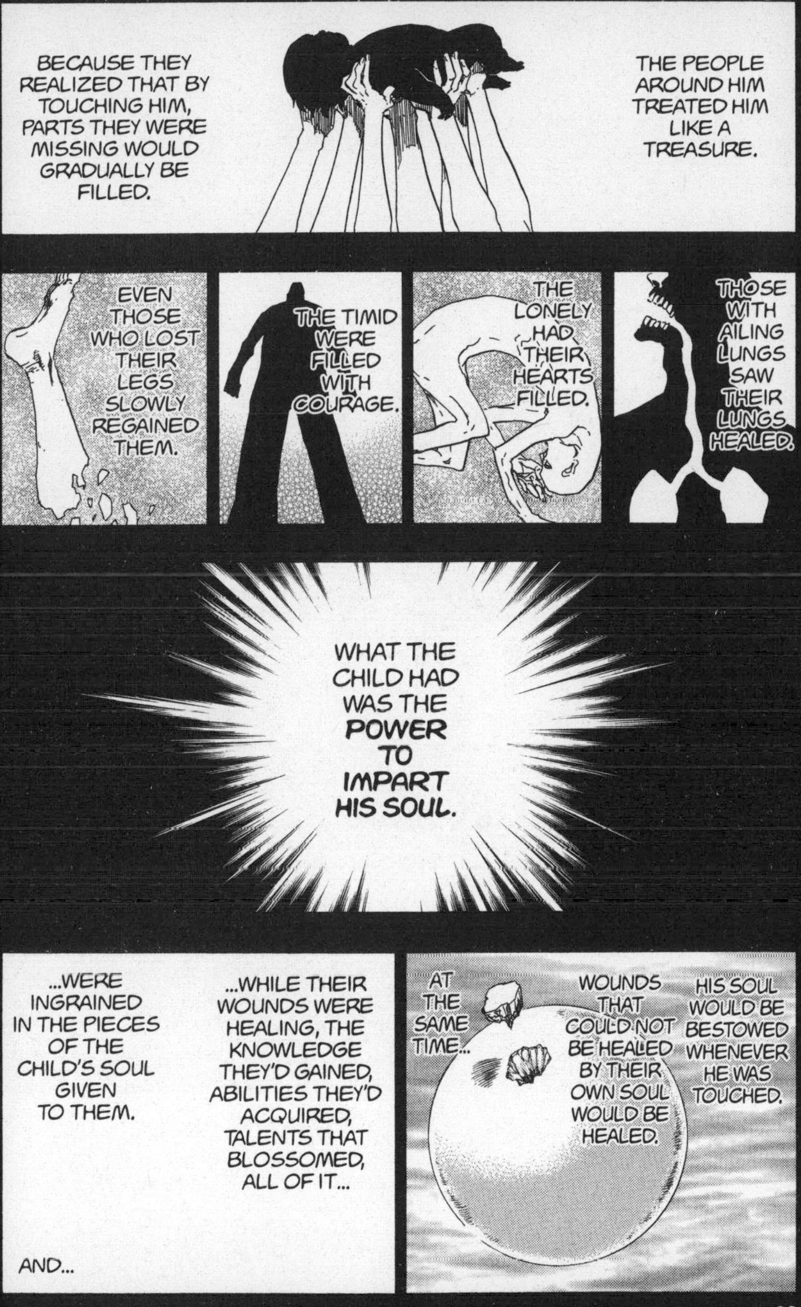
THE PEOPLE AROUND HIM TREATED HIM LIKE A TREASURE.
BECAUSE THEY REALIZED THAT BY TOUCHING HIM, PARTS THEY WERE MISSING WOULD GRADUALLY BE FILLED.
THOSE WITH AILING LUNGS SAW THEIR LUNGS HEALED.
THE LONELY HAD THEIR HEARTS FILLED.
THE TIMID WERE FILLED WITH COURAGE.
EVEN THOSE WHO LOST THEIR LEGS SLOWLY REGAINED THEM.
WHAT THE CHILD HAD WAS THE **POWER TO IMPART HIS SOUL.**
HIS SOUL WOULD BE BESTOWED WHENEVER HE WAS TOUCHED.
WOUNDS THAT COULD NOT BE HEALED BY THEIR OWN SOUL WOULD BE HEALED.
AT THE SAME TIME...
...WHILE THEIR WOUNDS WERE HEALING, THE KNOWLEDGE THEY'D GAINED, ABILITIES THEY'D ACQUIRED, TALENTS THAT BLOSSOMED, ALL OF IT...
...WERE INGRAINED IN THE PIECES OF THE CHILD'S SOUL GIVEN TO THEM.
AND...

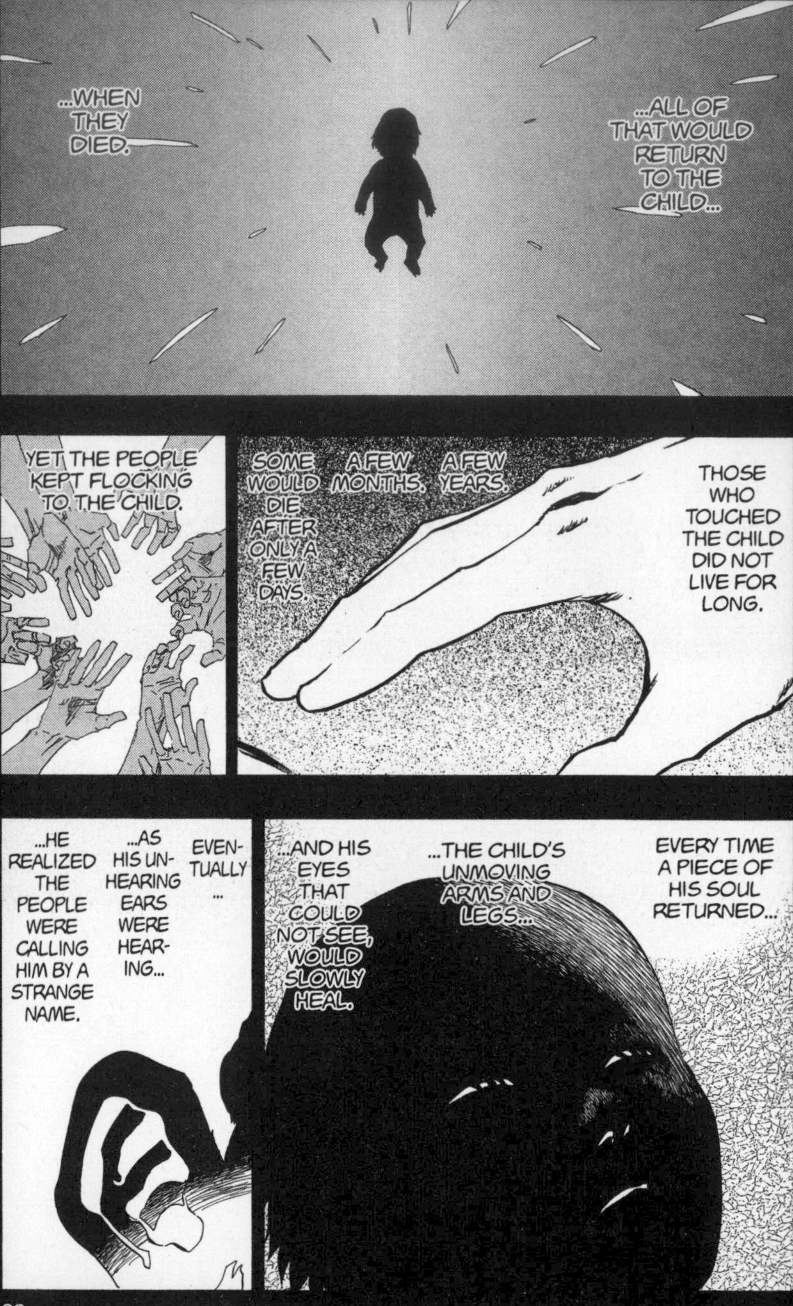

...ALL OF THAT WOULD RETURN TO THE CHILD...
...WHEN THEY DIED.
THOSE WHO TOUCHED THE CHILD DID NOT LIVE FOR LONG.
A FEW YEARS.
A FEW MONTHS.
SOME WOULD DIE AFTER ONLY A FEW DAYS.
YET THE PEOPLE KEPT FLOCKING TO THE CHILD.
EVERY TIME A PIECE OF HIS SOUL RETURNED...
...THE CHILD'S UNMOVING ARMS AND LEGS...
...AND HIS EYES THAT COULD NOT SEE, WOULD SLOWLY HEAL.
EVEN-TUALLY...
...AS HIS UN-HEARING EARS WERE HEAR-ING...
...HE REALIZED THE PEOPLE WERE CALLING HIM BY A STRANGE NAME.

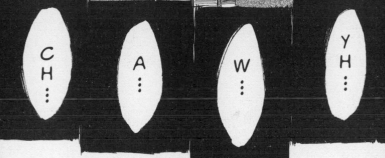

HE KNEW THAT NAME WAS THE NAME OF THE GOD THEY WORSHIPPED.
HE DECIDED TO MAKE THAT NAME HIS OWN.
YH...
W...
A...
CH...

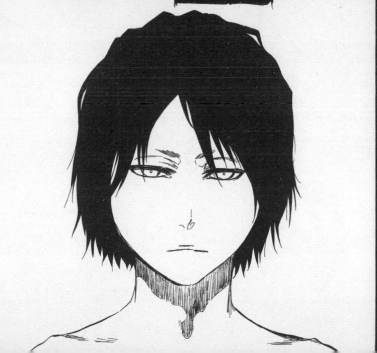

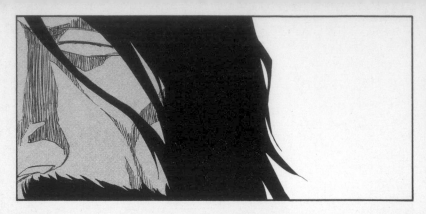

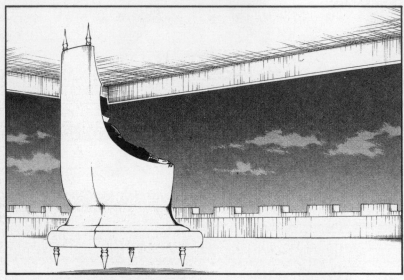

YOU DID WELL.

SO JAMES IS DEAD...

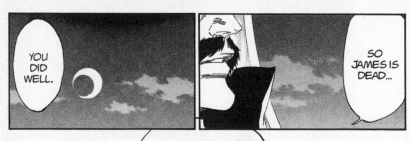

NOW RETURN.

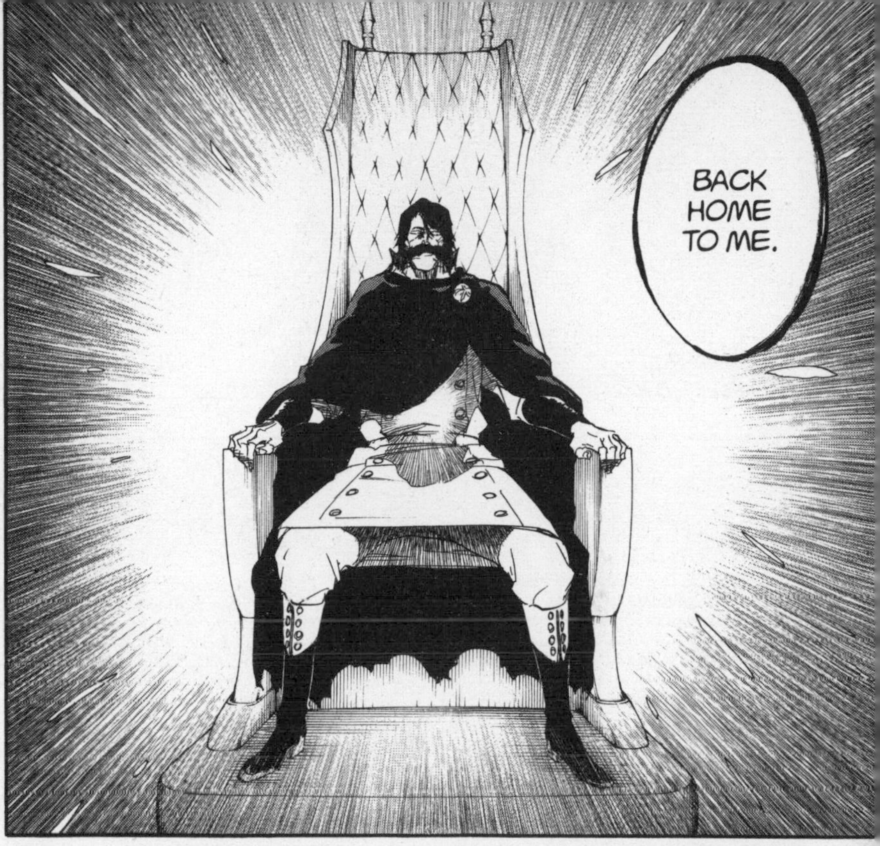
BACK HOME TO ME.
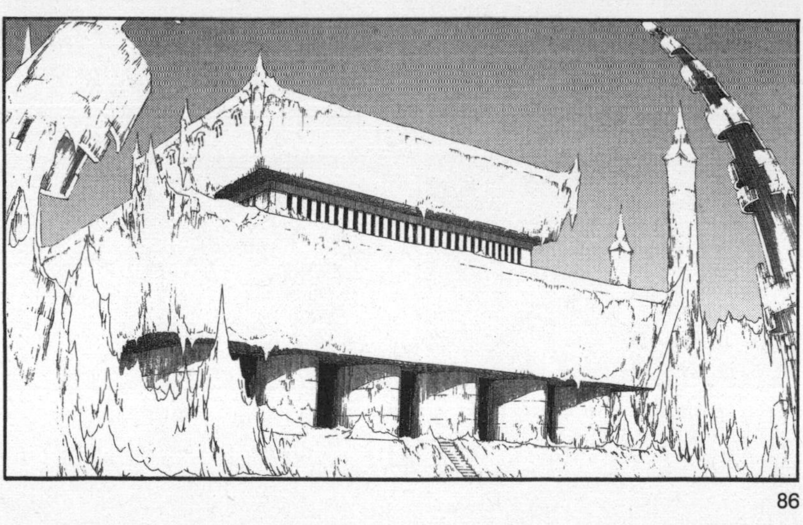

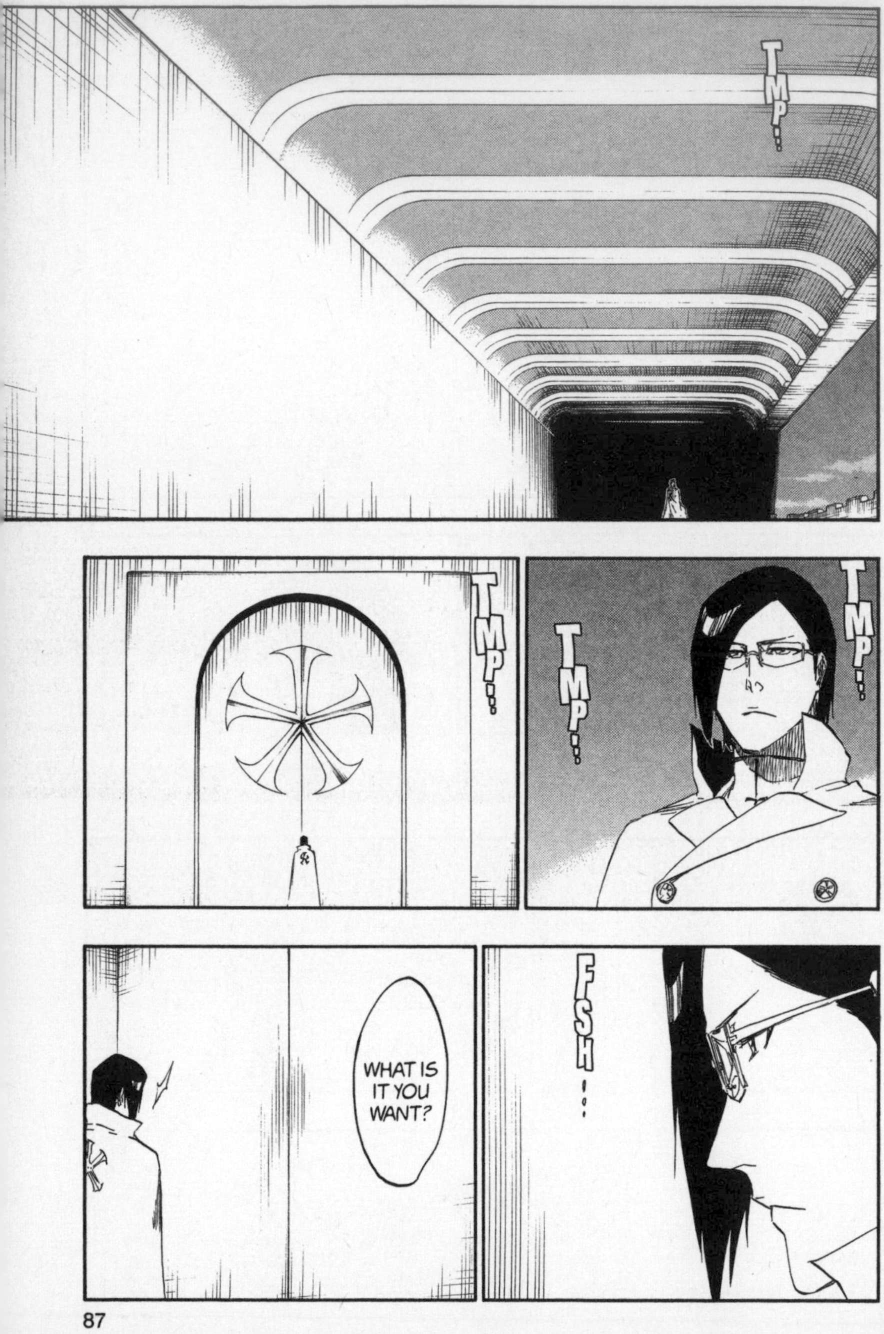
TMP..
TMP..
TMP..
TMP..
FSH..
WHAT IS IT YOU WANT?

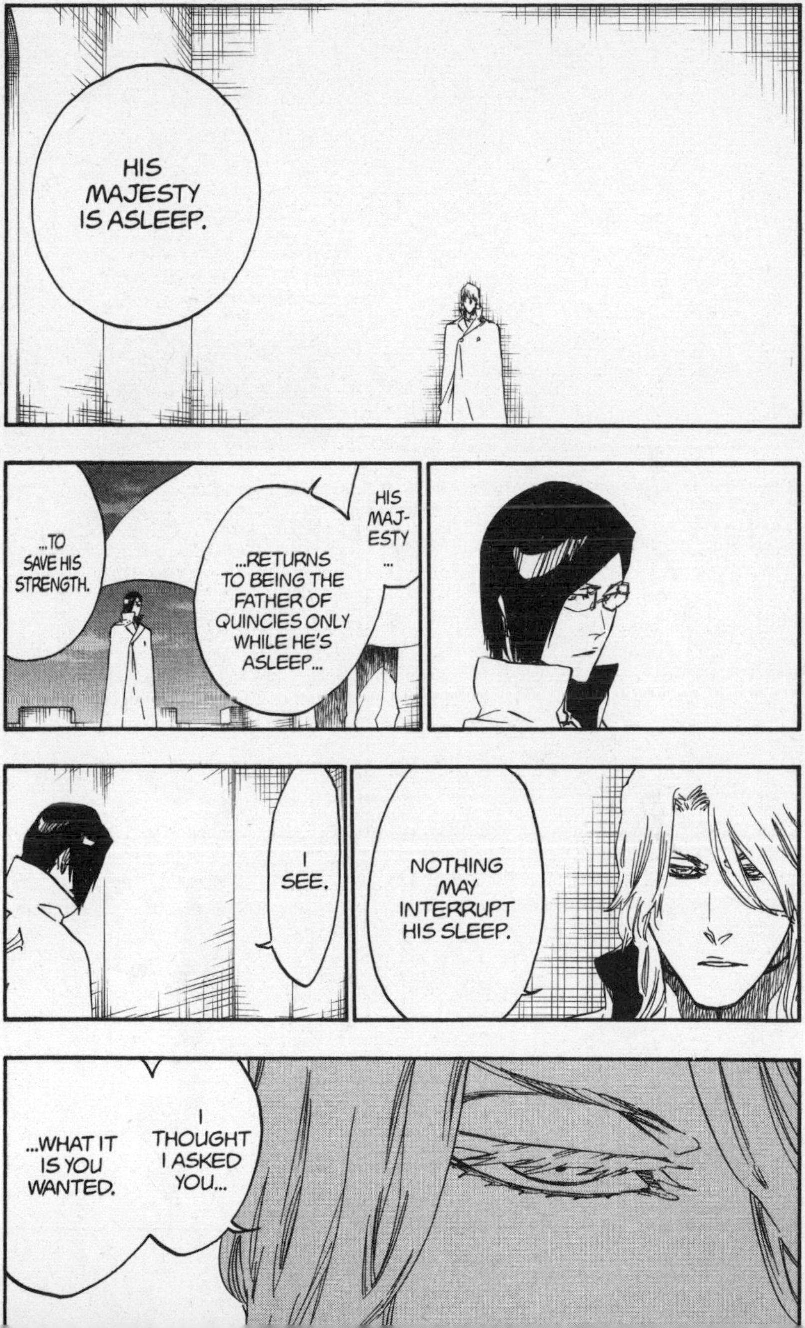
HIS MAJESTY IS ASLEEP.
HIS MAJ-ESTY ...
...RETURNS TO BEING THE FATHER OF QUINCIES ONLY WHILE HE'S ASLEEP...
...TO SAVE HIS STRENGTH.
NOTHING MAY INTERRUPT HIS SLEEP.
I SEE.
I THOUGHT I ASKED YOU...
...WHAT IT IS YOU WANTED.

READ THIS WAY

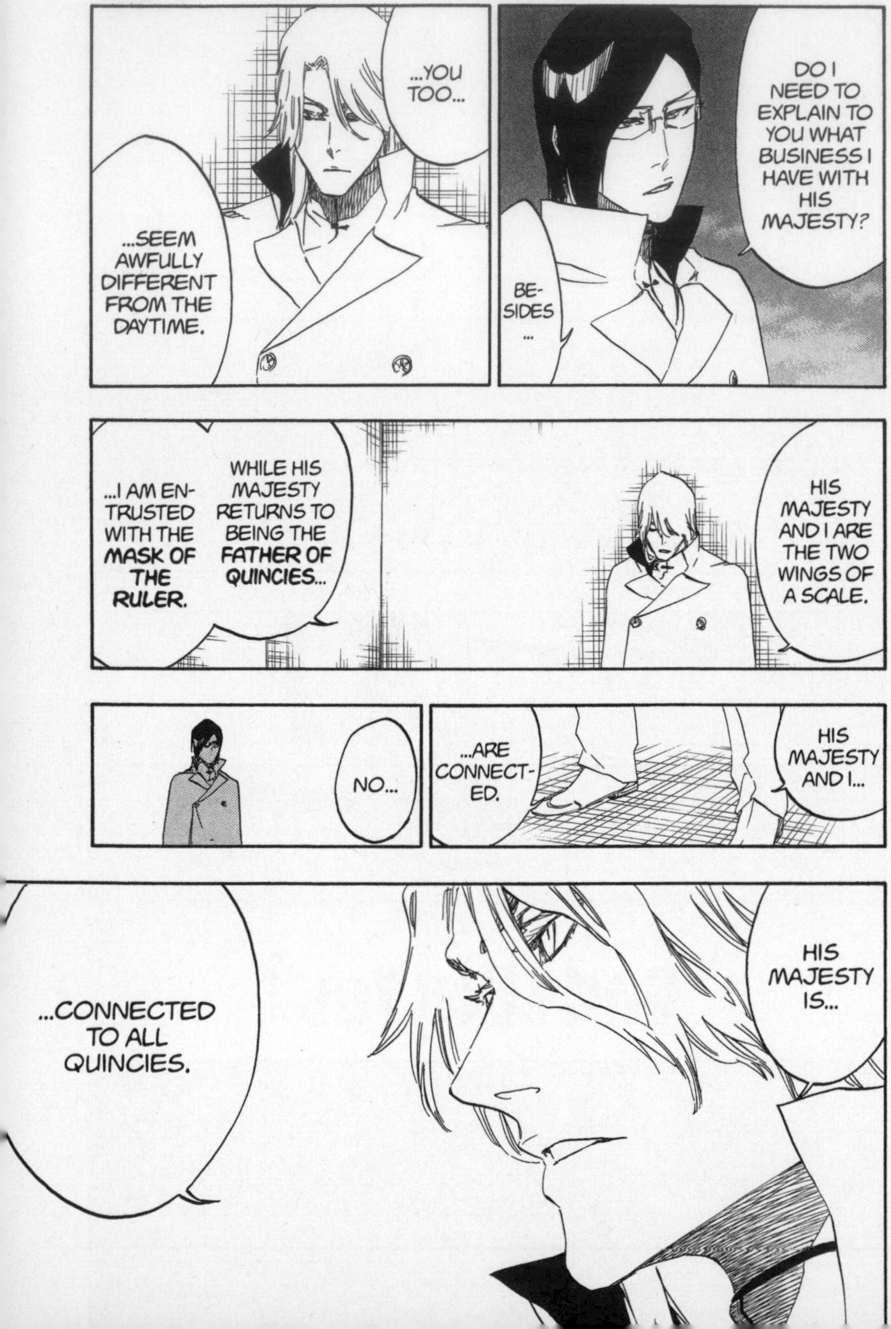
DO I NEED TO EXPLAIN TO YOU WHAT BUSINESS I HAVE WITH HIS MAJESTY?
BE-SIDES...
...YOU TOO...
...SEEM AWFULLY DIFFERENT FROM THE DAYTIME.
HIS MAJESTY AND I ARE THE TWO WINGS OF A SCALE.
WHILE HIS MAJESTY RETURNS TO BEING THE **FATHER OF QUINCIES**...
...I AM EN-TRUSTED WITH THE **MASK OF THE RULER.**
HIS MAJESTY AND I...
...ARE CONNECT-ED.
NO...
HIS MAJESTY IS...
...CONNECTED TO ALL QUINCIES.

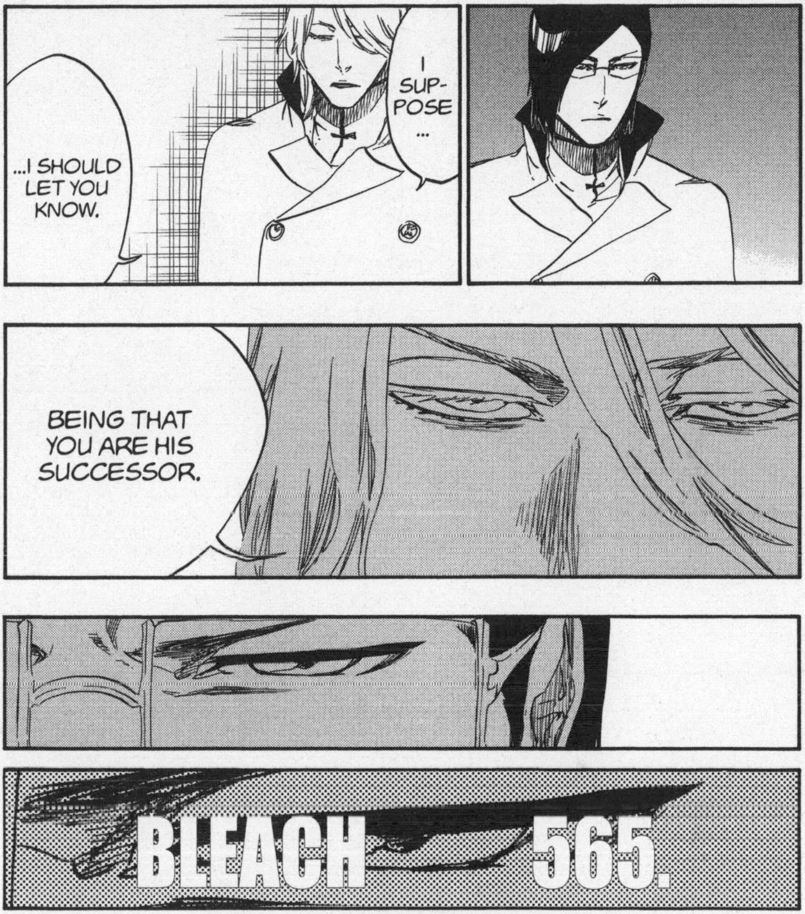
I SUP-POSE ...
...I SHOULD LET YOU KNOW.
BEING THAT YOU ARE HIS SUCCESSOR.
BLEACH 565.

God Like You

READ THIS WAY

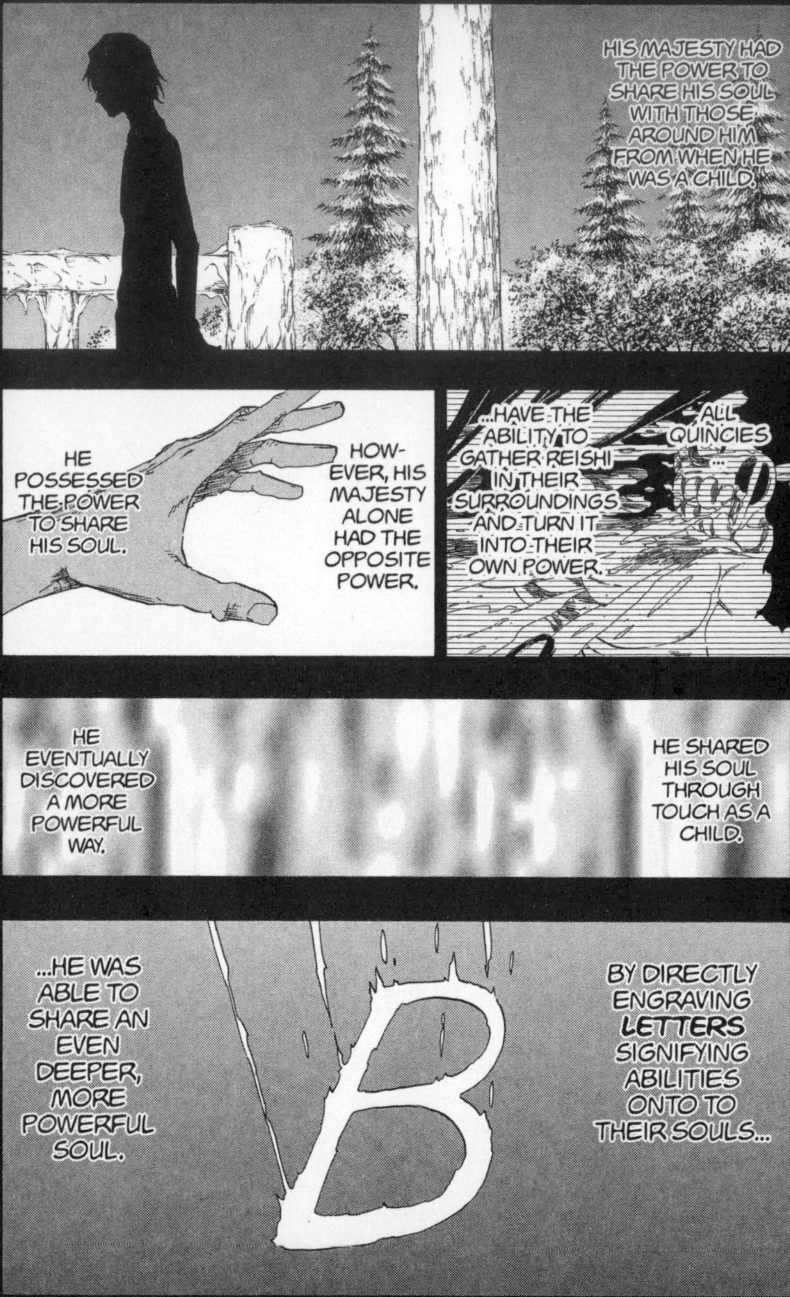
HIS MAJESTY HAD THE POWER TO SHARE HIS SOUL WITH THOSE AROUND HIM FROM WHEN HE WAS A CHILD.
ALL QUINCIES...
...HAVE THE ABILITY TO GATHER REISHI IN THEIR SURROUNDINGS AND TURN IT INTO THEIR OWN POWER.
HOW-EVER, HIS MAJESTY ALONE HAD THE OPPOSITE POWER.
HE POSSESSED THE POWER TO SHARE HIS SOUL.
HE SHARED HIS SOUL THROUGH TOUCH AS A CHILD.
HE EVENTUALLY DISCOVERED A MORE POWERFUL WAY.
BY DIRECTLY ENGRAVING **LETTERS** SIGNIFYING ABILITIES ONTO TO THEIR SOULS...
...HE WAS ABLE TO SHARE AN EVEN DEEPER, MORE POWERFUL SOUL.

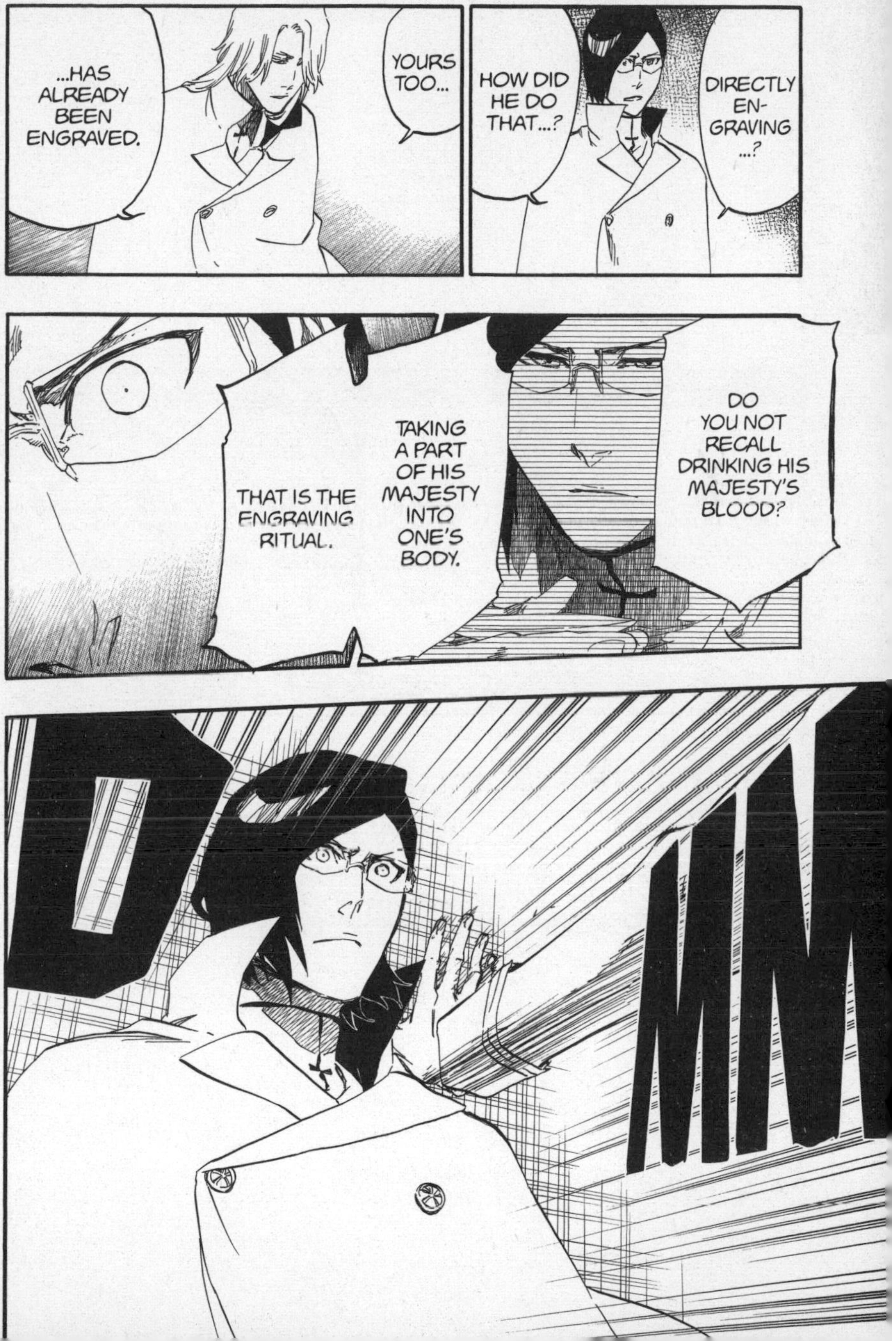
DIRECTLY EN-GRAVING ...?
HOW DID HE DO THAT...?
YOURS TOO...
...HAS ALREADY BEEN ENGRAVED.
DO YOU NOT RECALL DRINKING HIS MAJESTY'S BLOOD?
TAKING A PART OF HIS MAJESTY INTO ONE'S BODY.
THAT IS THE ENGRAVING RITUAL.
!

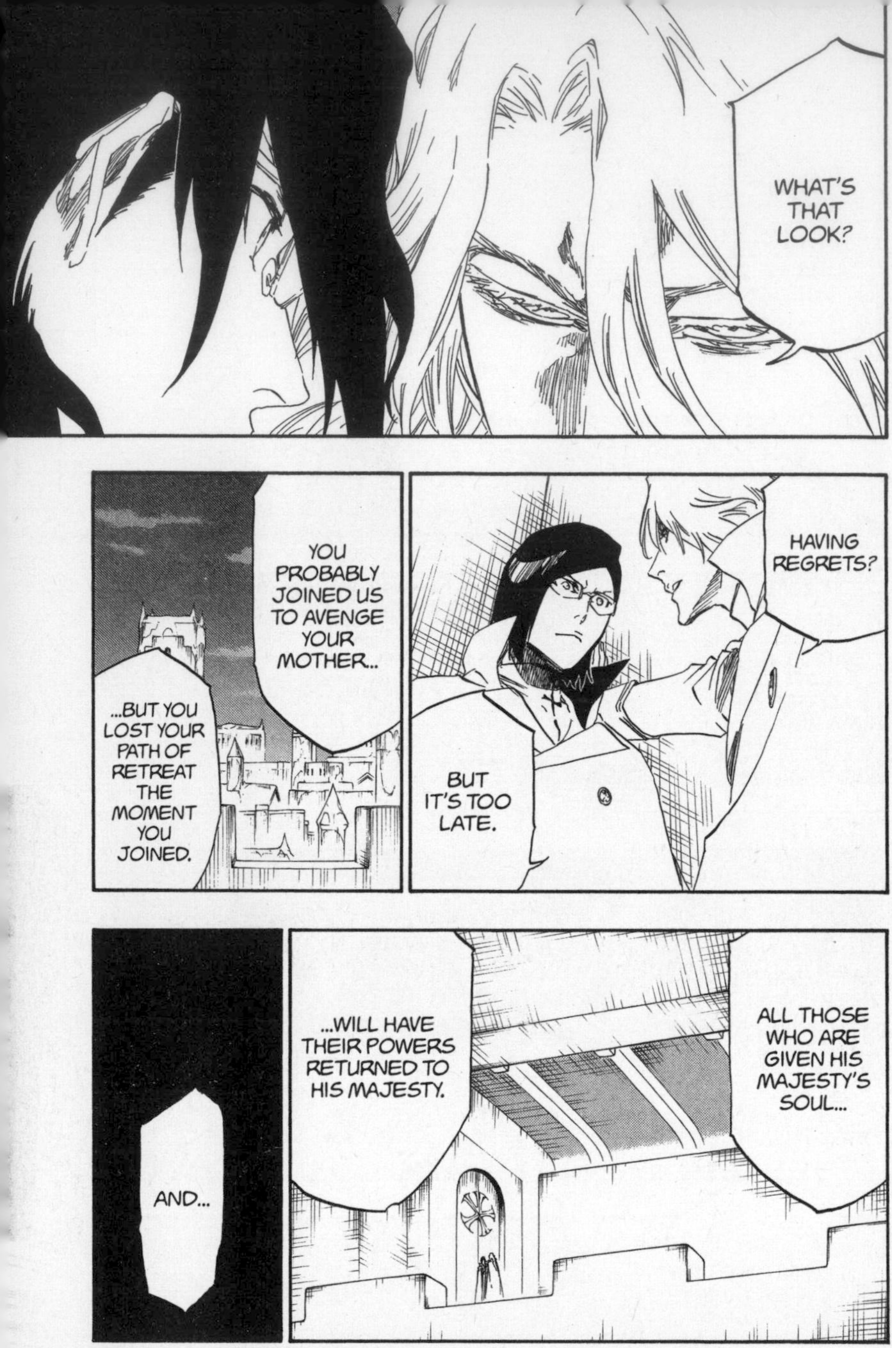
WHAT'S THAT LOOK?
HAVING REGRETS?
BUT IT'S TOO LATE.
YOU PROBABLY JOINED US TO AVENGE YOUR MOTHER...
...BUT YOU LOST YOUR PATH OF RETREAT THE MOMENT YOU JOINED.
ALL THOSE WHO ARE GIVEN HIS MAJESTY'S SOUL...
...WILL HAVE THEIR POWERS RETURNED TO HIS MAJESTY.
AND...

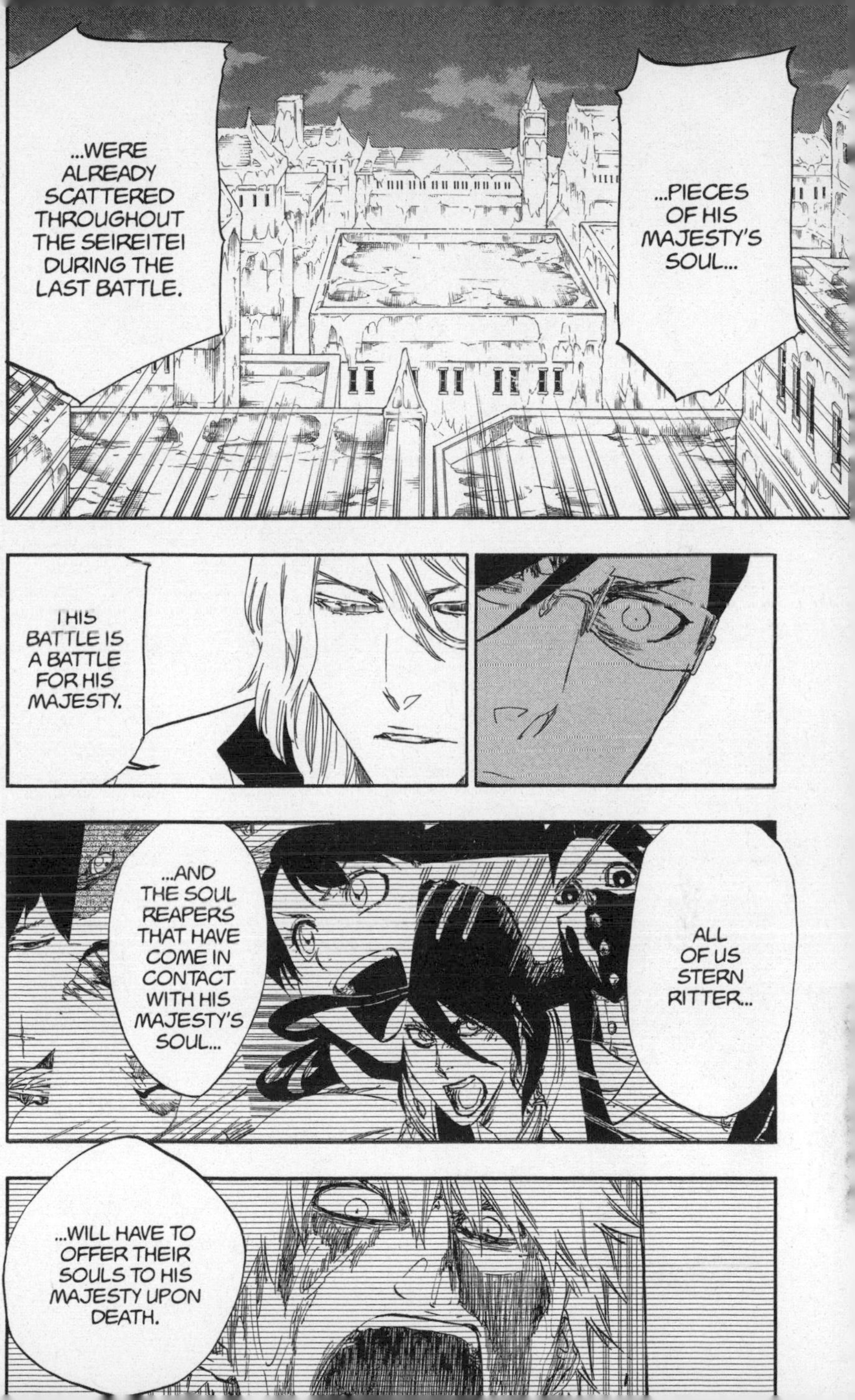
...PIECES OF HIS MAJESTY'S SOUL...
...WERE ALREADY SCATTERED THROUGHOUT THE SEIREITEI DURING THE LAST BATTLE.
THIS BATTLE IS A BATTLE FOR HIS MAJESTY.
ALL OF US STERN RITTER...
...AND THE SOUL REAPERS THAT HAVE COME IN CONTACT WITH HIS MAJESTY'S SOUL...
...WILL HAVE TO OFFER THEIR SOULS TO HIS MAJESTY UPON DEATH.

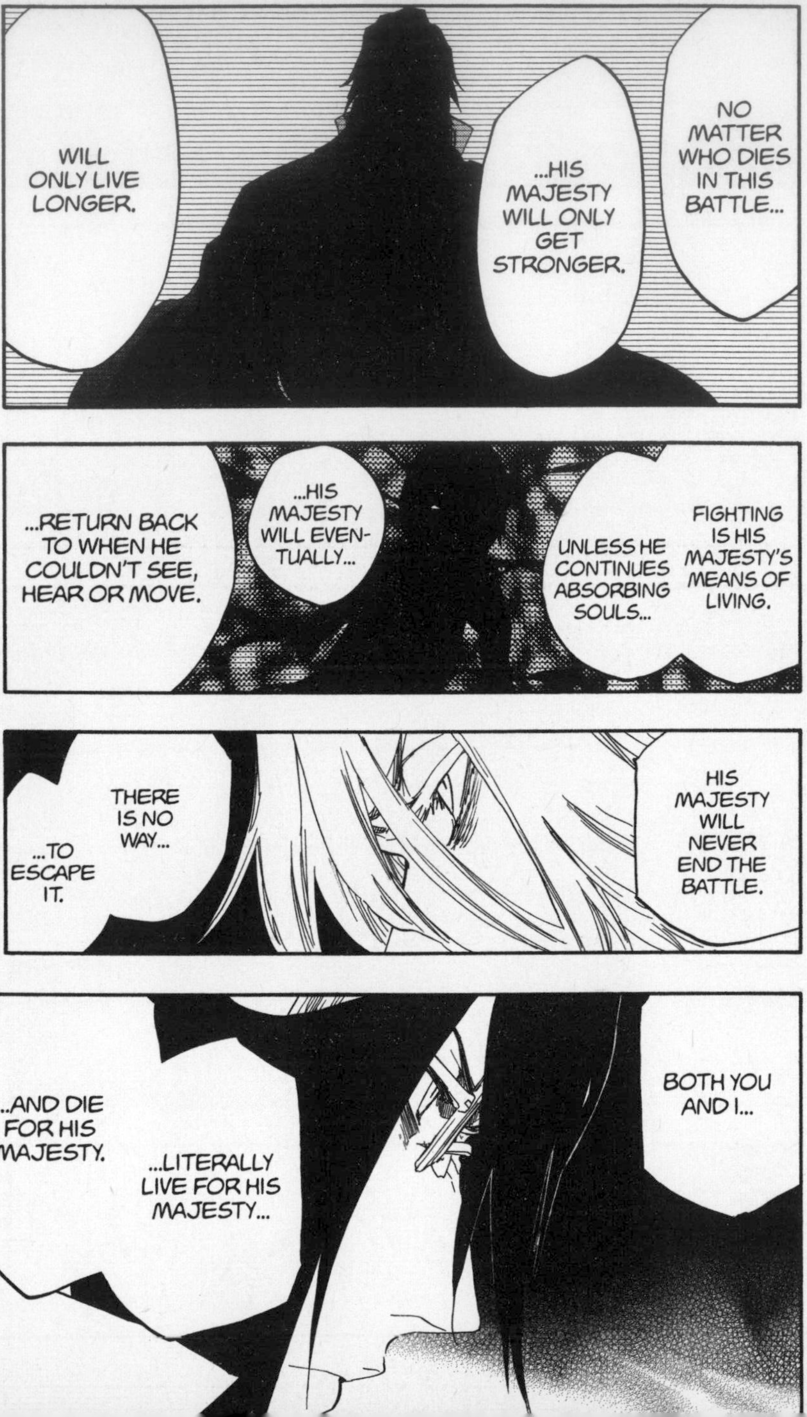
NO MATTER WHO DIES IN THIS BATTLE...
...HIS MAJESTY WILL ONLY GET STRONGER.
WILL ONLY LIVE LONGER.
FIGHTING IS HIS MAJESTY'S MEANS OF LIVING.
UNLESS HE CONTINUES ABSORBING SOULS...
...HIS MAJESTY WILL EVEN-TUALLY...
...RETURN BACK TO WHEN HE COULDN'T SEE, HEAR OR MOVE.
HIS MAJESTY WILL NEVER END THE BATTLE.
THERE IS NO WAY...
...TO ESCAPE IT.
BOTH YOU AND I...
...LITERALLY LIVE FOR HIS MAJESTY...
...AND DIE FOR HIS MAJESTY.

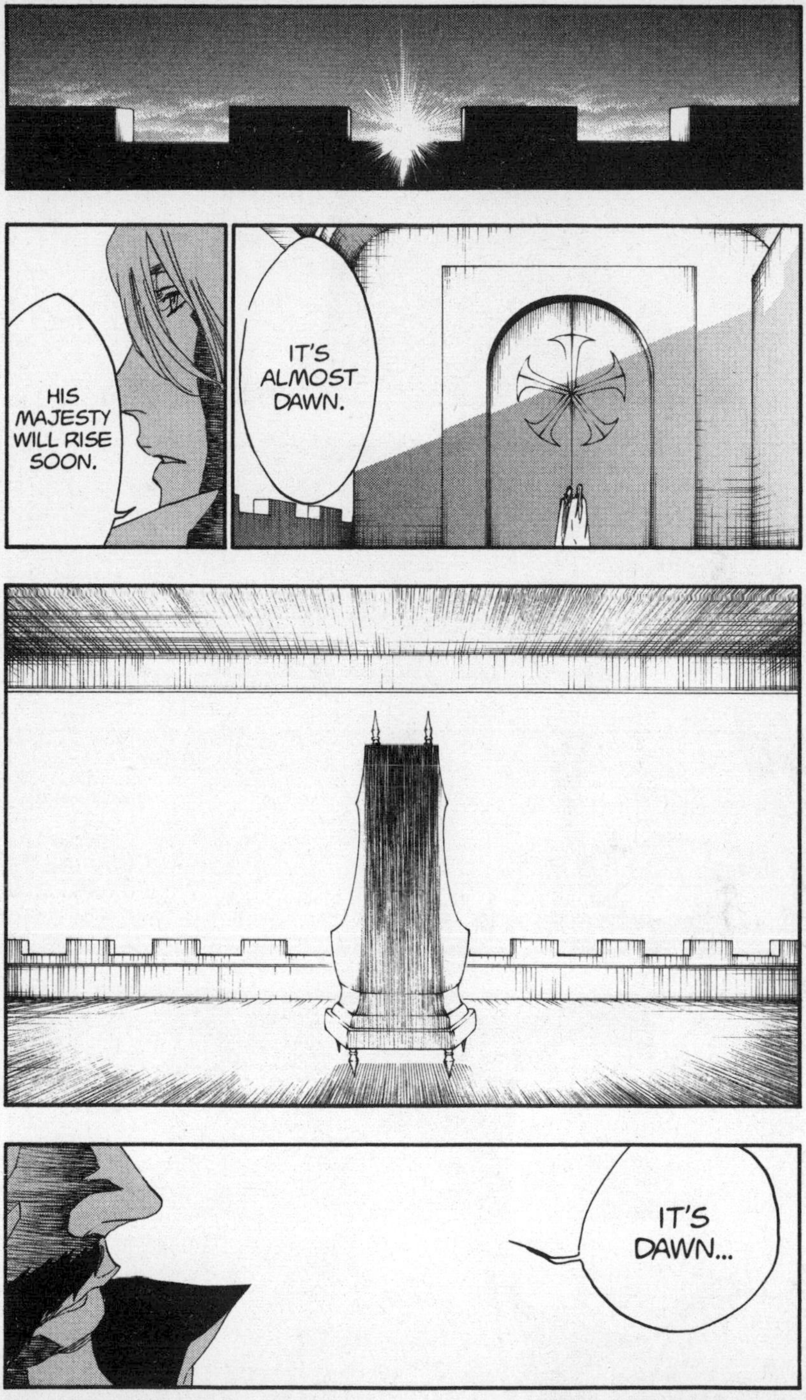
IT'S ALMOST DAWN.
HIS MAJESTY WILL RISE SOON.
IT'S DAWN...

READ THIS WAY

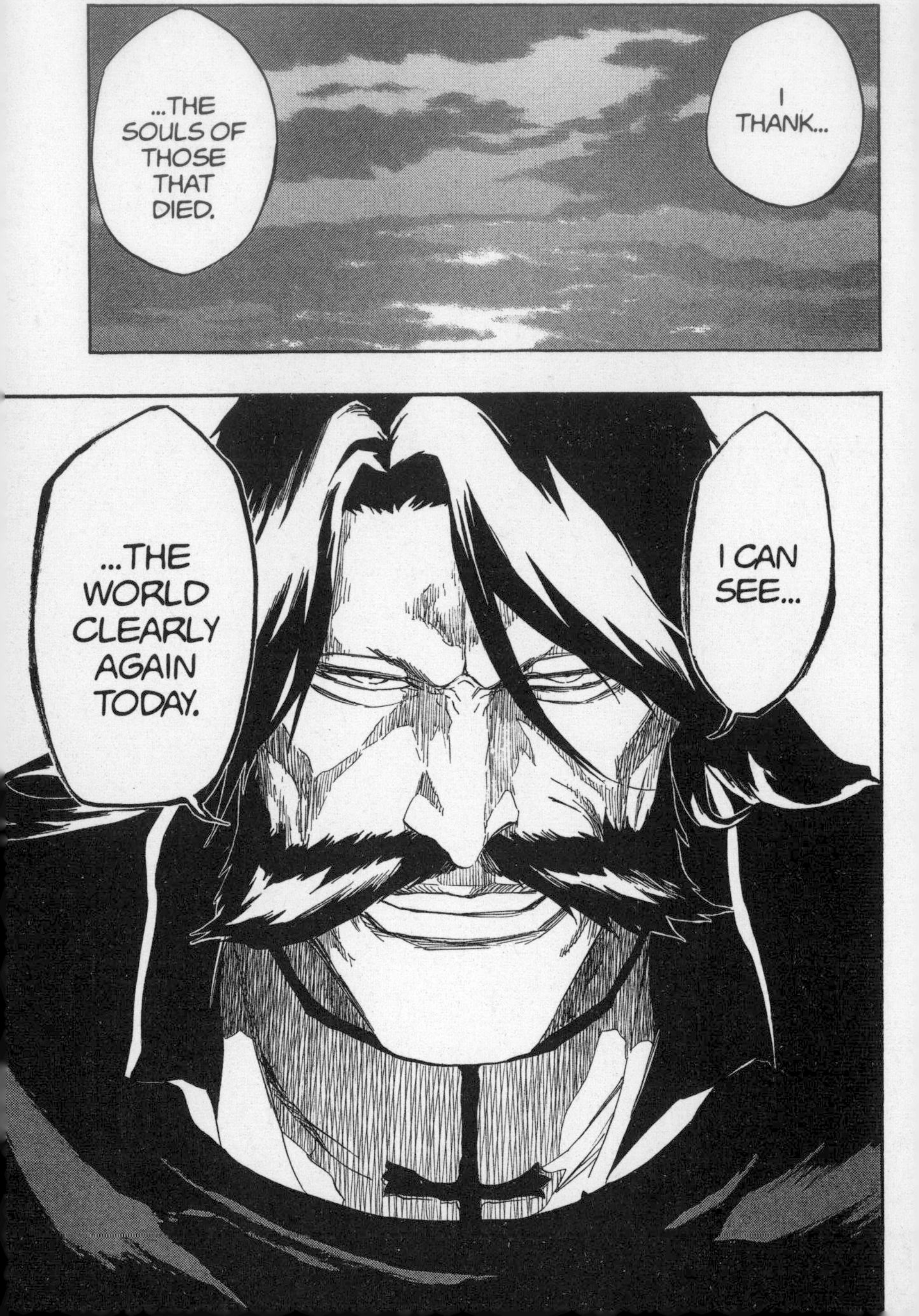
I THANK...
...THE SOULS OF THOSE THAT DIED.
I CAN SEE...
...THE WORLD CLEARLY AGAIN TODAY.

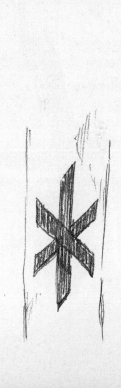

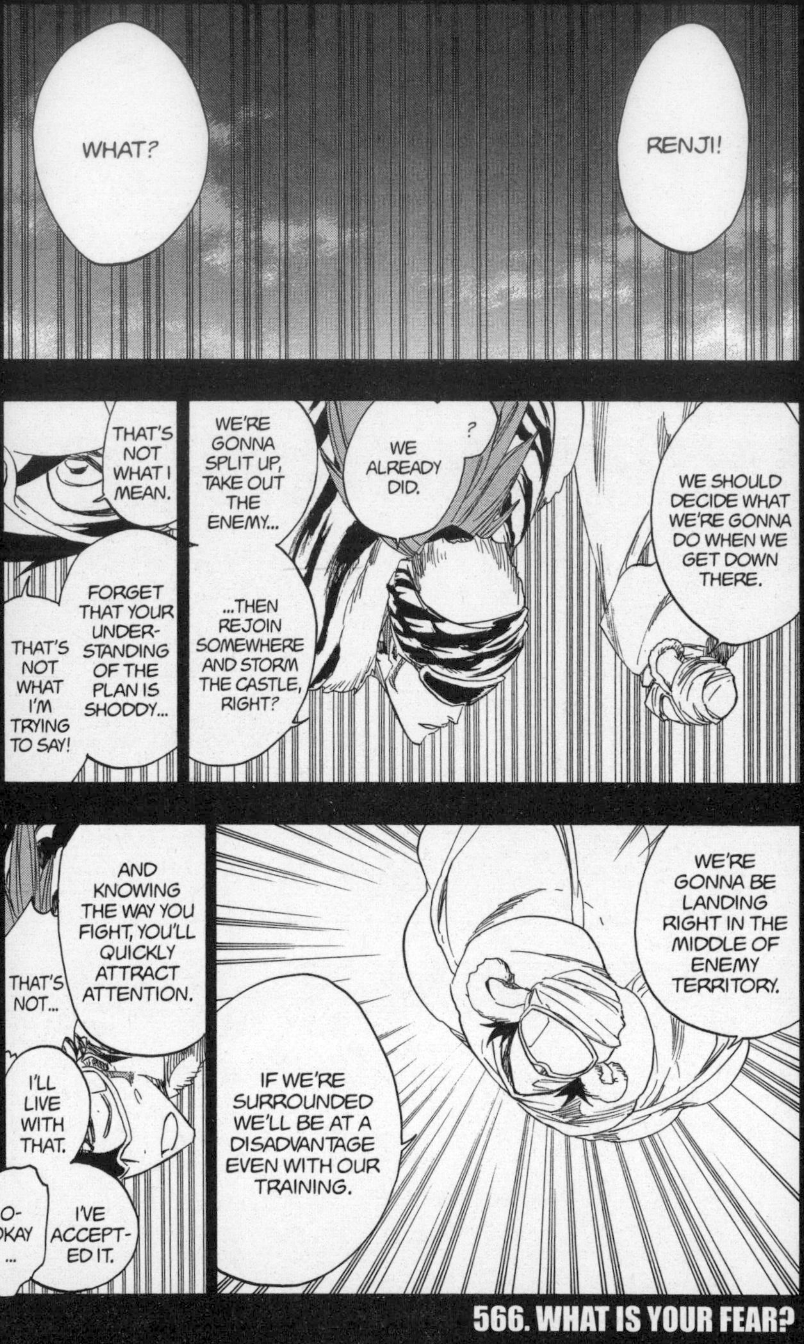
RENJI!
WHAT?
WE SHOULD DECIDE WHAT WE'RE GONNA DO WHEN WE GET DOWN THERE.
?
WE ALREADY DID.
WE'RE GONNA SPLIT UP, TAKE OUT THE ENEMY...
...THEN REJOIN SOMEWHERE AND STORM THE CASTLE, RIGHT?
THAT'S NOT WHAT I MEAN.
FORGET THAT YOUR UNDER-STANDING OF THE PLAN IS SHODDY...
THAT'S NOT WHAT I'M TRYING TO SAY!
WE'RE GONNA BE LANDING RIGHT IN THE MIDDLE OF ENEMY TERRITORY.
IF WE'RE SURROUNDED WE'LL BE AT A DISADVANTAGE EVEN WITH OUR TRAINING.
AND KNOWING THE WAY YOU FIGHT, YOU'LL QUICKLY ATTRACT ATTENTION.
THAT'S NOT...
I'LL LIVE WITH THAT.
I'VE ACCEPT-ED IT.
O-OKAY...

566. WHAT IS YOUR FEAR?

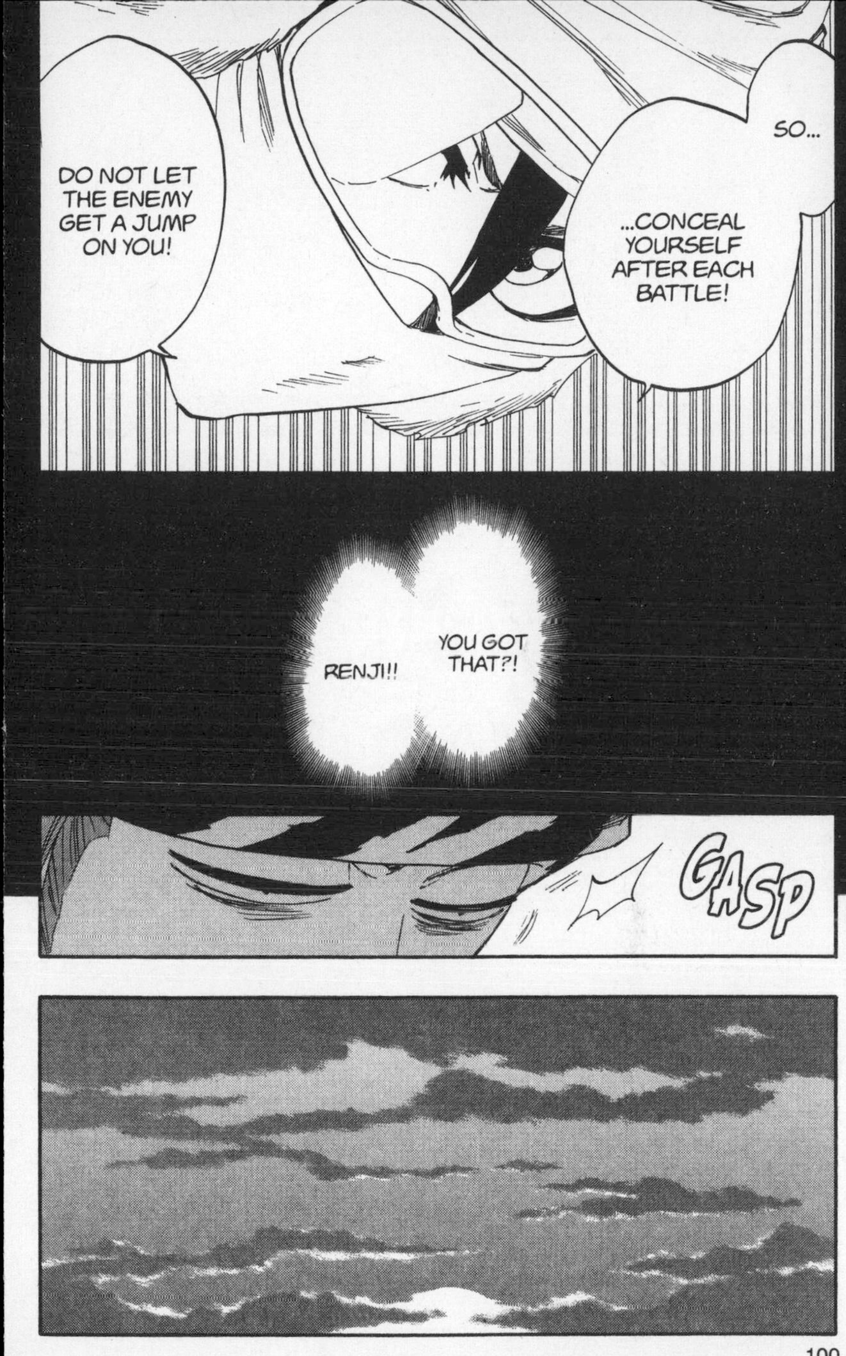
SO...
...CONCEAL YOURSELF AFTER EACH BATTLE!
DO NOT LET THE ENEMY GET A JUMP ON YOU!
YOU GOT THAT?!
RENJI!!
GASP

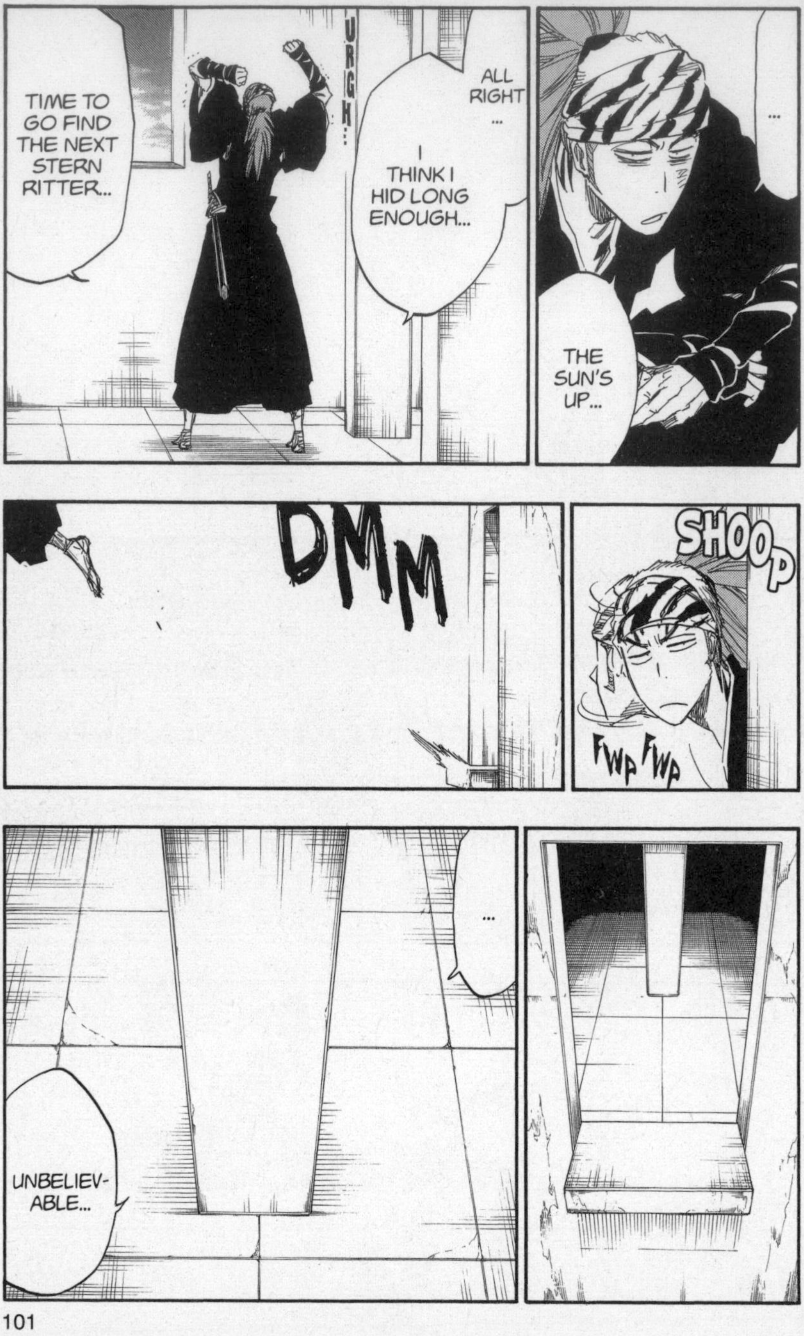
...
THE SUN'S UP...
URGH...
ALL RIGHT...
I THINK I HID LONG ENOUGH...
TIME TO GO FIND THE NEXT STERN RITTER...
SHOOP
FWP FWP
DMM
...
UNBELIEV-ABLE...

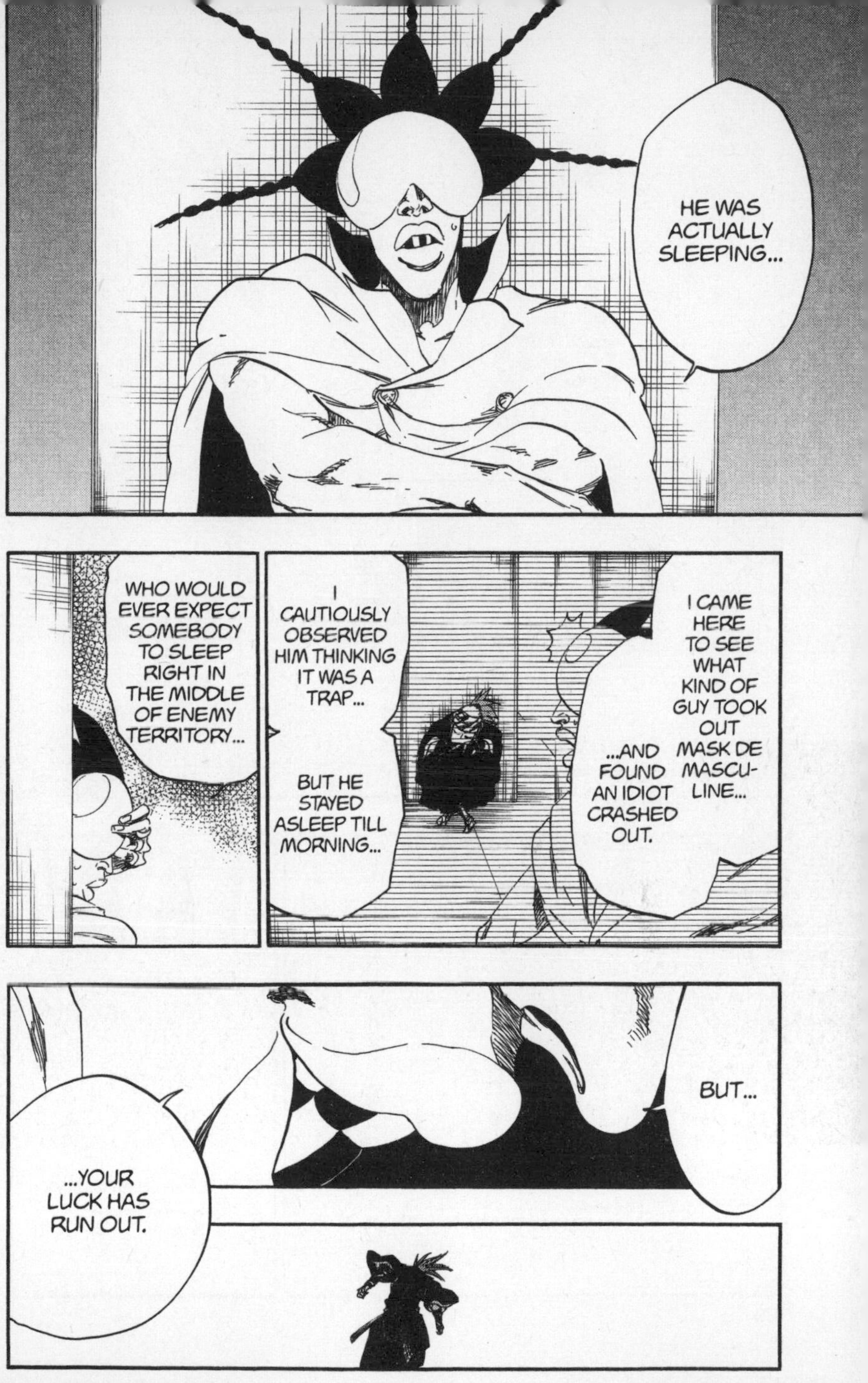
HE WAS ACTUALLY SLEEPING...
I CAME HERE TO SEE WHAT KIND OF GUY TOOK OUT MASK DE MASCU-LINE...
...AND FOUND AN IDIOT CRASHED OUT.
I CAUTIOUSLY OBSERVED HIM THINKING IT WAS A TRAP...
BUT HE STAYED ASLEEP TILL MORNING...
WHO WOULD EVER EXPECT SOMEBODY TO SLEEP RIGHT IN THE MIDDLE OF ENEMY TERRITORY...
BUT...
...YOUR LUCK HAS RUN OUT.

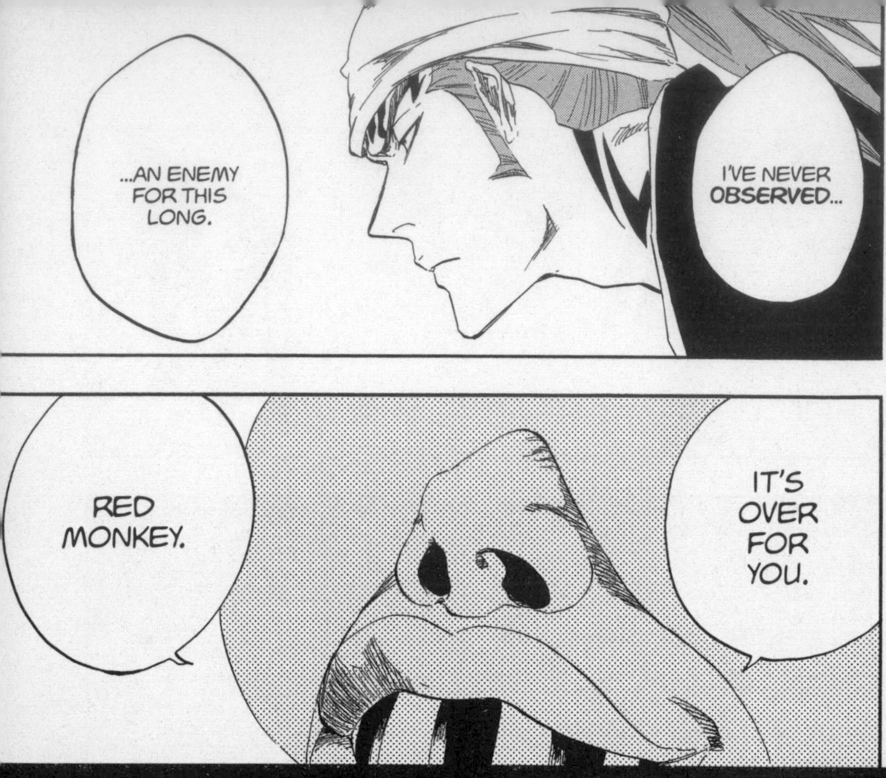
I'VE NEVER OBSERVED...
...AN ENEMY FOR THIS LONG.
IT'S OVER FOR YOU.
RED MONKEY.

BLEACH 566.

What is Your Fear?

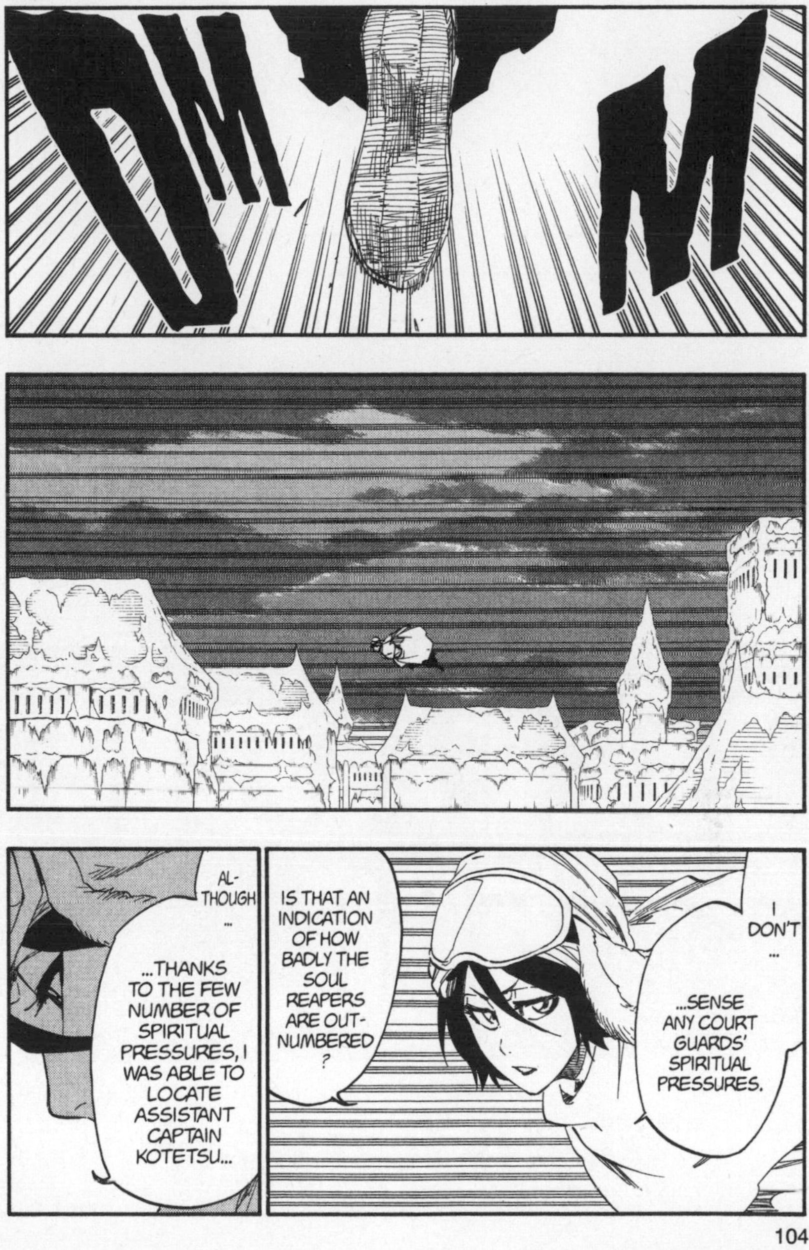
DMM
I DON'T...
...SENSE ANY COURT GUARDS' SPIRITUAL PRESSURES.
IS THAT AN INDICATION OF HOW BADLY THE SOUL REAPERS ARE OUT-NUMBERED?
AL-THOUGH...
...THANKS TO THE FEW NUMBER OF SPIRITUAL PRESSURES, I WAS ABLE TO LOCATE ASSISTANT CAPTAIN KOTETSU...

READ THIS WAY

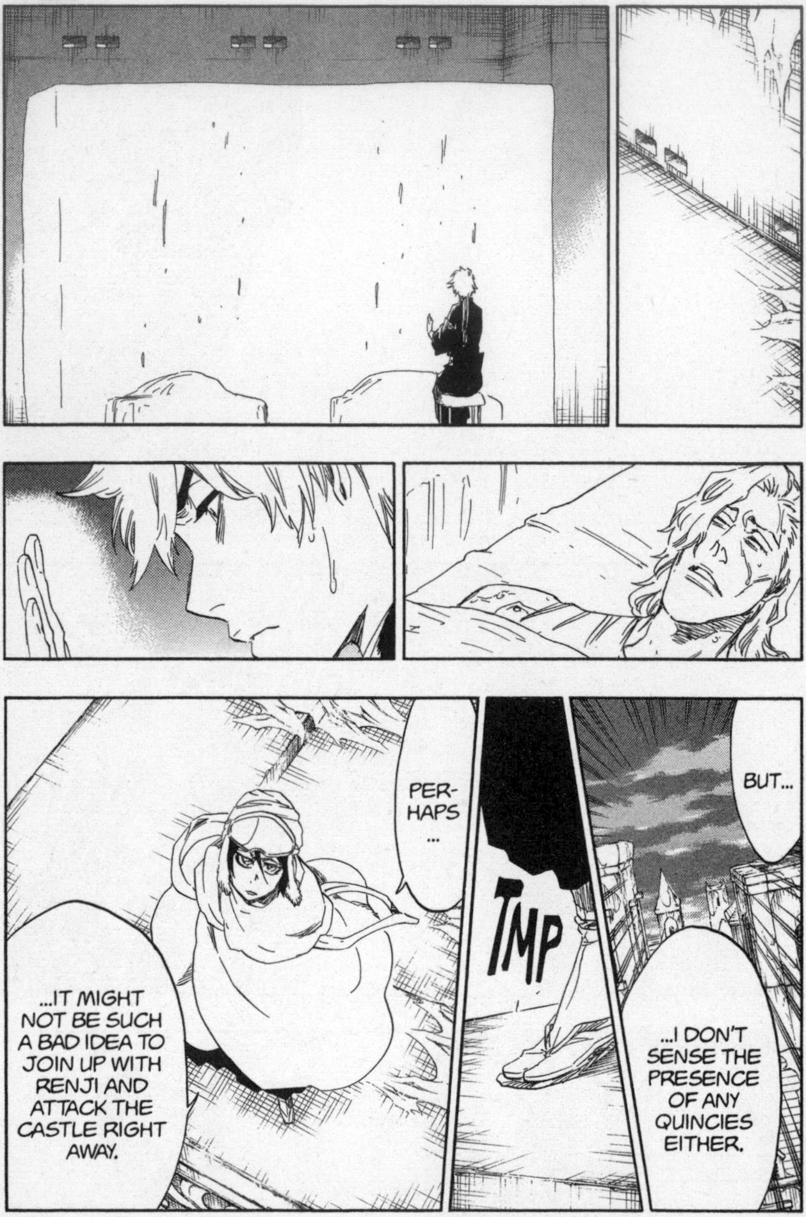
BUT...
...I DON'T SENSE THE PRESENCE OF ANY QUINCIES EITHER.
TMP
PER-HAPS...
...IT MIGHT NOT BE SUCH A BAD IDEA TO JOIN UP WITH RENJI AND ATTACK THE CASTLE RIGHT AWAY.

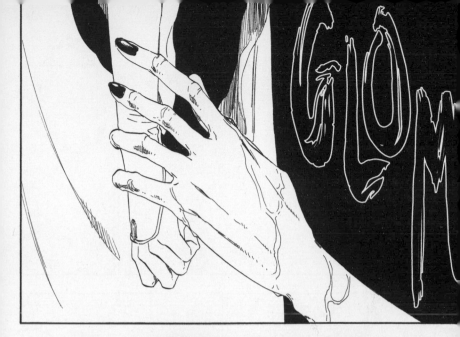

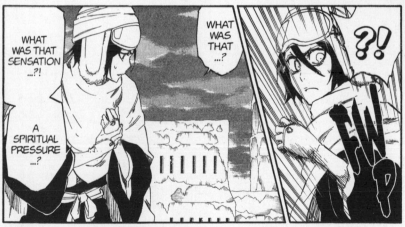

WHAT
WAS THAT
SENSATION
...?!

A
SPIRITUAL
PRESSURE
...?

WHAT
WAS
THAT
...?

?!

FWP

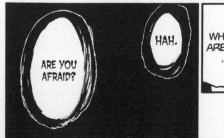

ARE YOU
AFRAID?

HAH.

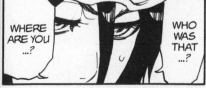

WHERE
ARE YOU
...?

WHO
WAS
THAT
...?

106

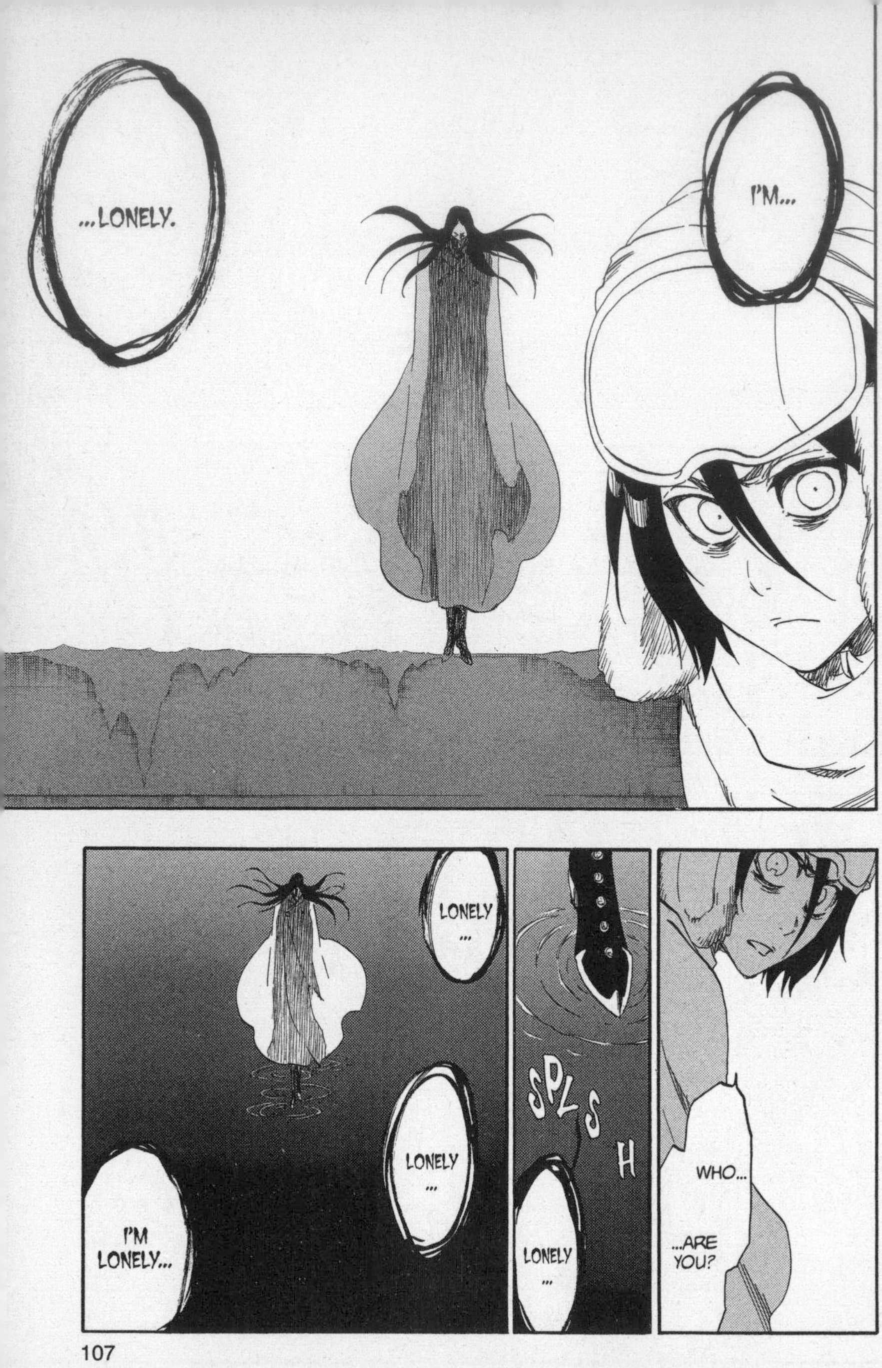
I'M...
...LONELY.
WHO...
...ARE YOU?
SPLSH
LONELY...
LONELY...
LONELY...
I'M LONELY...

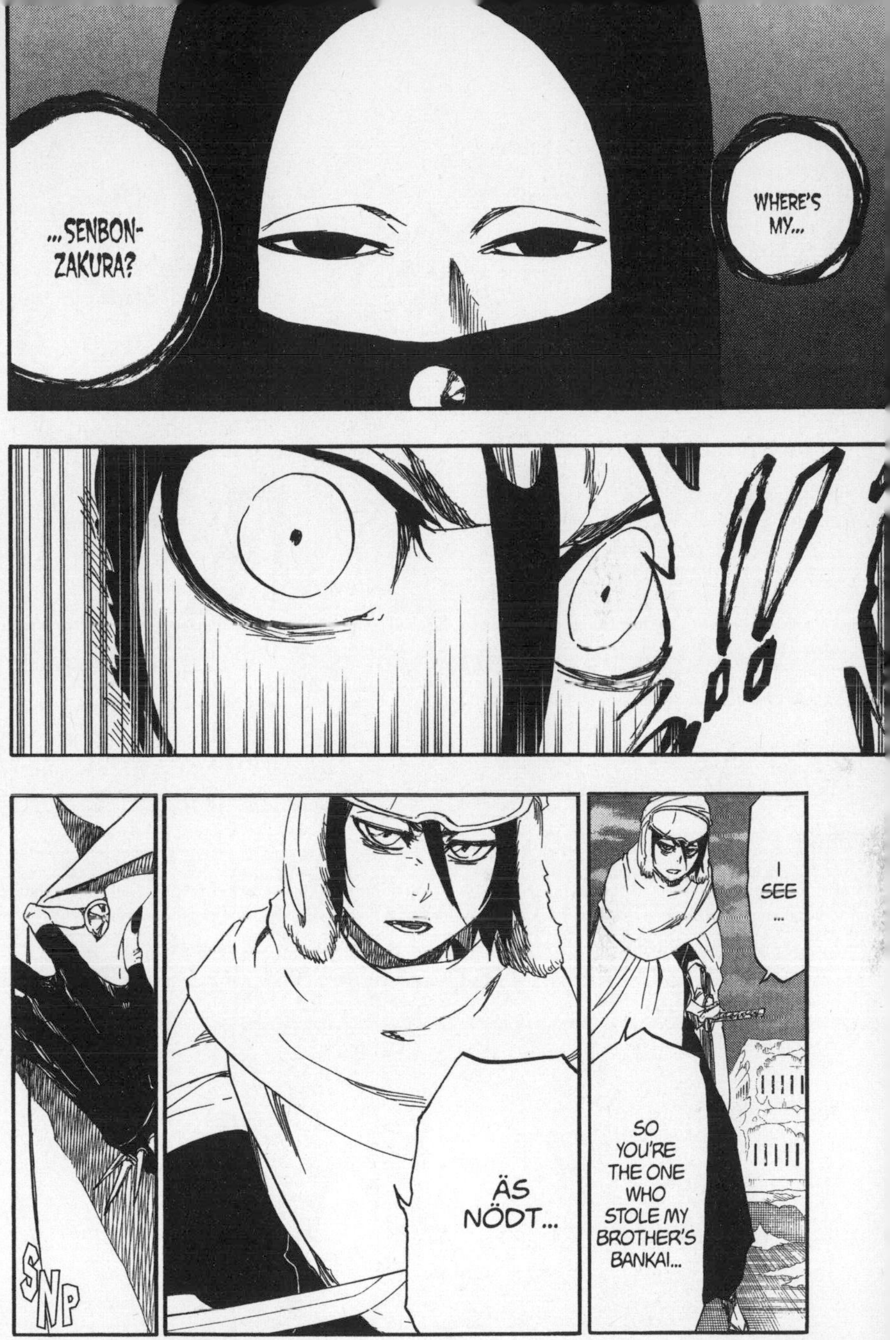
WHERE'S MY...
...SENBON-ZAKURA?
I SEE...
SO YOU'RE THE ONE WHO STOLE MY BROTHER'S BANKAI...
ÄS NÖDT...
SNP

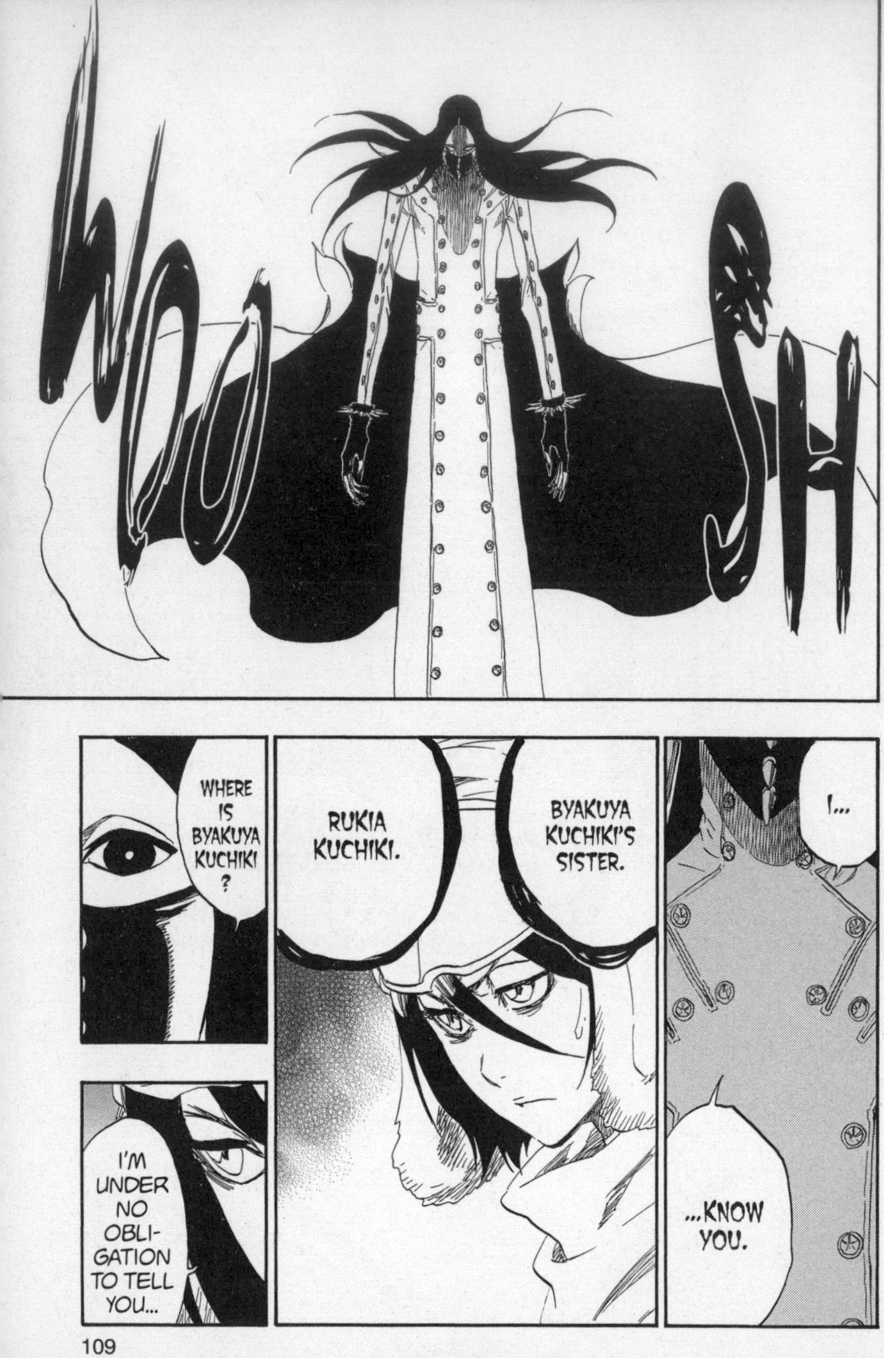
WHOOSH
I...
...KNOW YOU.
BYAKUYA KUCHIKI'S SISTER.
RUKIA KUCHIKI.
WHERE IS BYAKUYA KUCHIKI?
I'M UNDER NO OBLIGATION TO TELL YOU...

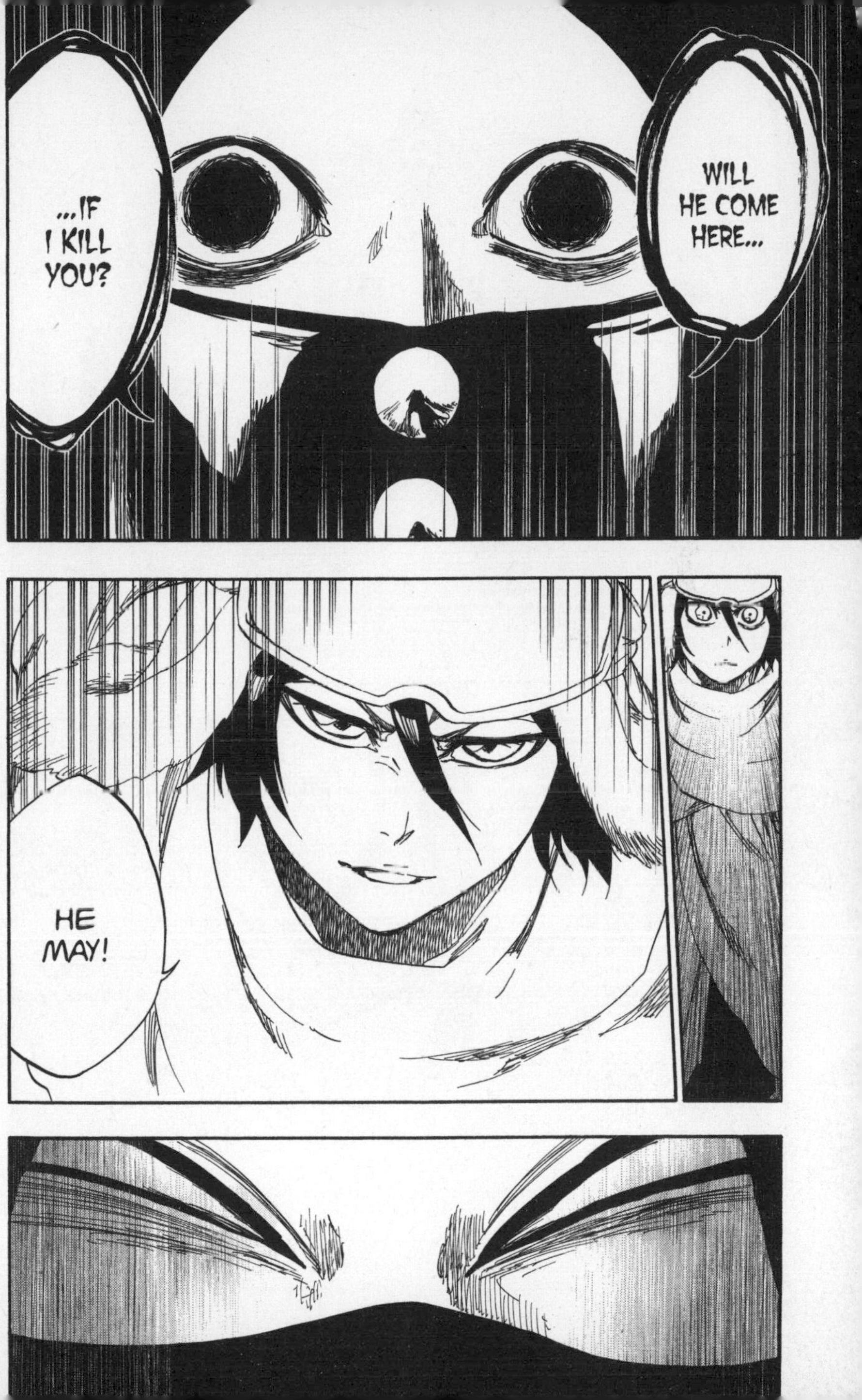
WILL HE COME HERE...
...IF I KILL YOU?
HE MAY!

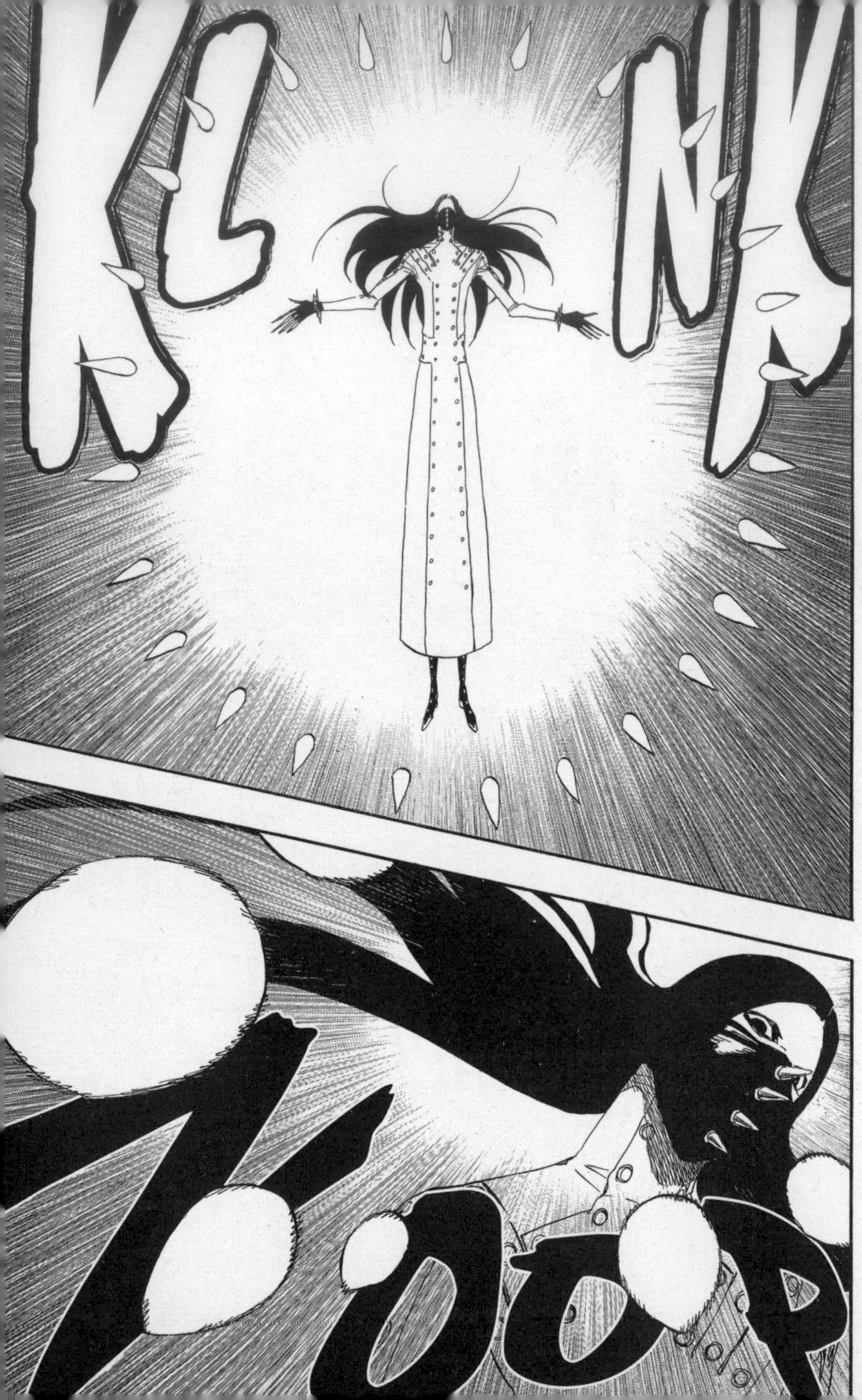
KLNK

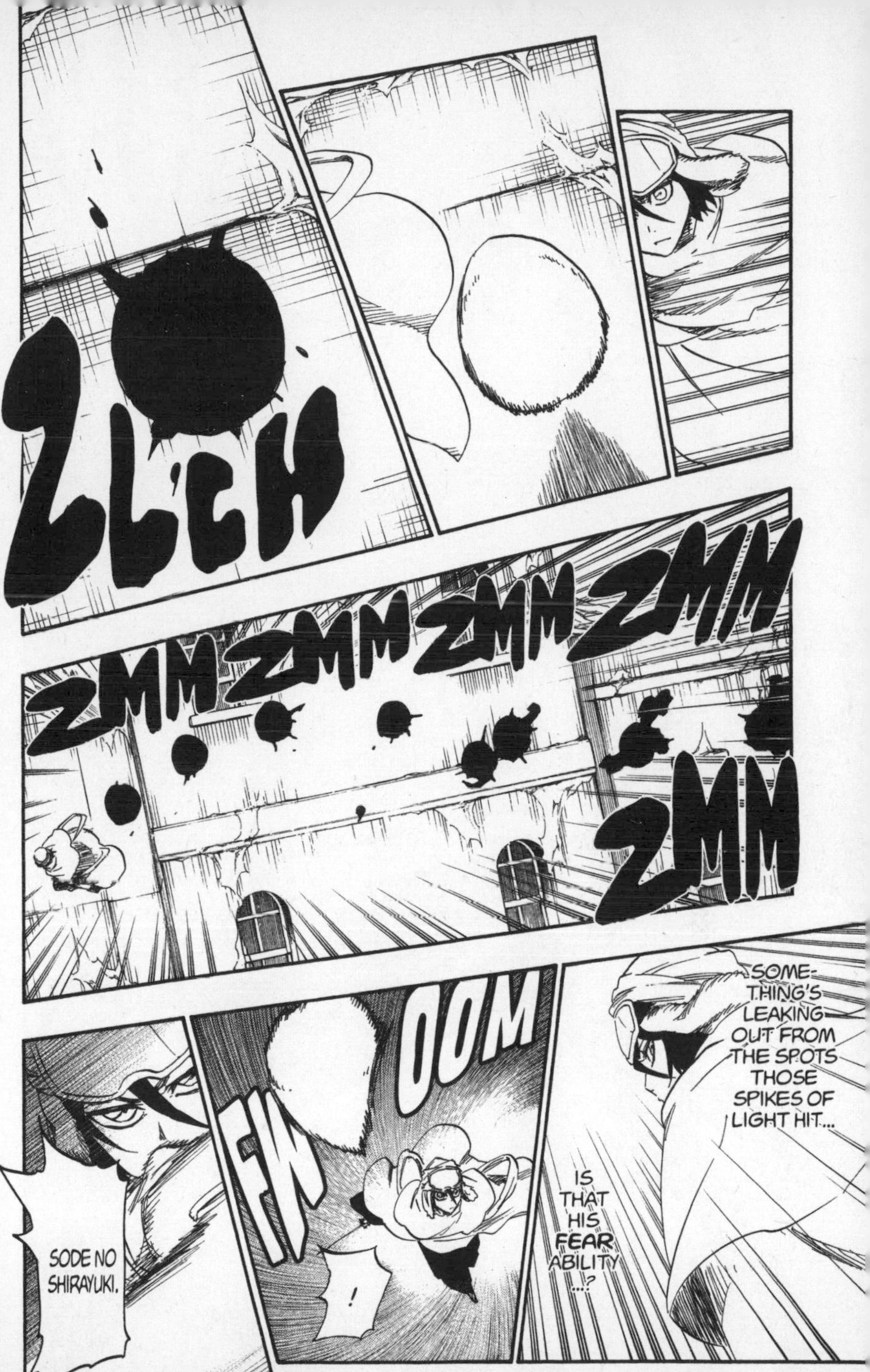
ZL'CH
ZMM ZMM ZMM ZMM ZMM
ZMM
SOME-THING'S LEAKING OUT FROM THE SPOTS THOSE SPIKES OF LIGHT HIT...
IS THAT HIS FEAR ABILITY...?
FWOOM
!
SODE NO SHIRAYUKI.

READ THIS WAY

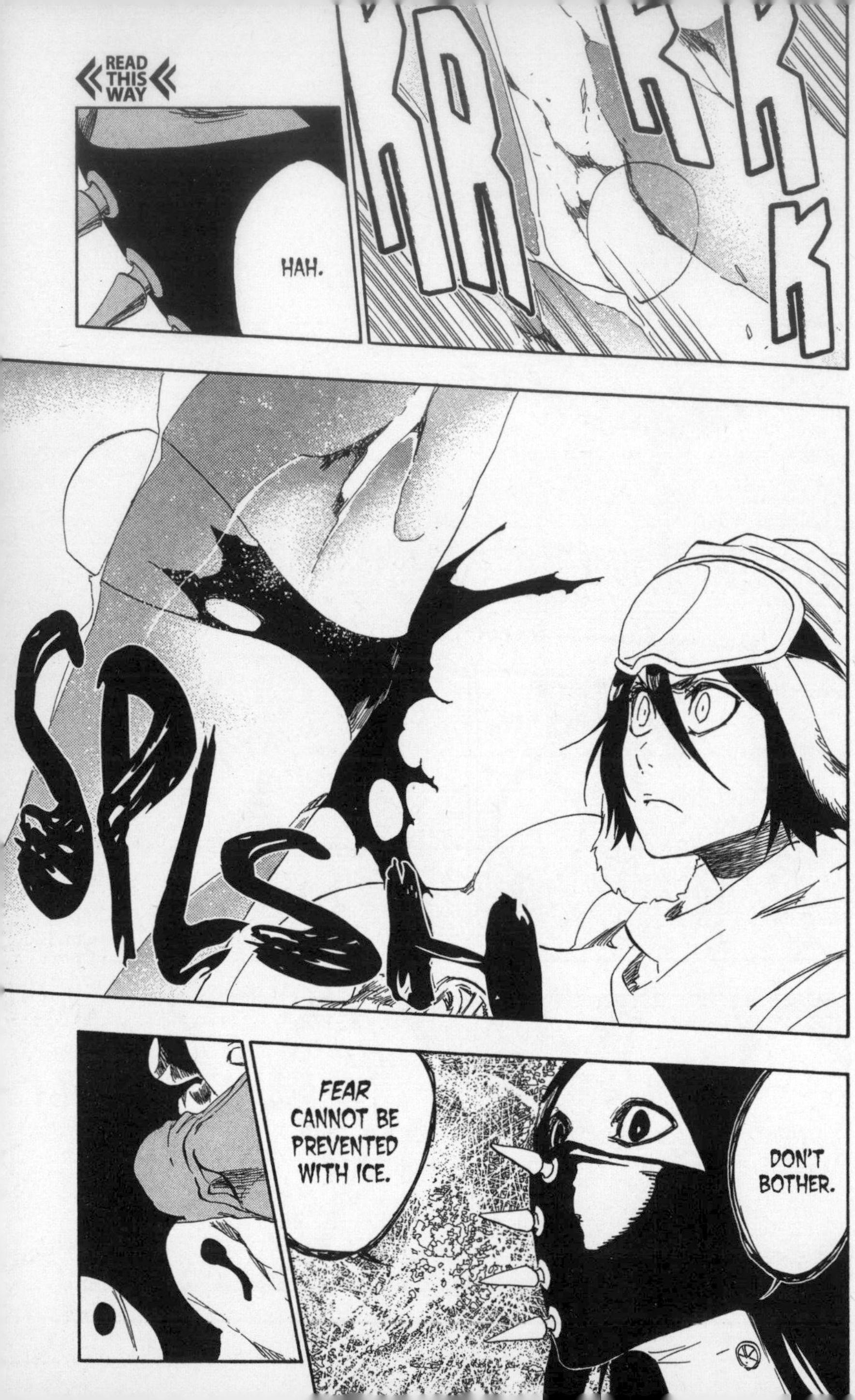
HAH.
SPLSH
DON'T BOTHER.
FEAR CANNOT BE PREVENTED WITH ICE.

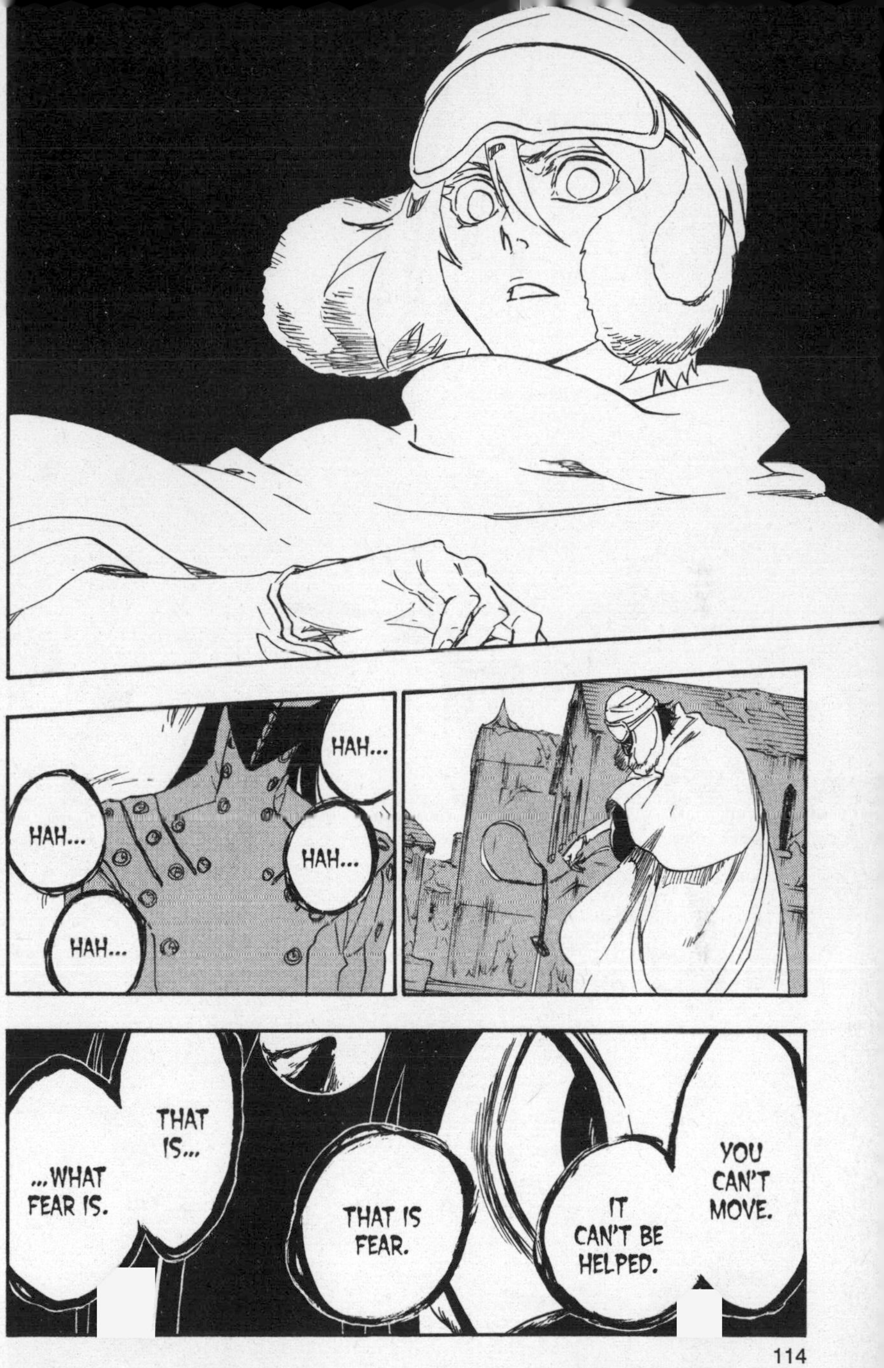
HAH...
HAH...
HAH...
HAH...
YOU CAN'T MOVE.
IT CAN'T BE HELPED.
THAT IS FEAR.
THAT IS...
...WHAT FEAR IS.

READ THIS WAY

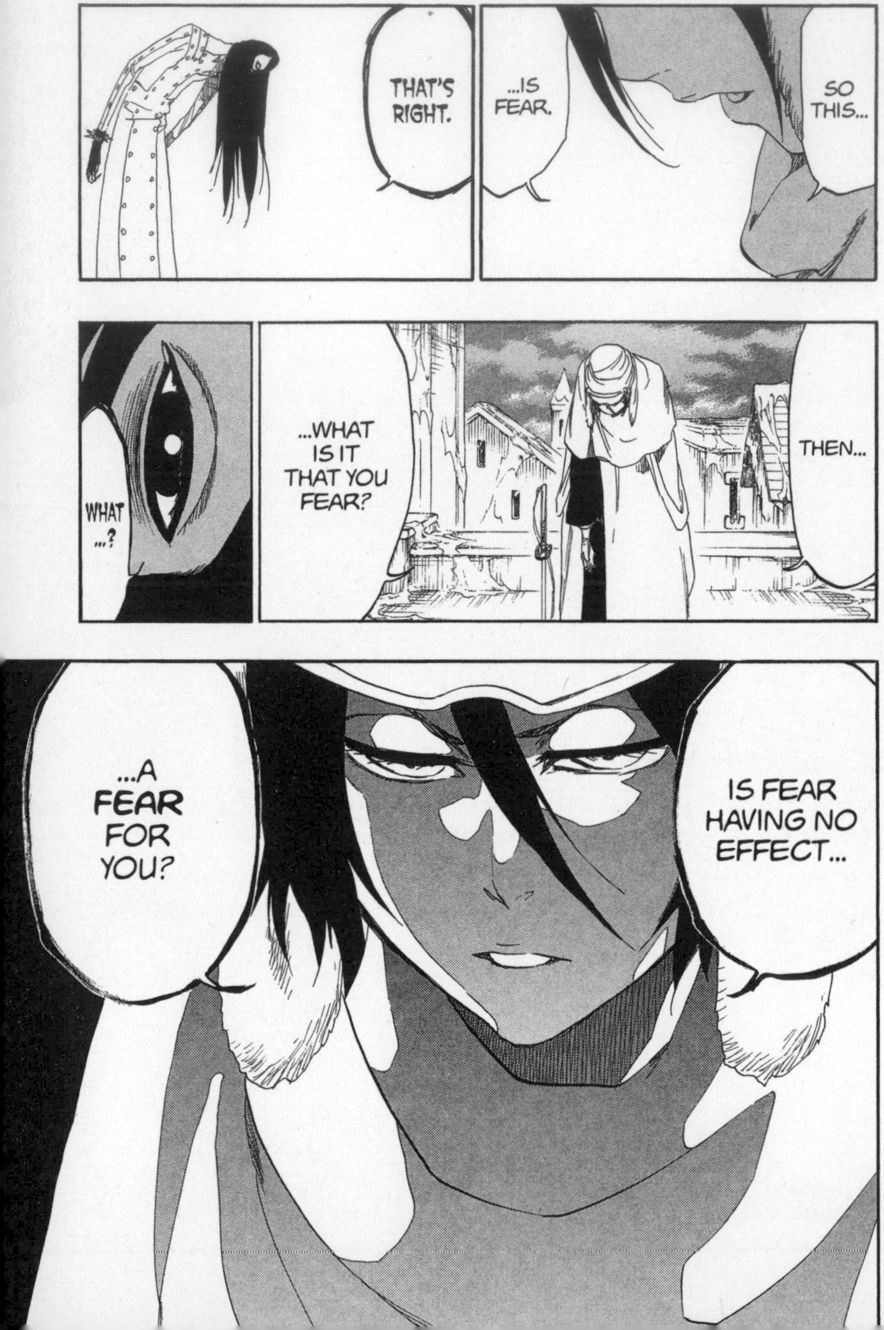
SO THIS...
...IS FEAR.
THAT'S RIGHT.
THEN...
...WHAT IS IT THAT YOU FEAR?
WHAT ...?
IS FEAR HAVING NO EFFECT...
...A FEAR FOR YOU?

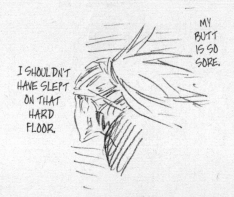

MY BUTT IS SO SORE.
I SHOULDN'T HAVE SLEPT ON THAT HARD FLOOR.

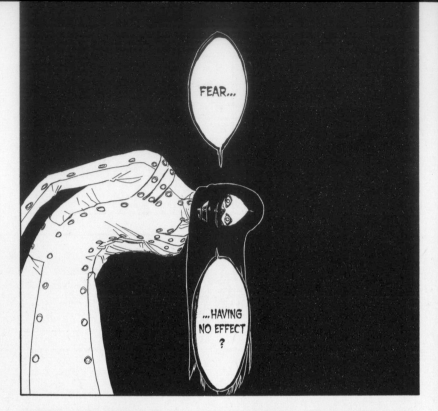

FEAR...

...HAVING
NO EFFECT
?

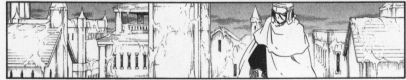

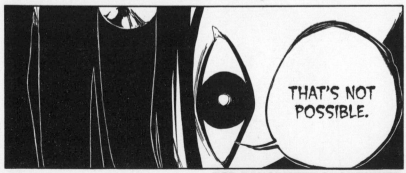

THAT'S NOT
POSSIBLE.

567. DANCE WITH SNOWWHITE

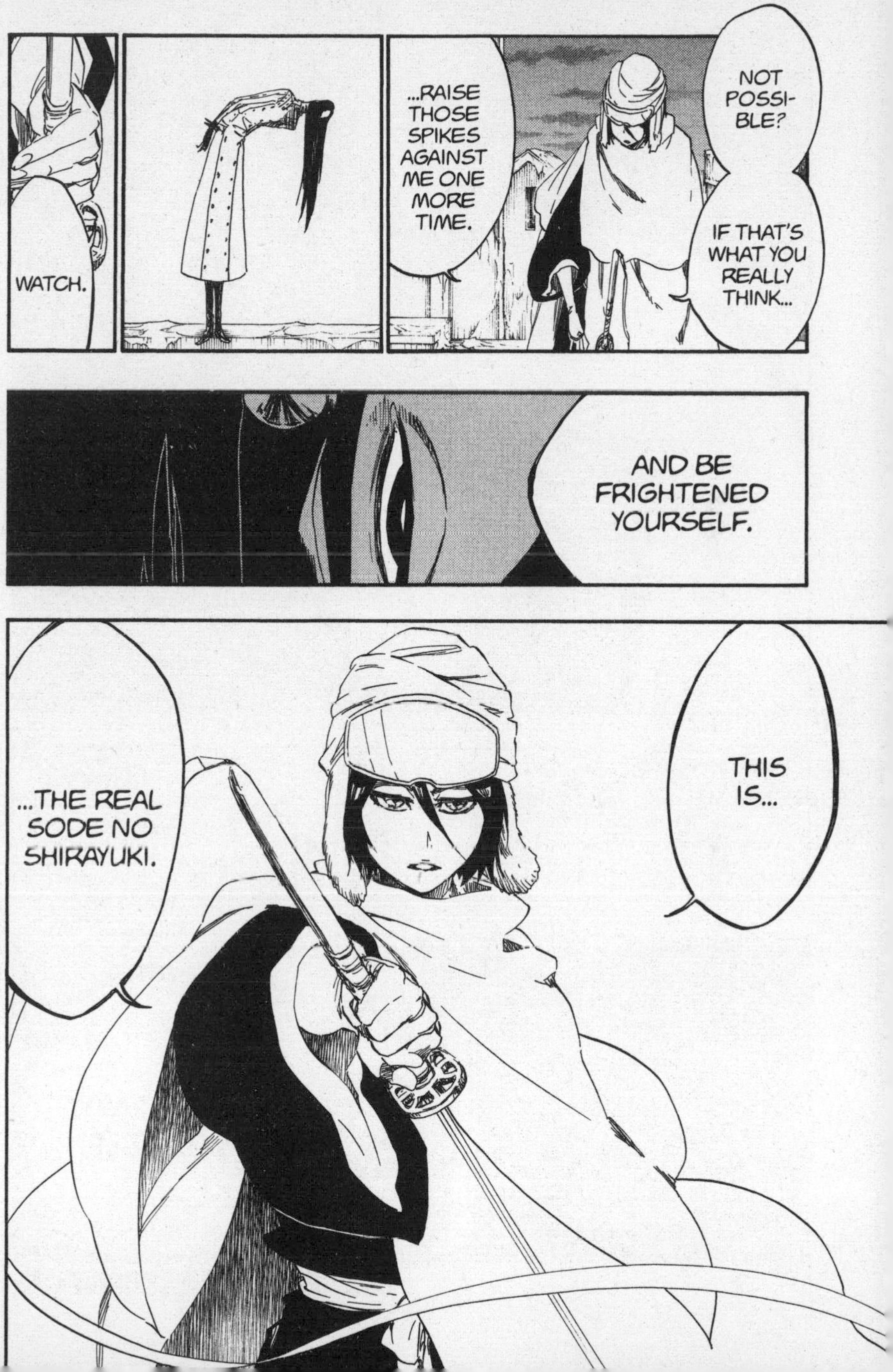
NOT POSSI-BLE?
IF THAT'S WHAT YOU REALLY THINK...
...RAISE THOSE SPIKES AGAINST ME ONE MORE TIME.
WATCH.
AND BE FRIGHTENED YOURSELF.
THIS IS...
...THE REAL SODE NO SHIRAYUKI.

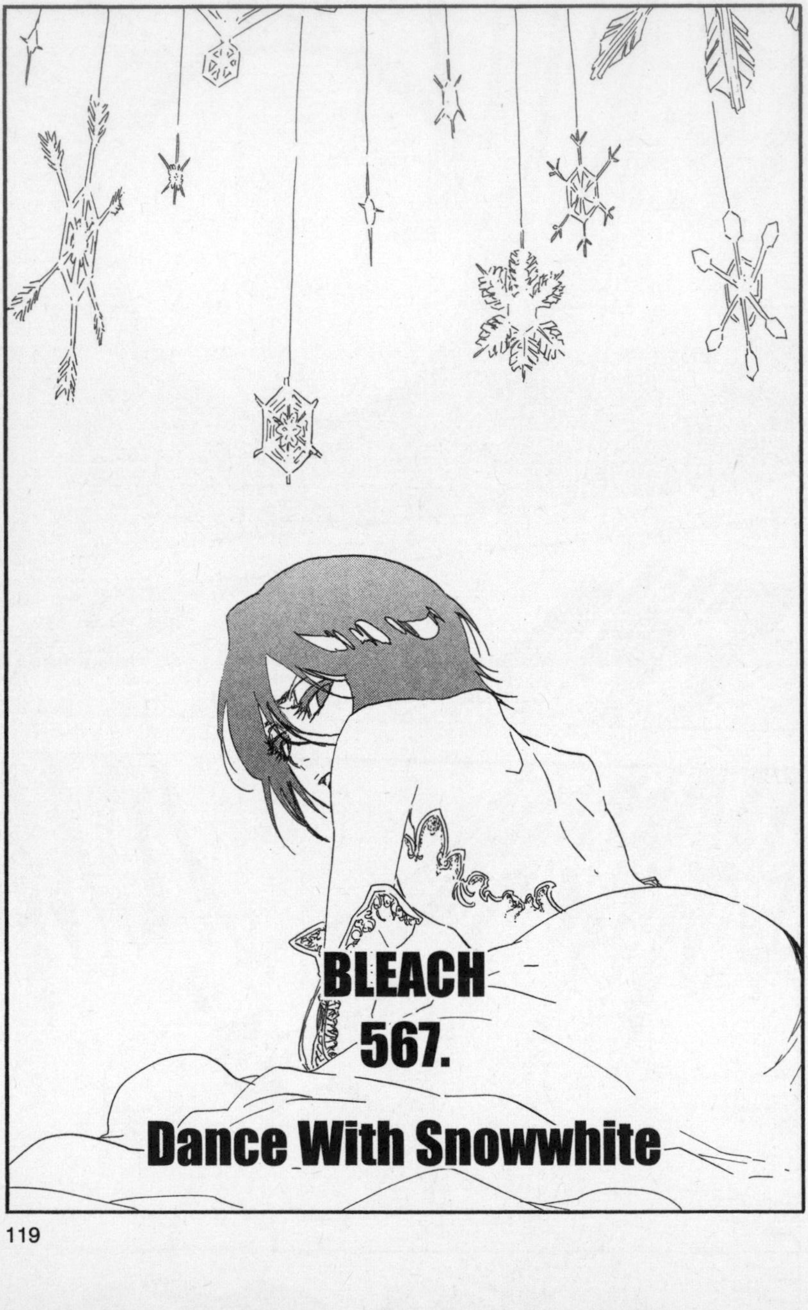
BLEACH
567.
Dance With Snowwhite

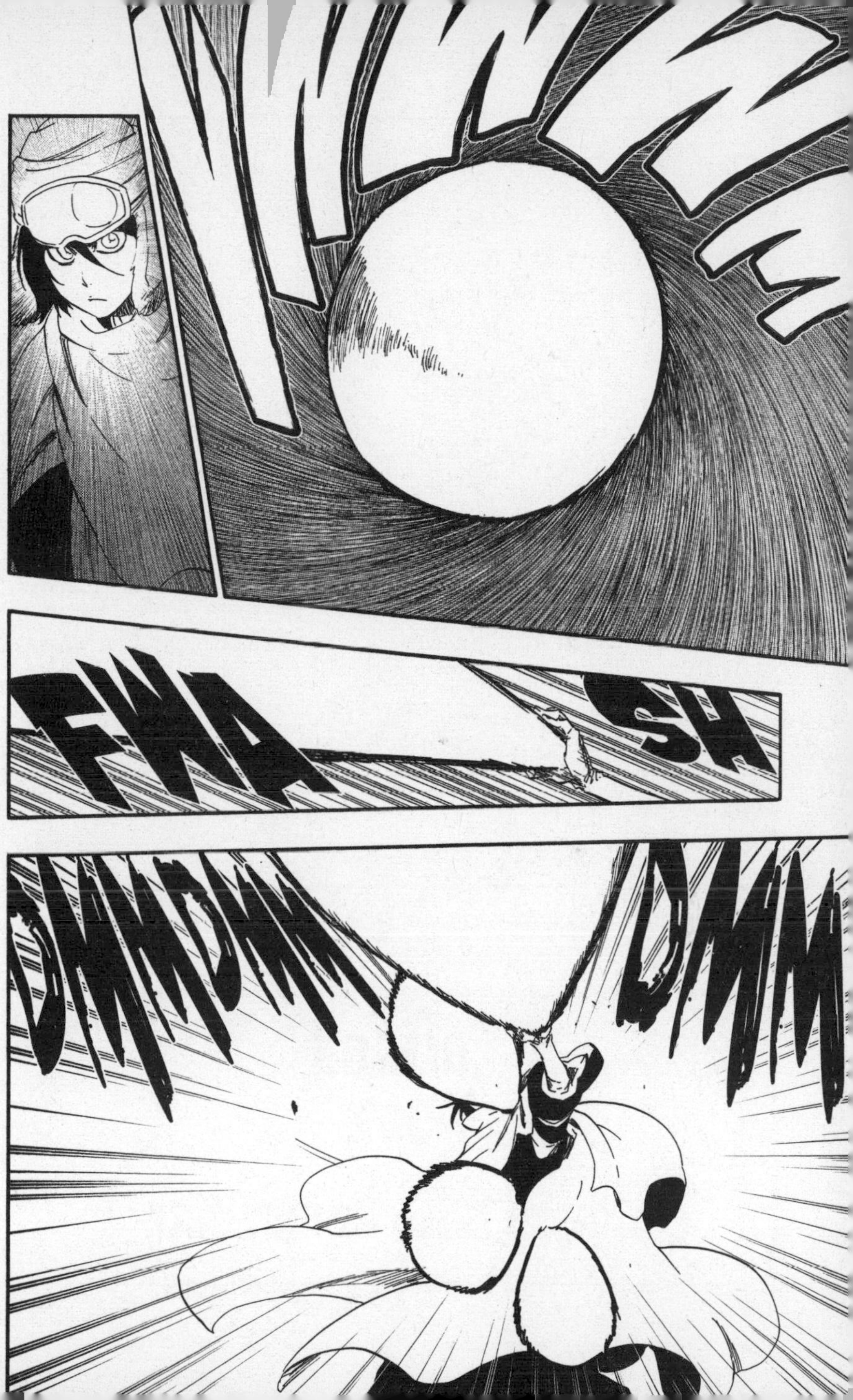
FWASH

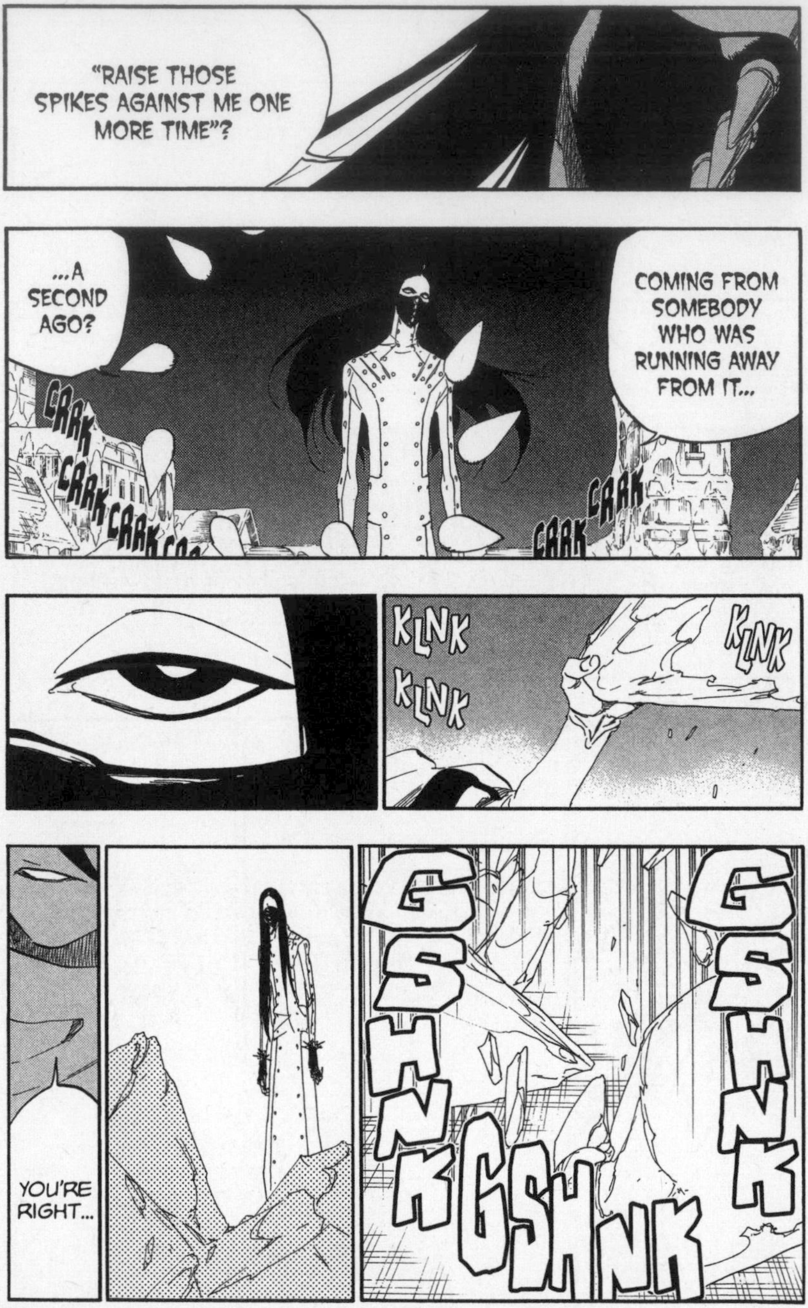
"RAISE THOSE SPIKES AGAINST ME ONE MORE TIME"?
COMING FROM SOMEBODY WHO WAS RUNNING AWAY FROM IT...
CRRK CRRK
...A SECOND AGO?
CRRK CRRK CRRK CRRK
KLNK
KLNK KLNK
GSHNK GSHNK GSHNK
YOU'RE RIGHT...

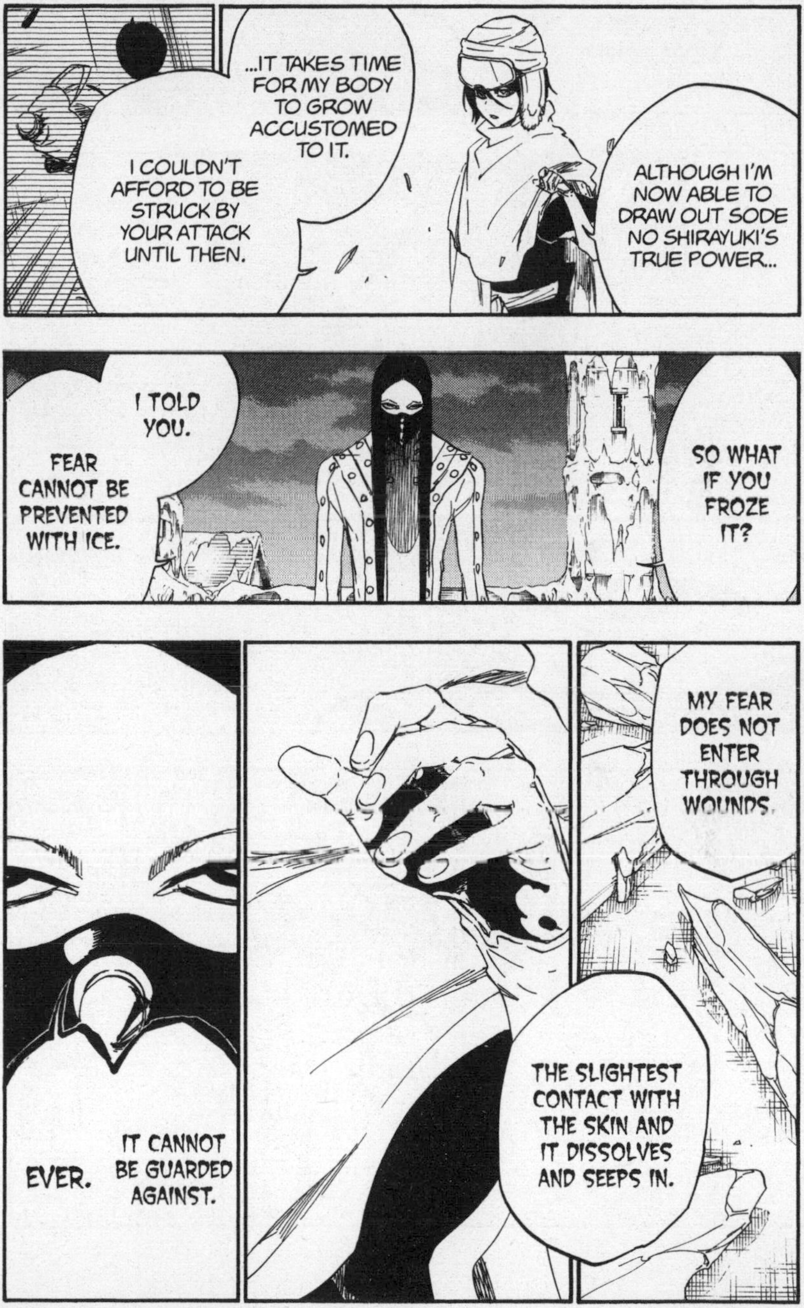
ALTHOUGH I'M NOW ABLE TO DRAW OUT SODE NO SHIRAYUKI'S TRUE POWER...
...IT TAKES TIME FOR MY BODY TO GROW ACCUSTOMED TO IT.
I COULDN'T AFFORD TO BE STRUCK BY YOUR ATTACK UNTIL THEN.
SO WHAT IF YOU FROZE IT?
I TOLD YOU.
FEAR CANNOT BE PREVENTED WITH ICE.
MY FEAR DOES NOT ENTER THROUGH WOUNDS.
THE SLIGHTEST CONTACT WITH THE SKIN AND IT DISSOLVES AND SEEPS IN.
IT CANNOT BE GUARDED AGAINST.
EVER.

READ THIS WAY

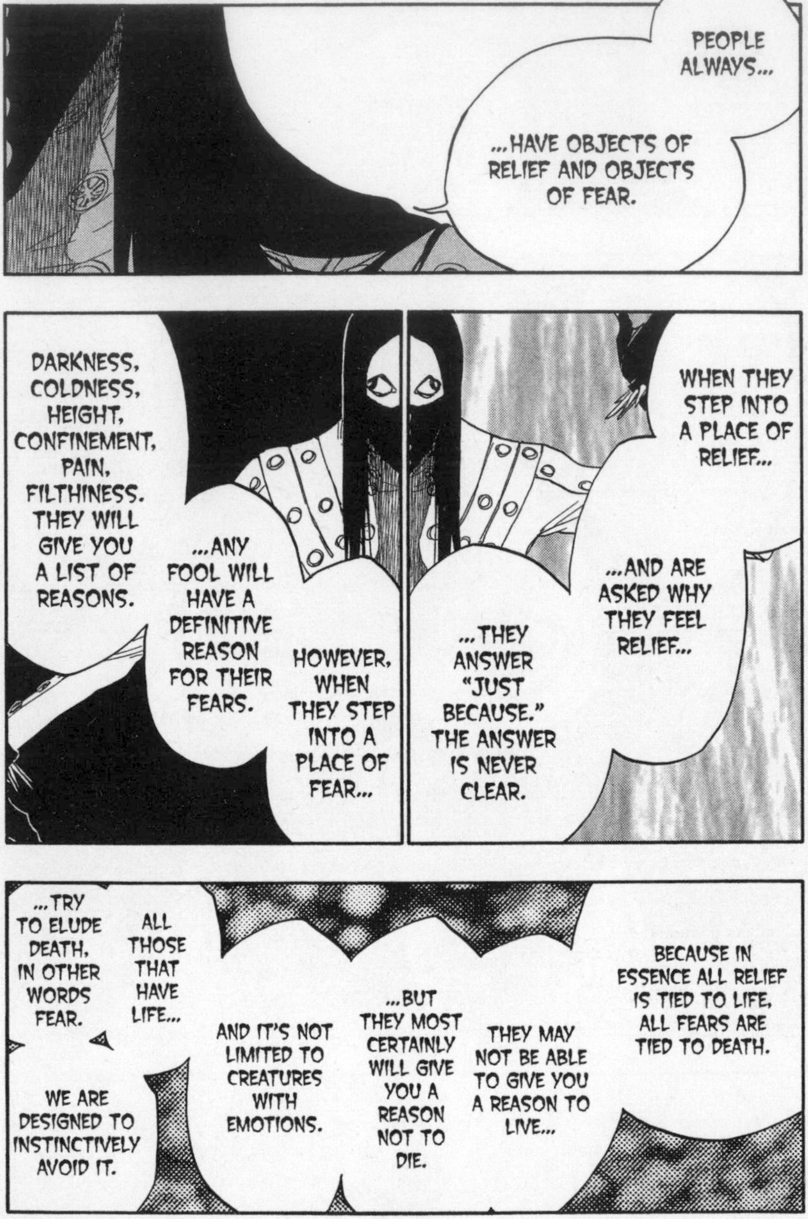
PEOPLE ALWAYS...
...HAVE OBJECTS OF RELIEF AND OBJECTS OF FEAR.
WHEN THEY STEP INTO A PLACE OF RELIEF...
...AND ARE ASKED WHY THEY FEEL RELIEF...
...THEY ANSWER "JUST BECAUSE." THE ANSWER IS NEVER CLEAR.
HOWEVER, WHEN THEY STEP INTO A PLACE OF FEAR...
...ANY FOOL WILL HAVE A DEFINITIVE REASON FOR THEIR FEARS.
DARKNESS, COLDNESS, HEIGHT, CONFINEMENT, PAIN, FILTHINESS. THEY WILL GIVE YOU A LIST OF REASONS.
BECAUSE IN ESSENCE ALL RELIEF IS TIED TO LIFE, ALL FEARS ARE TIED TO DEATH.
THEY MAY NOT BE ABLE TO GIVE YOU A REASON TO LIVE...
...BUT THEY MOST CERTAINLY WILL GIVE YOU A REASON NOT TO DIE.
AND IT'S NOT LIMITED TO CREATURES WITH EMOTIONS.
ALL THOSE THAT HAVE LIFE...
...TRY TO ELUDE DEATH, IN OTHER WORDS FEAR.
WE ARE DESIGNED TO INSTINCTIVELY AVOID IT.

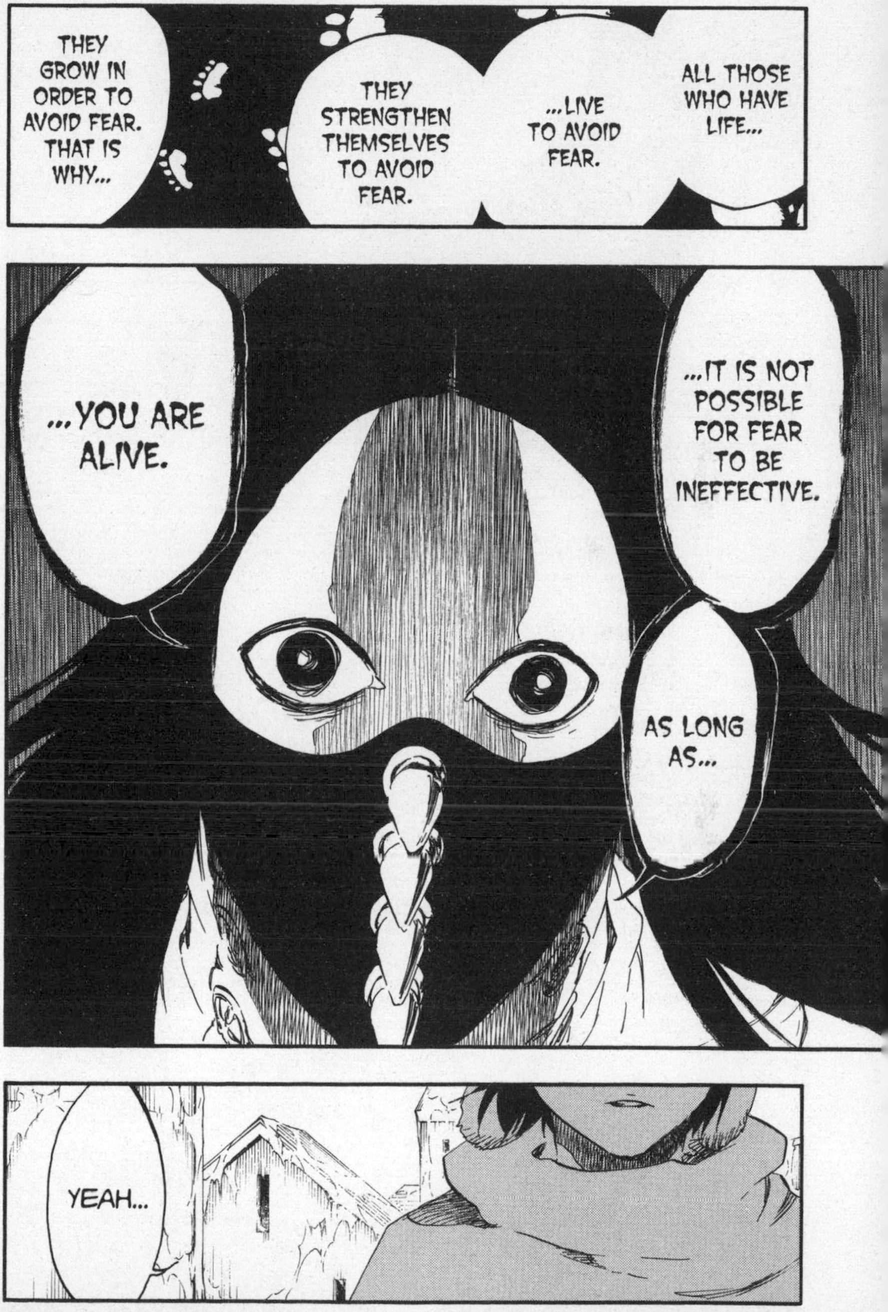
ALL THOSE WHO HAVE LIFE...
...LIVE TO AVOID FEAR.
THEY STRENGTHEN THEMSELVES TO AVOID FEAR.
THEY GROW IN ORDER TO AVOID FEAR. THAT IS WHY...
...IT IS NOT POSSIBLE FOR FEAR TO BE INEFFECTIVE.
AS LONG AS...
...YOU ARE ALIVE.
YEAH...

READ THIS WAY

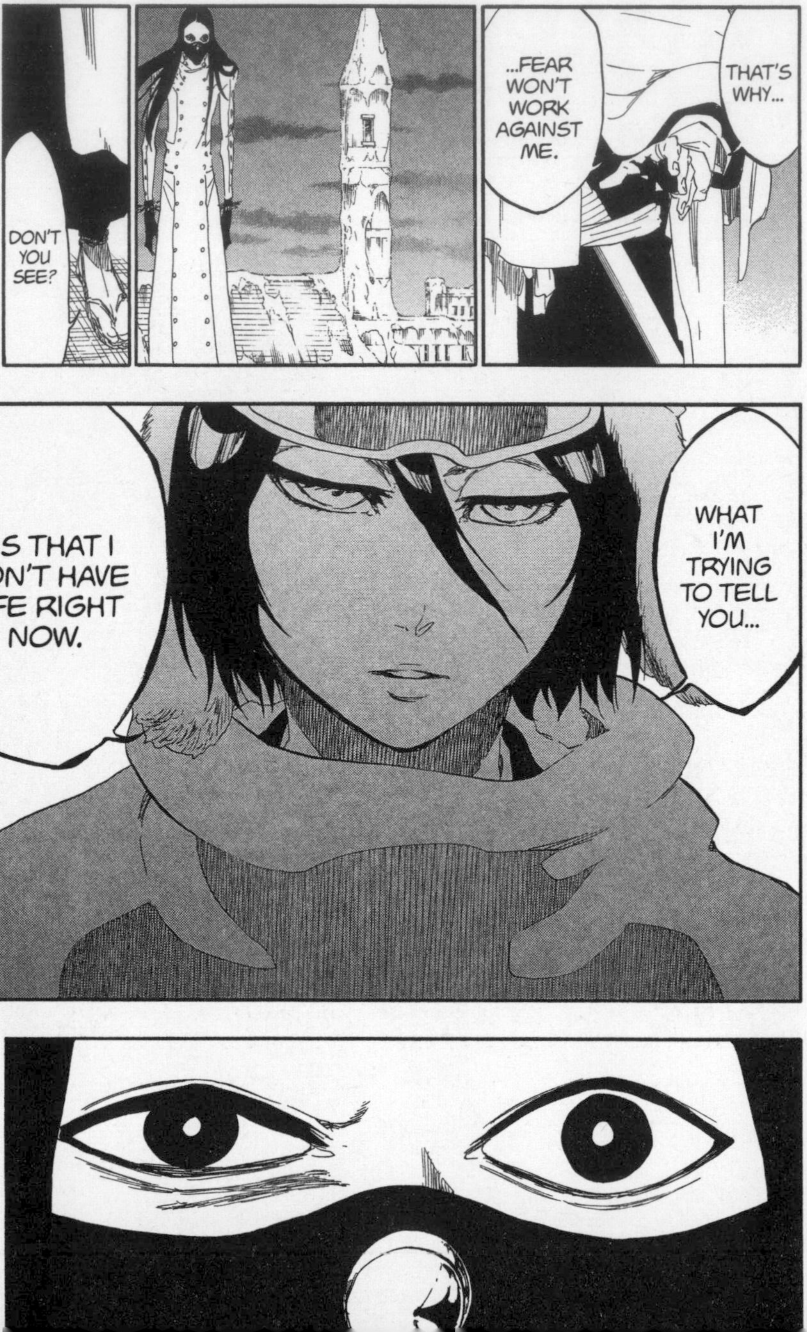
THAT'S WHY...
...FEAR WON'T WORK AGAINST ME.
DON'T YOU SEE?
WHAT I'M TRYING TO TELL YOU...
...IS THAT I DON'T HAVE LIFE RIGHT NOW.

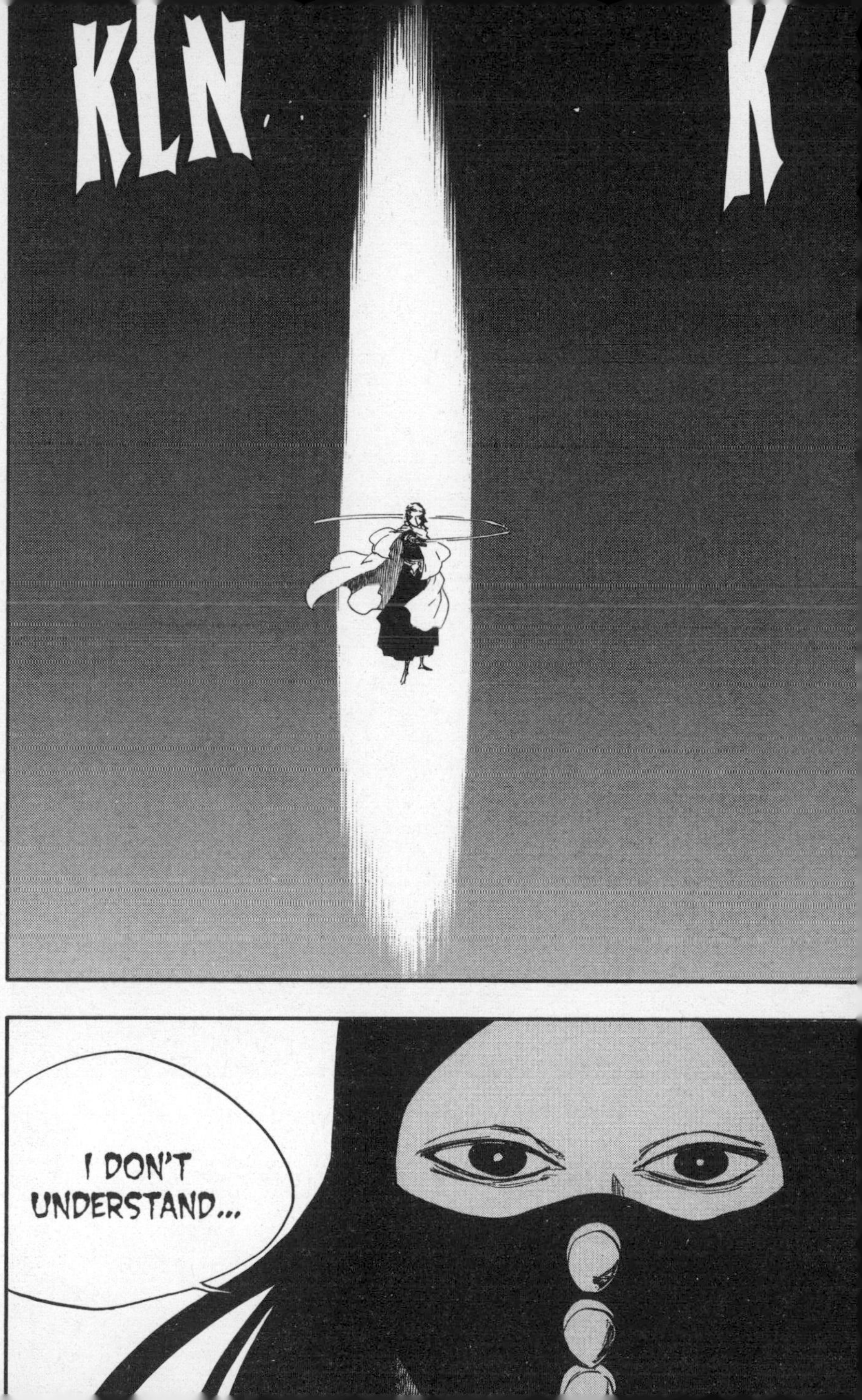
KLN
K
I DON'T UNDERSTAND...

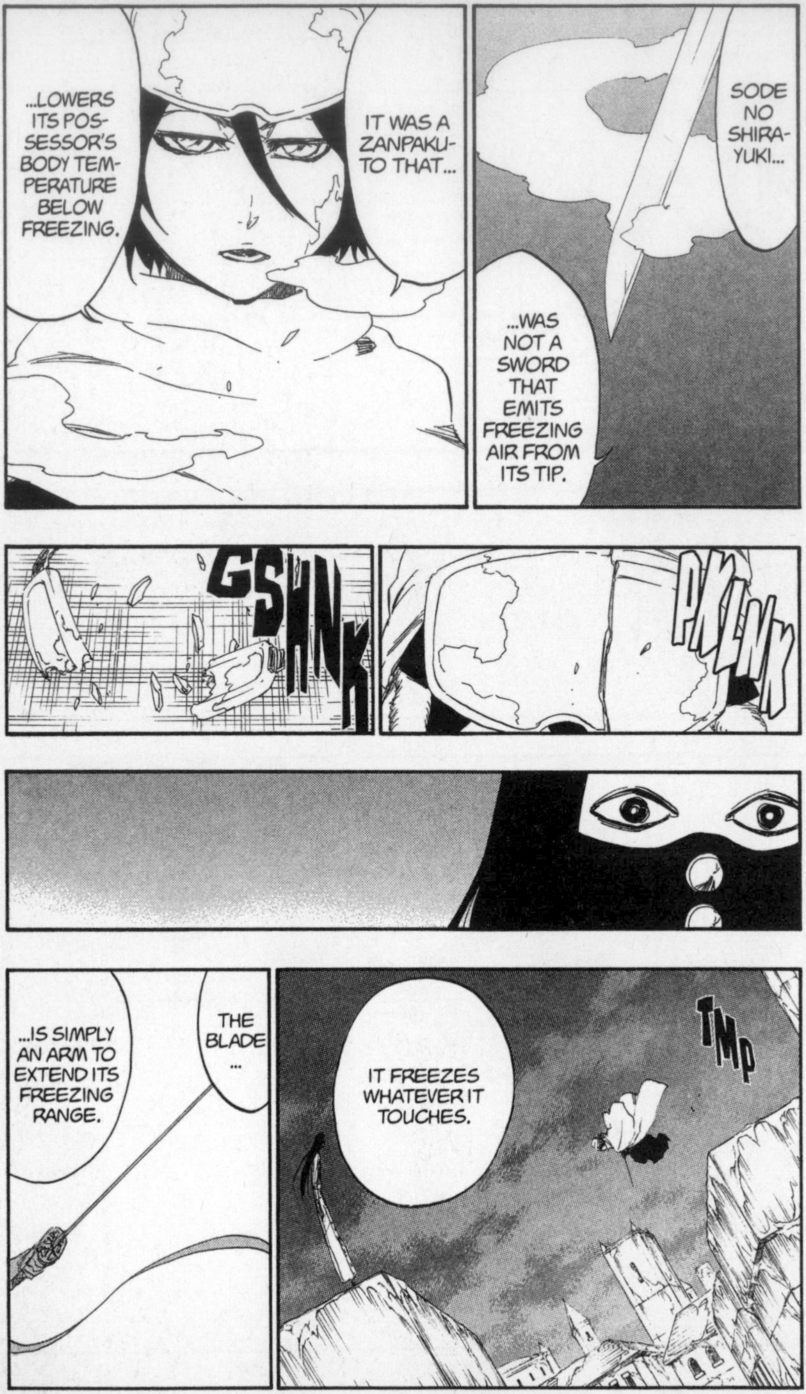
SODE NO SHIRAYUKI...
...WAS NOT A SWORD THAT EMITS FREEZING AIR FROM ITS TIP.
IT WAS A ZANPAKUTO THAT...
...LOWERS ITS POSSESSOR'S BODY TEMPERATURE BELOW FREEZING.
PKLNK
GSHNK
TMP
IT FREEZES WHATEVER IT TOUCHES.
THE BLADE...
...IS SIMPLY AN ARM TO EXTEND ITS FREEZING RANGE.

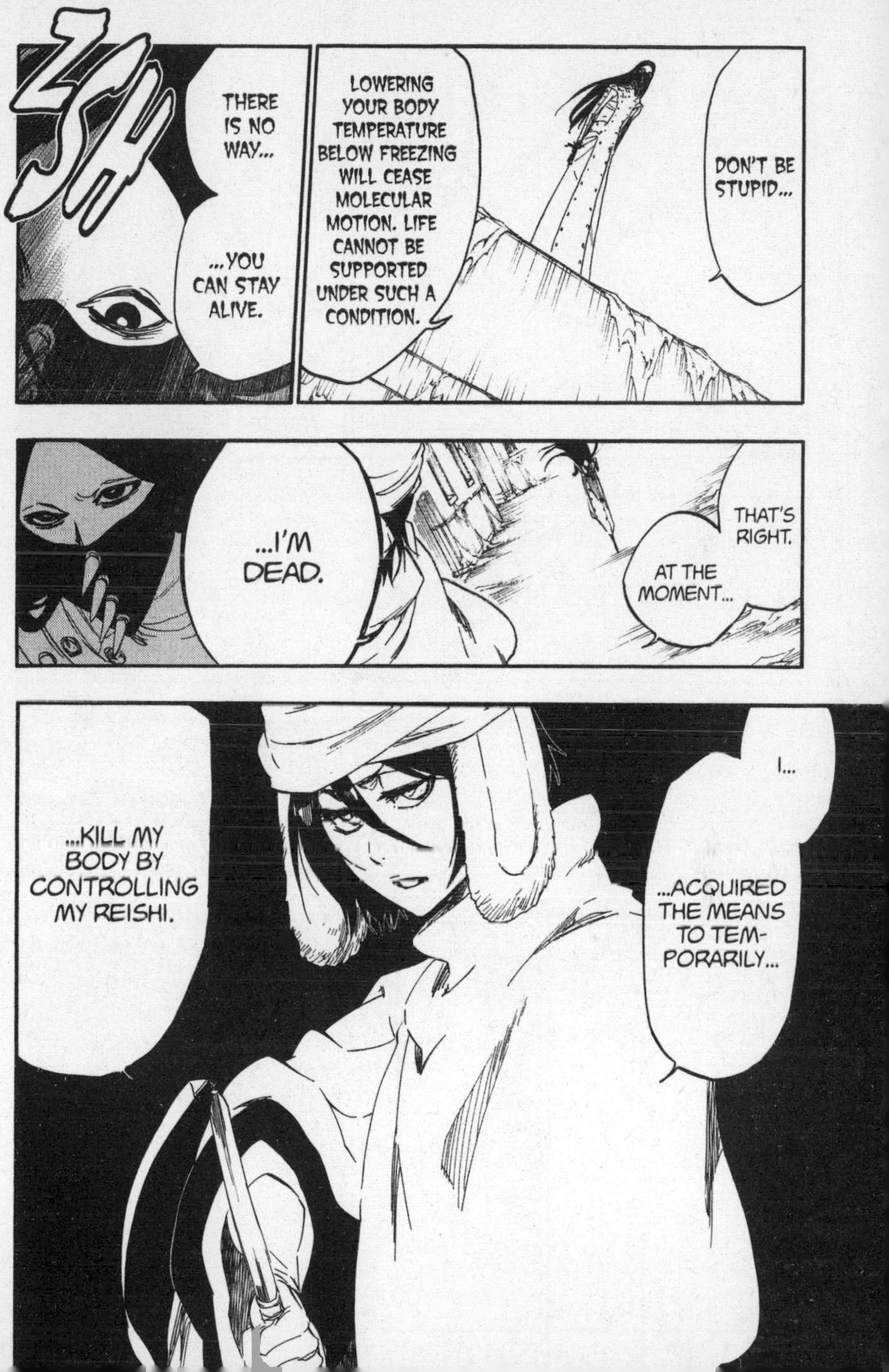
DON'T BE STUPID...
LOWERING YOUR BODY TEMPERATURE BELOW FREEZING WILL CEASE MOLECULAR MOTION. LIFE CANNOT BE SUPPORTED UNDER SUCH A CONDITION.
ZSH
THERE IS NO WAY...
...YOU CAN STAY ALIVE.
THAT'S RIGHT.
AT THE MOMENT...
...I'M DEAD.
I...
...ACQUIRED THE MEANS TO TEMPORARILY...
...KILL MY BODY BY CONTROLLING MY REISHI.

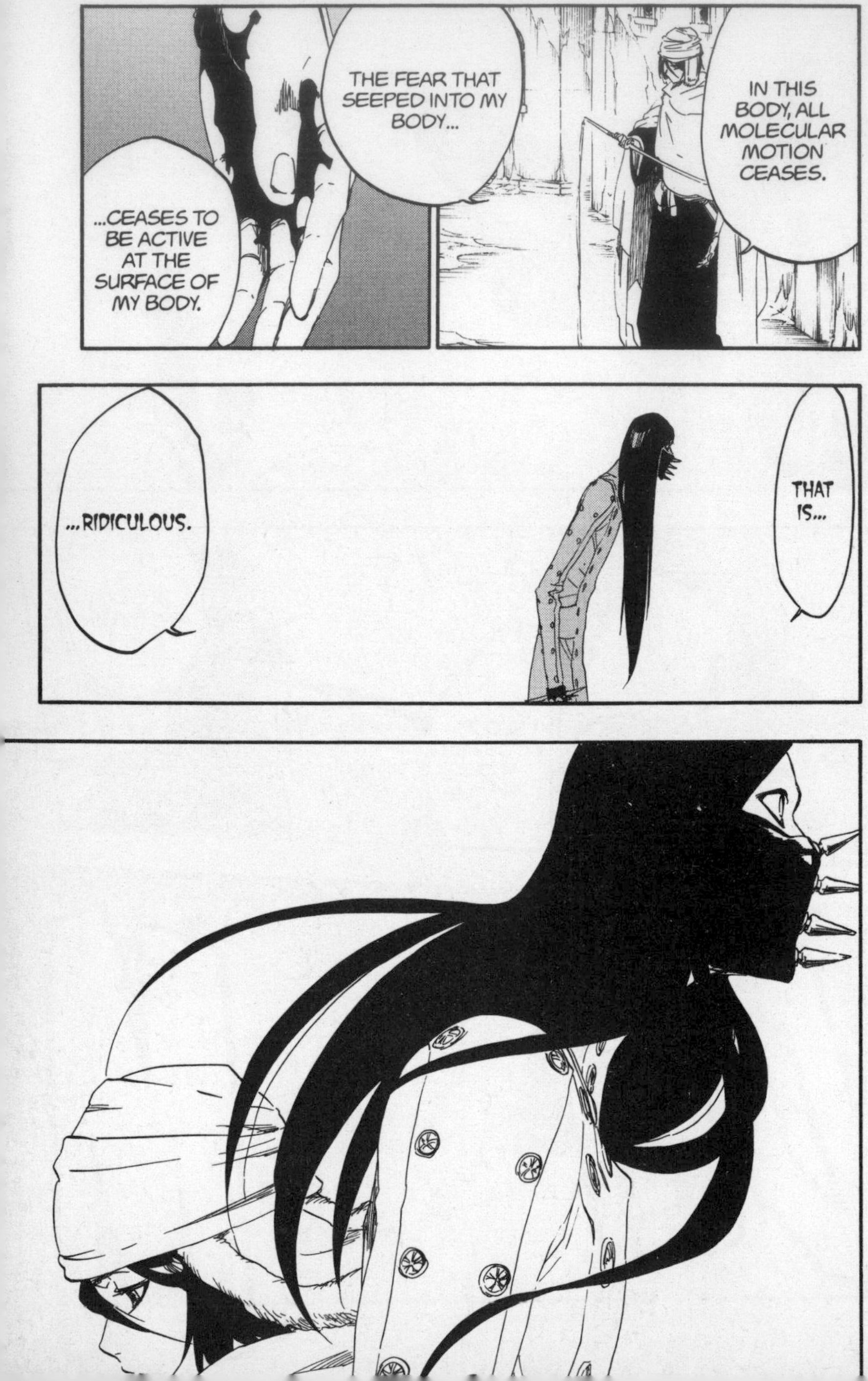
IN THIS BODY, ALL MOLECULAR MOTION CEASES.
THE FEAR THAT SEEPED INTO MY BODY...
...CEASES TO BE ACTIVE AT THE SURFACE OF MY BODY.
THAT IS...
...RIDICULOUS.

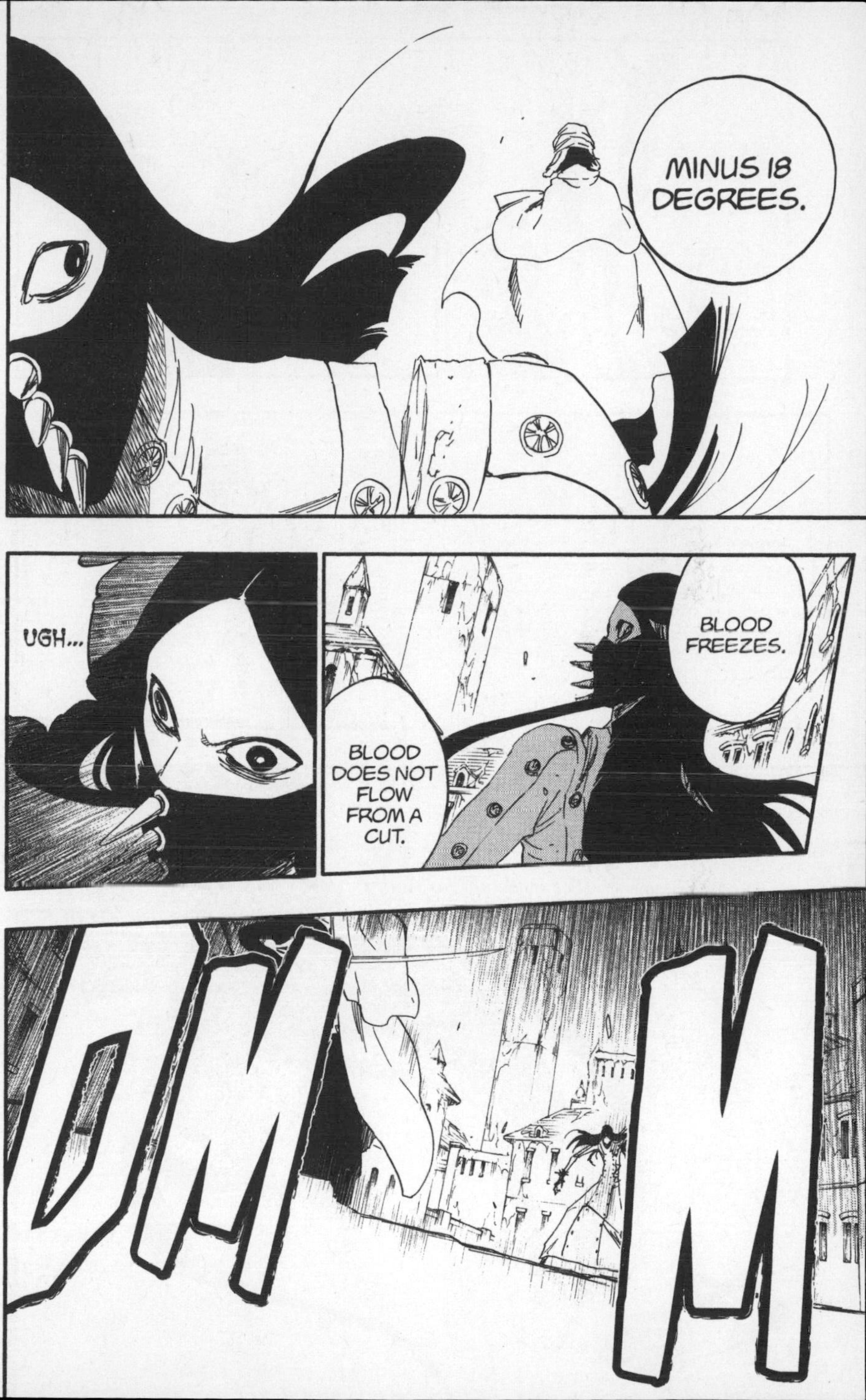
MINUS 18 DEGREES.
BLOOD FREEZES.
BLOOD DOES NOT FLOW FROM A CUT.
UGH...

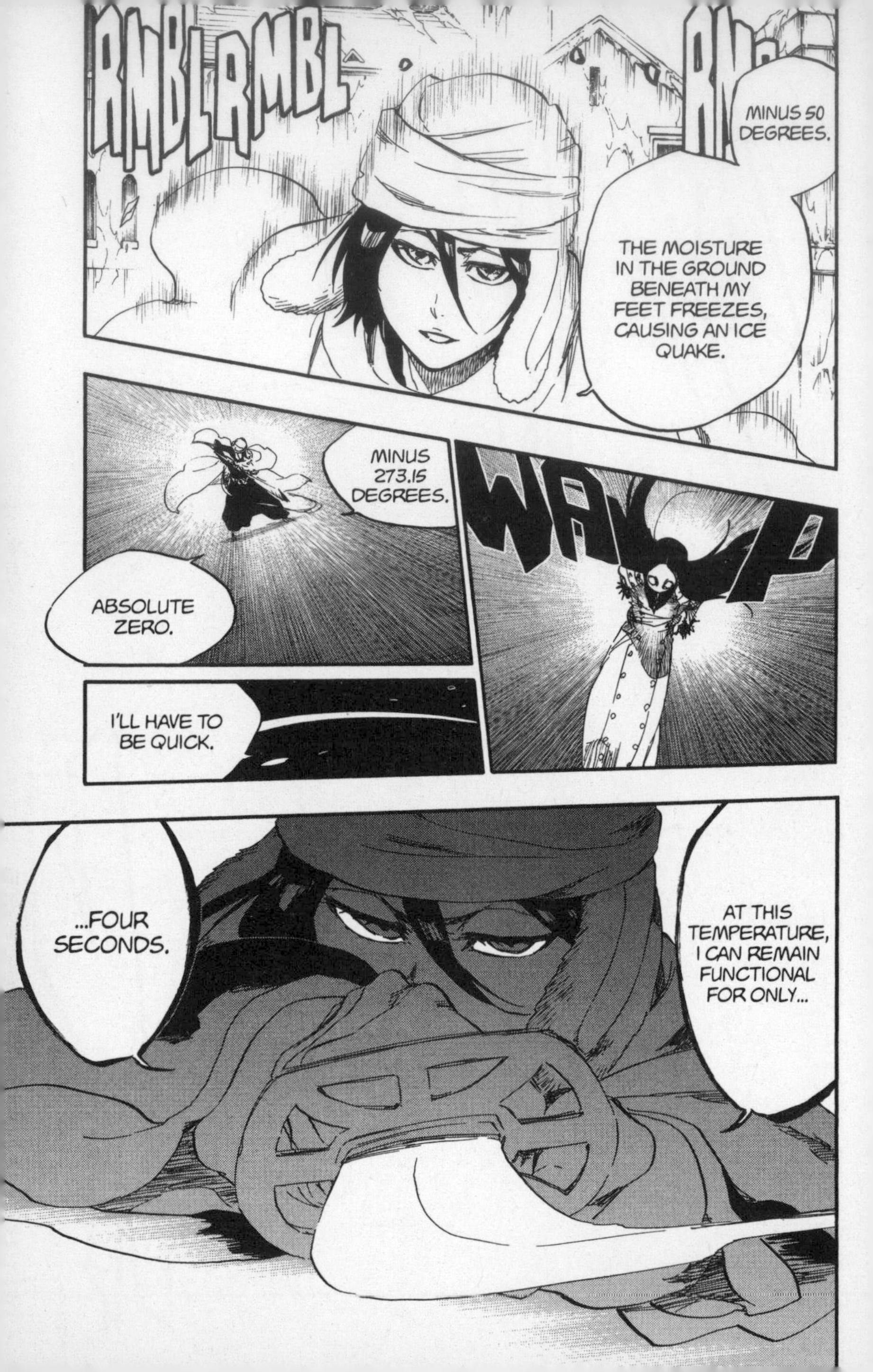
MINUS 50 DEGREES.
THE MOISTURE IN THE GROUND BENEATH MY FEET FREEZES, CAUSING AN ICE QUAKE.
RMBL RMBL
MINUS 273.15 DEGREES.
ABSOLUTE ZERO.
I'LL HAVE TO BE QUICK.
AT THIS TEMPERATURE, I CAN REMAIN FUNCTIONAL FOR ONLY...
...FOUR SECONDS.

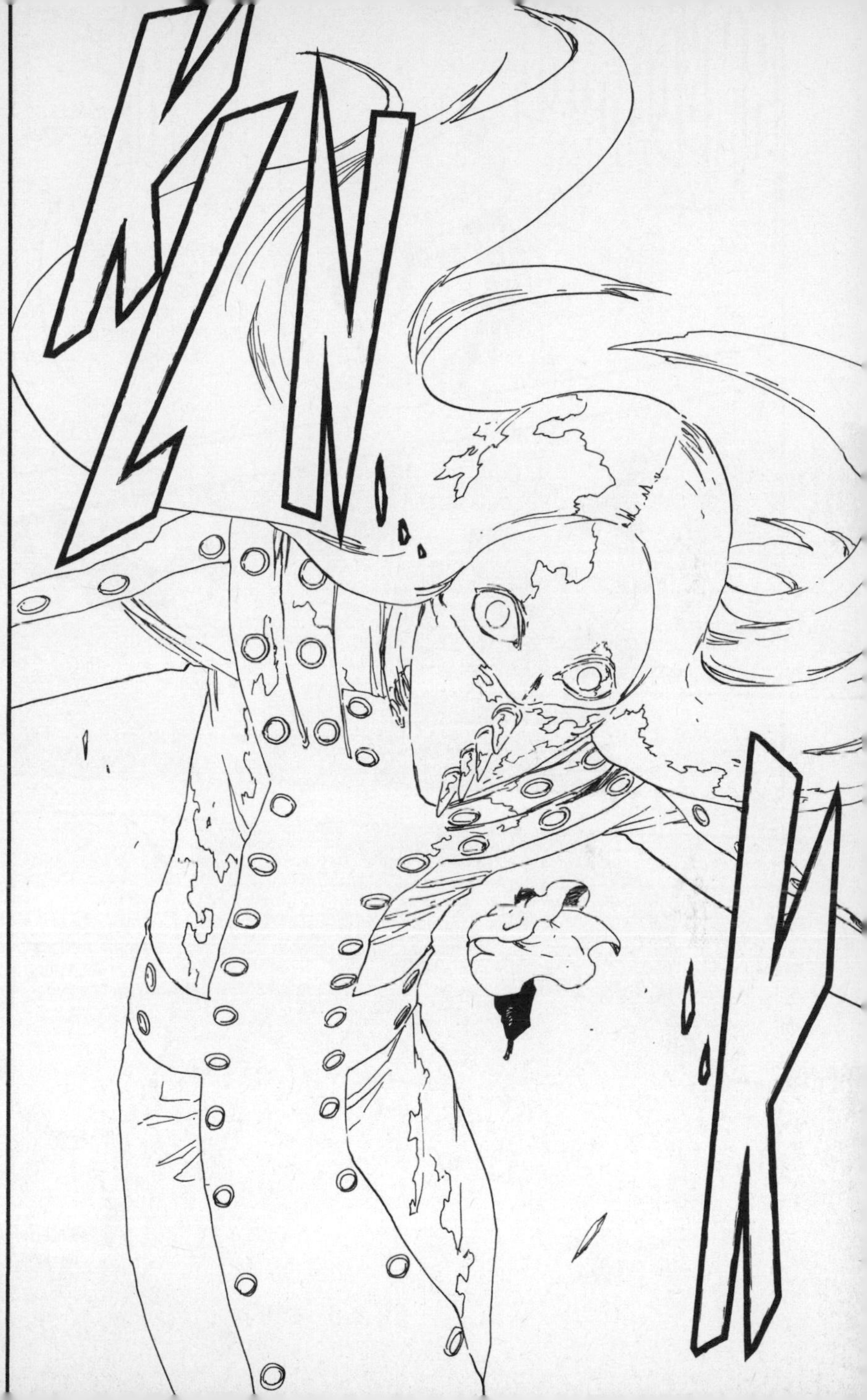

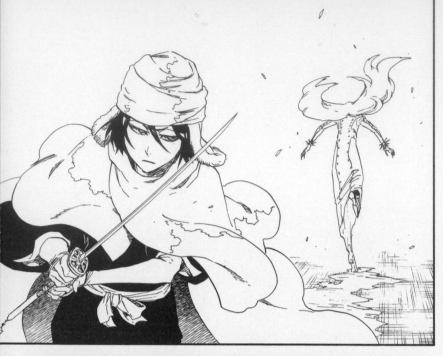

FEAR...

IS
THIS...

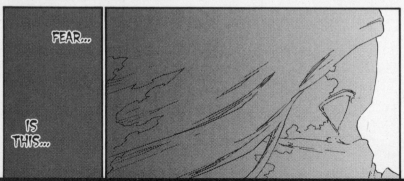

...FEAR
IS?

IS THIS
WHAT...

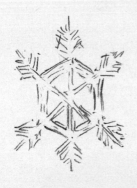

568. HEAR, FEAR, HERE 2

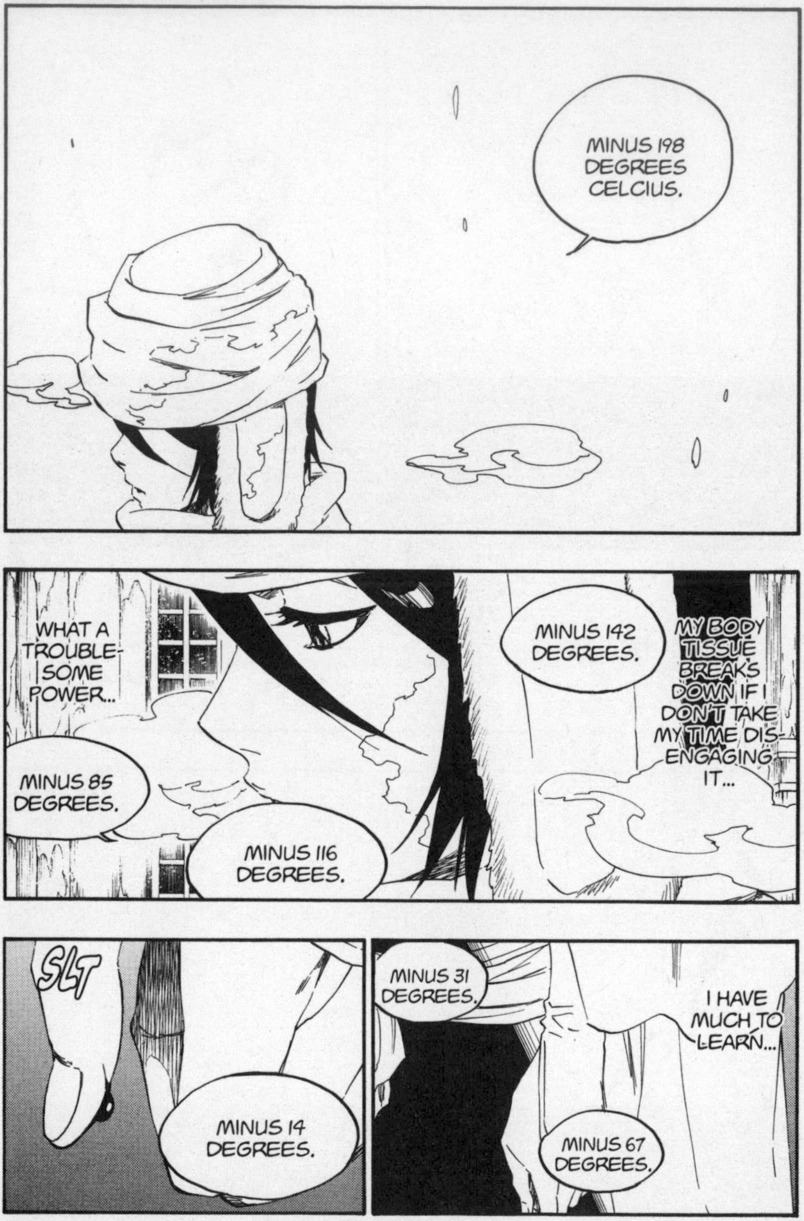
MINUS 198 DEGREES CELCIUS.
MY BODY TISSUE BREAKS DOWN IF I DON'T TAKE MY TIME DIS-ENGAGING IT...
MINUS 142 DEGREES.
WHAT A TROUBLE-SOME POWER...
MINUS 116 DEGREES.
MINUS 85 DEGREES.
I HAVE MUCH TO LEARN...
MINUS 67 DEGREES.
MINUS 31 DEGREES.
SLT
MINUS 14 DEGREES.

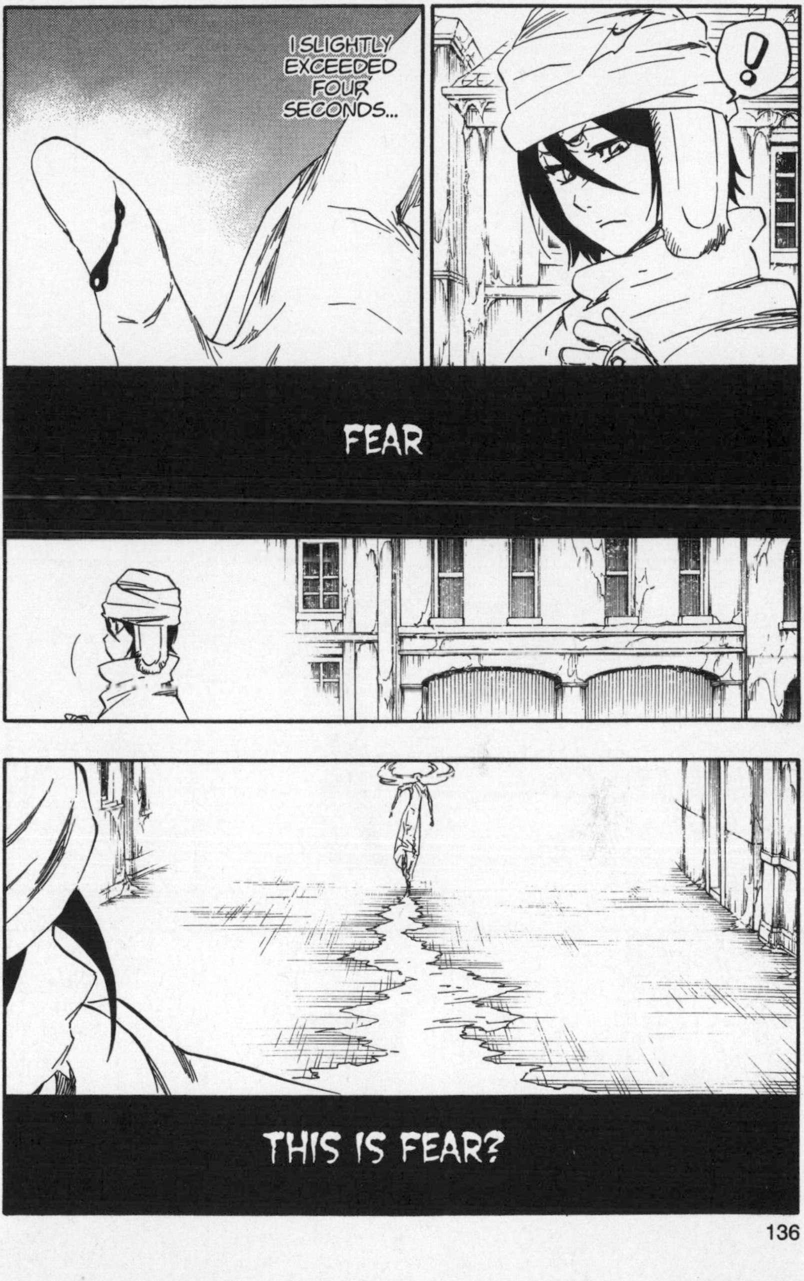
!
I SLIGHTLY EXCEEDED FOUR SECONDS...
FEAR
THIS IS FEAR?

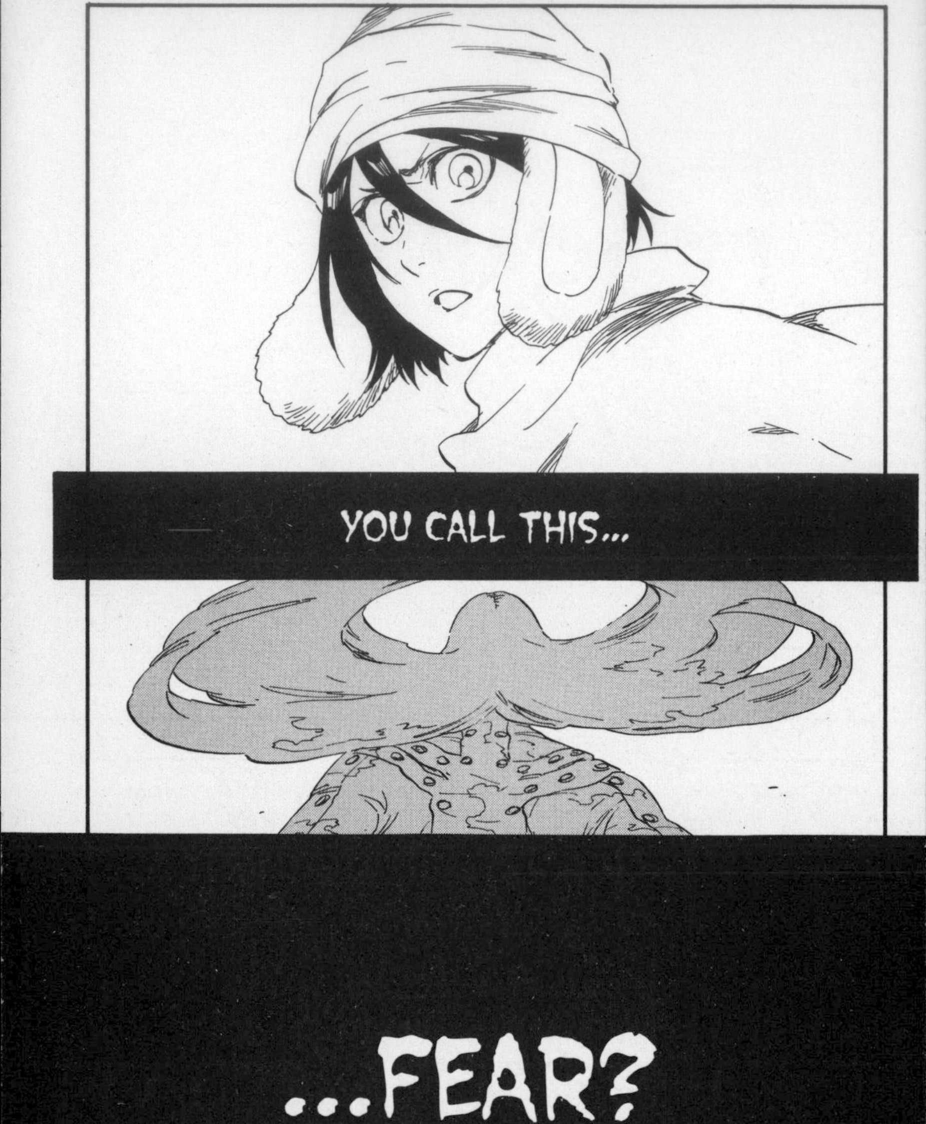
YOU CALL THIS...
...FEAR?

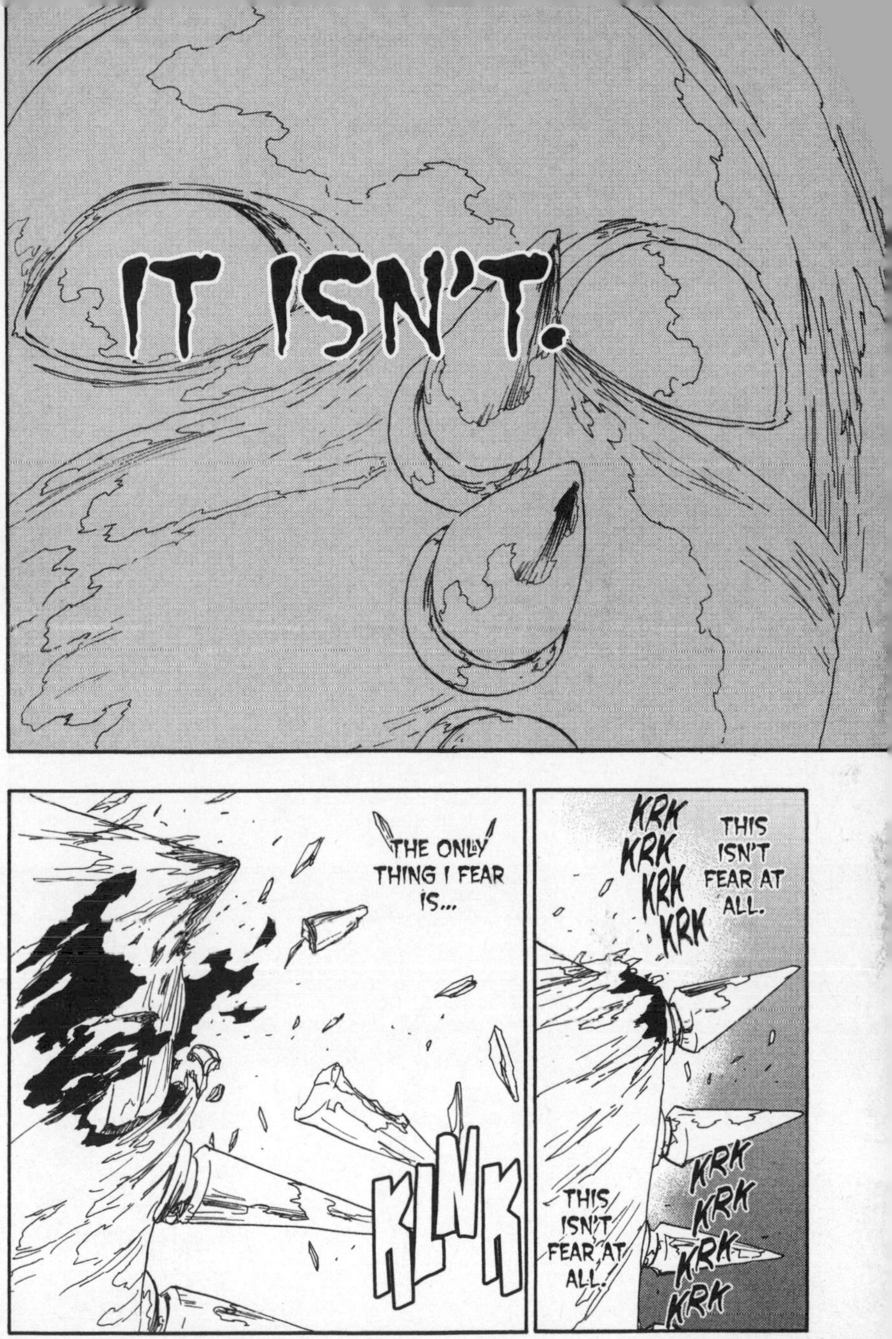
IT ISN'T!
KRK KRK KRK KRK
THIS ISN'T FEAR AT ALL.
THIS ISN'T FEAR AT ALL.
KRK KRK KRK KRK
THE ONLY THING I FEAR IS...
KLNK

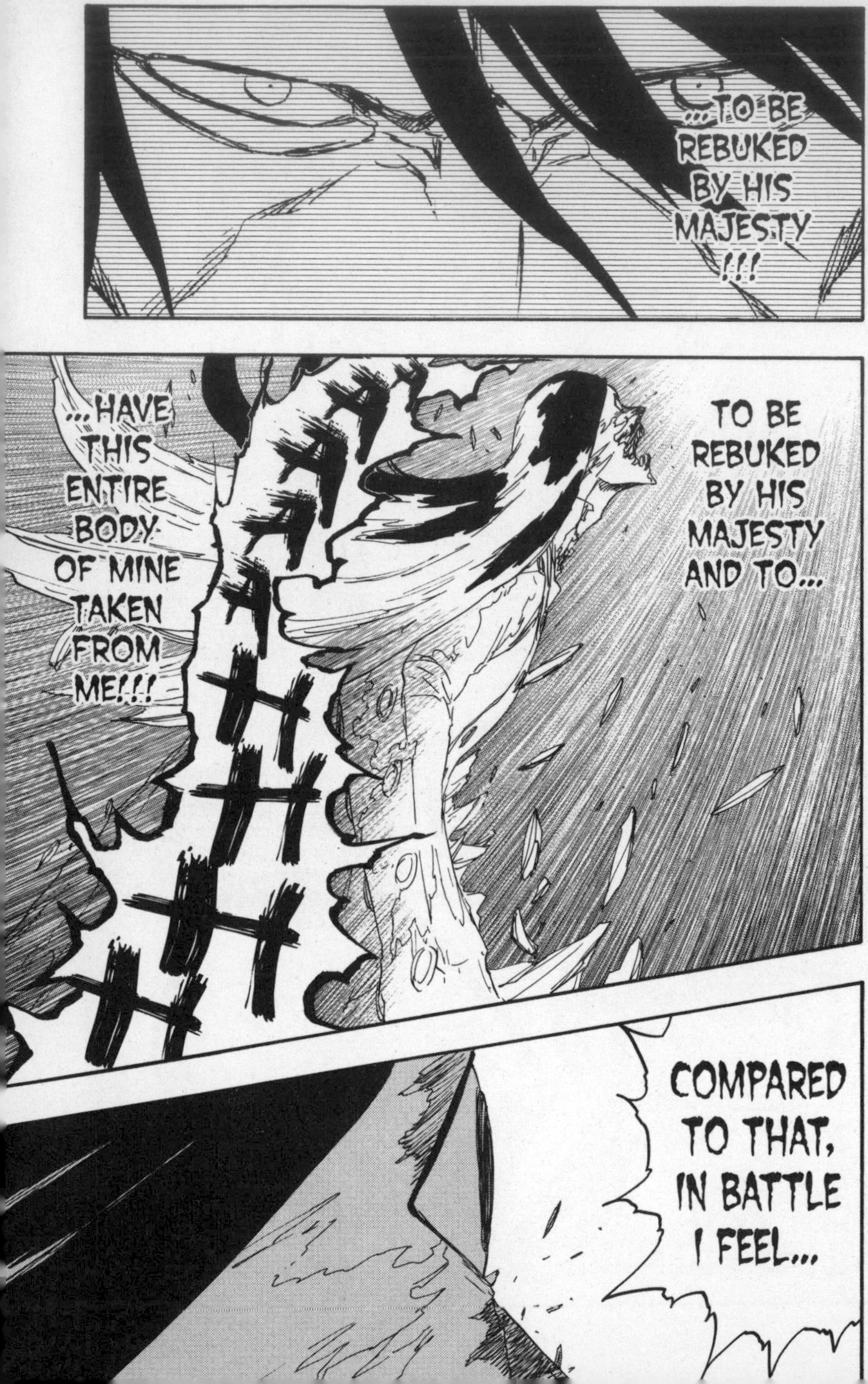
...TO BE REBUKED BY HIS MAJESTY !!!
TO BE REBUKED BY HIS MAJESTY AND TO...
...HAVE THIS ENTIRE BODY OF MINE TAKEN FROM ME!!!
COMPARED TO THAT, IN BATTLE I FEEL...

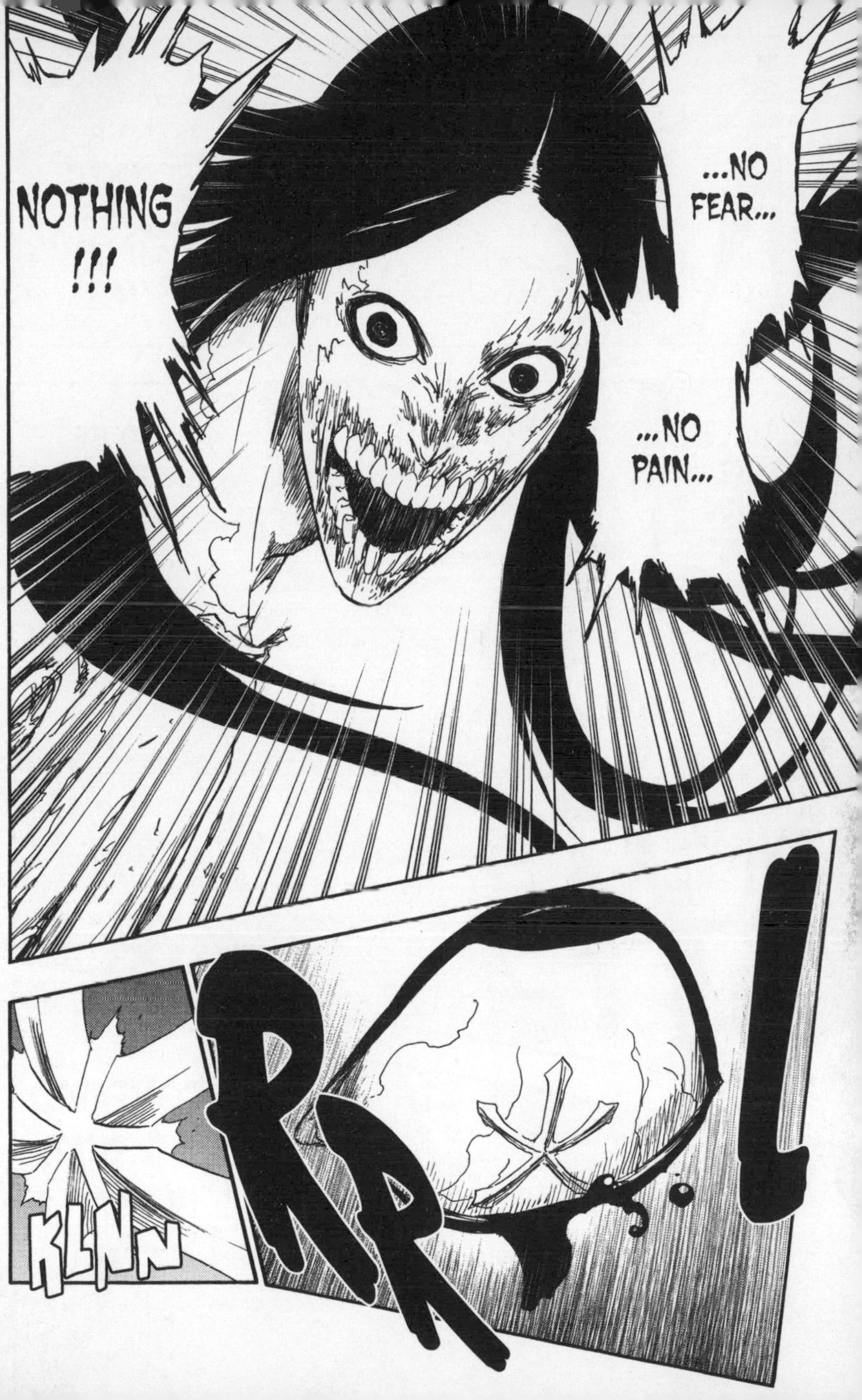
...NO FEAR...
...NO PAIN...
NOTHING !!!
RR..!
KLNN

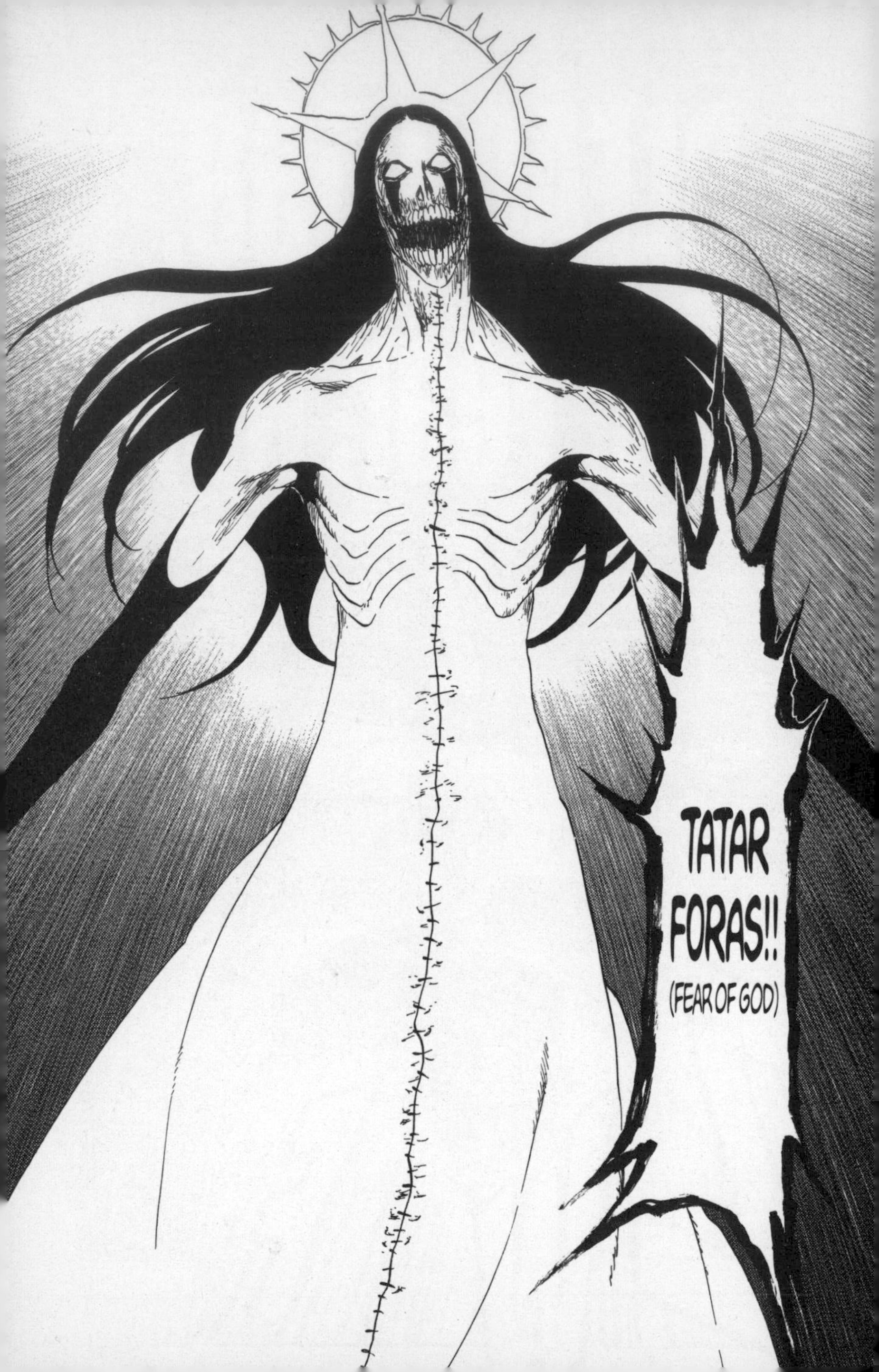
TATAR FORAS!!
(FEAR OF GOD)

BLEACH 568. Hear. Fear. Here 2

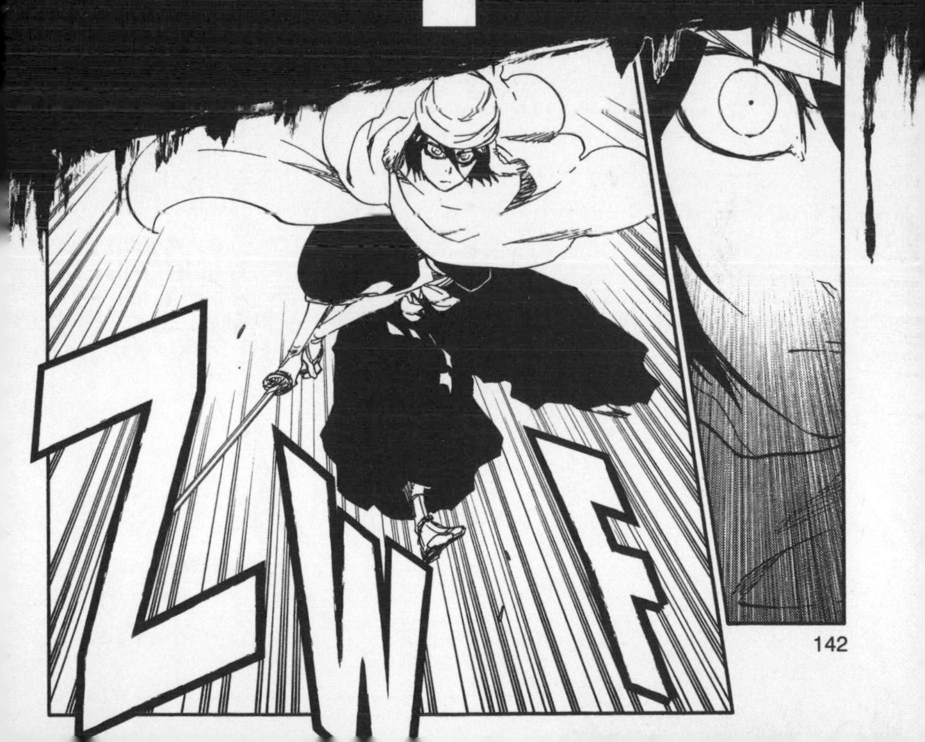
ZWE

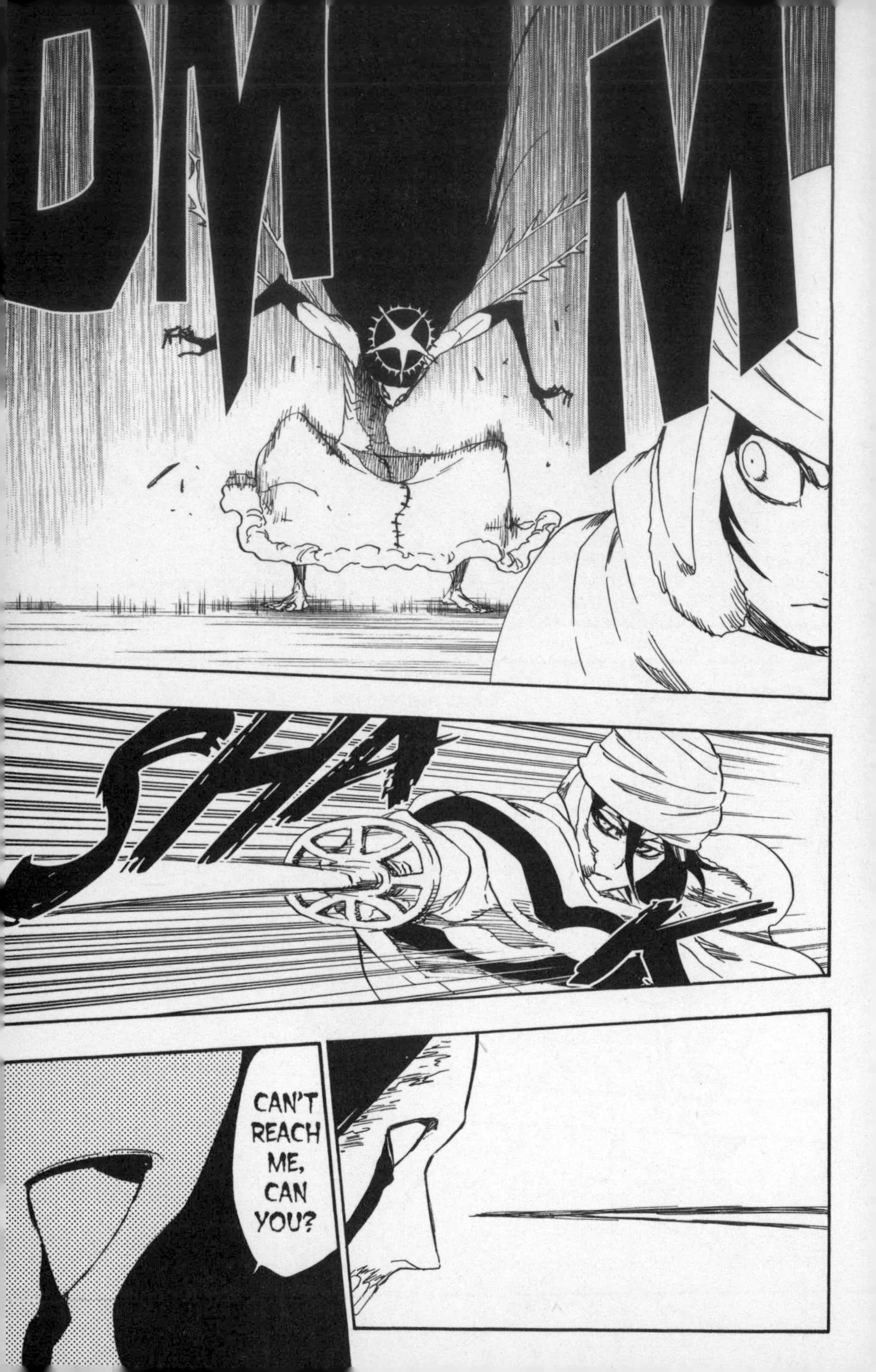
DMM
SHA
CAN'T REACH ME, CAN YOU?

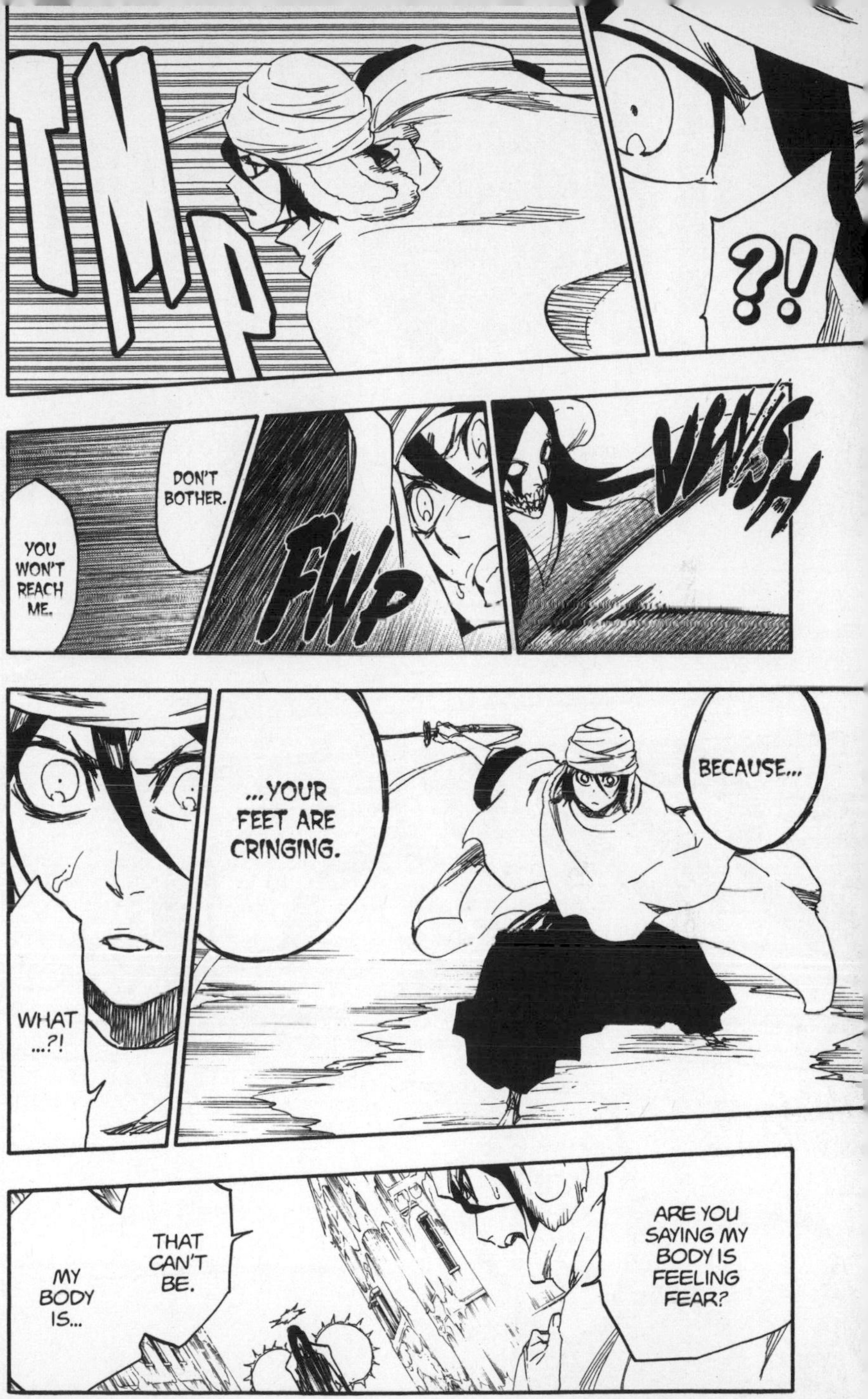
?!
TMP
VMSH
FWP
DON'T BOTHER.
YOU WON'T REACH ME.
BECAUSE...
...YOUR FEET ARE CRINGING.
WHAT ...?!
ARE YOU SAYING MY BODY IS FEELING FEAR?
THAT CAN'T BE.
MY BODY IS...

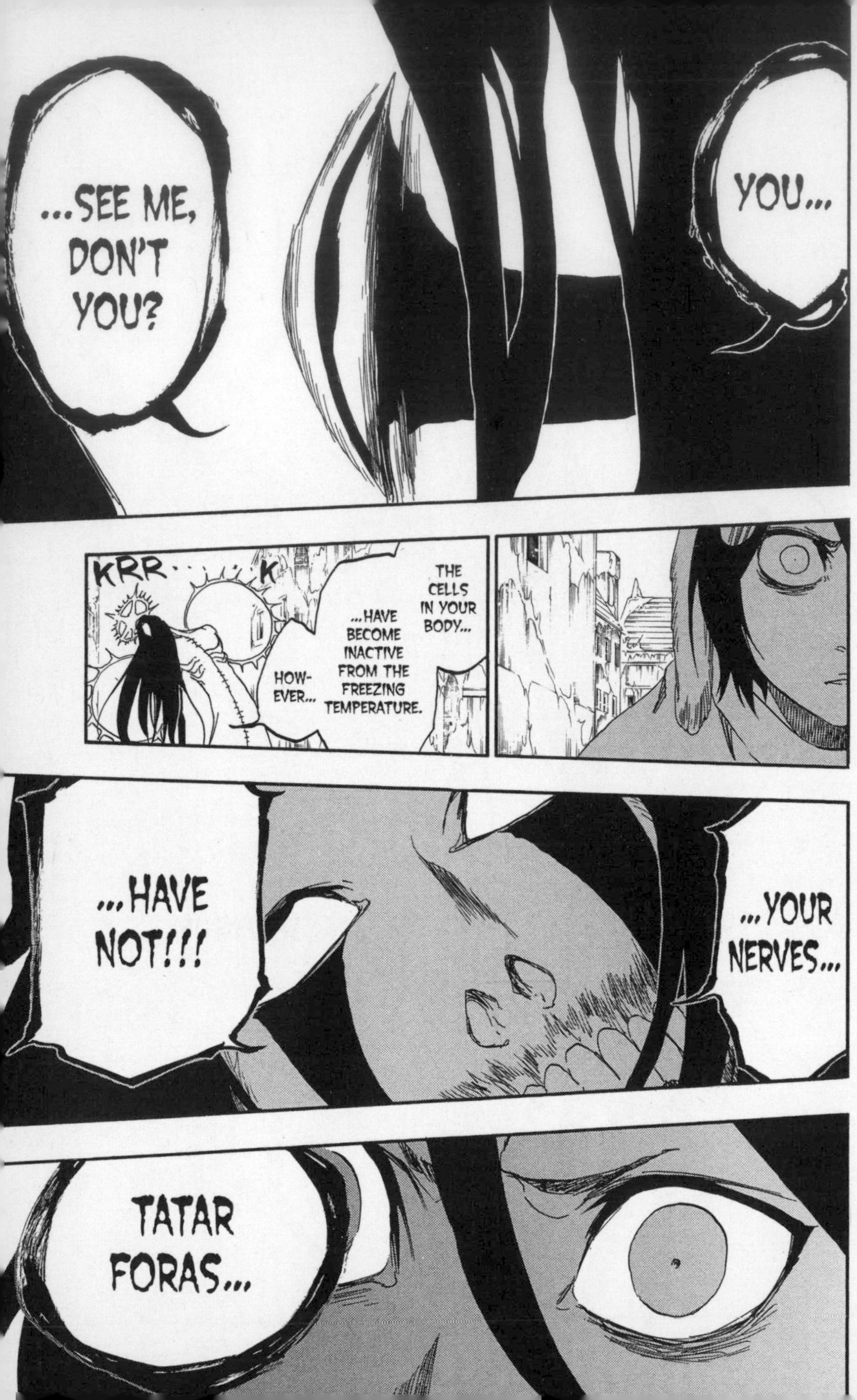
YOU...
...SEE ME, DON'T YOU?
KRR.....K
THE CELLS IN YOUR BODY...
...HAVE BECOME INACTIVE FROM THE FREEZING TEMPERATURE.
HOW-EVER...
...YOUR NERVES...
...HAVE NOT!!!
TATAR FORAS...

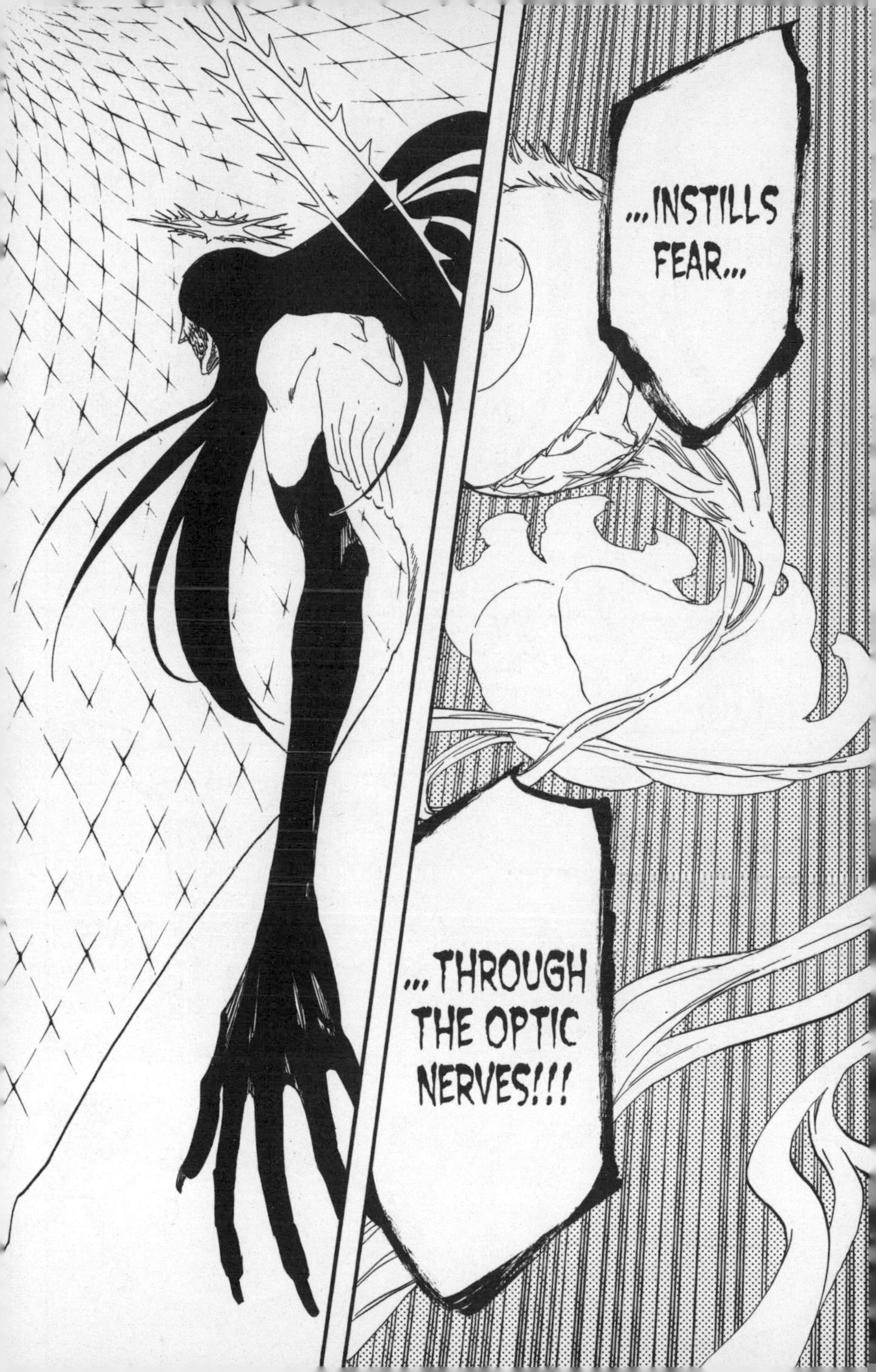
...INSTILLS FEAR...
...THROUGH THE OPTIC NERVES!!!

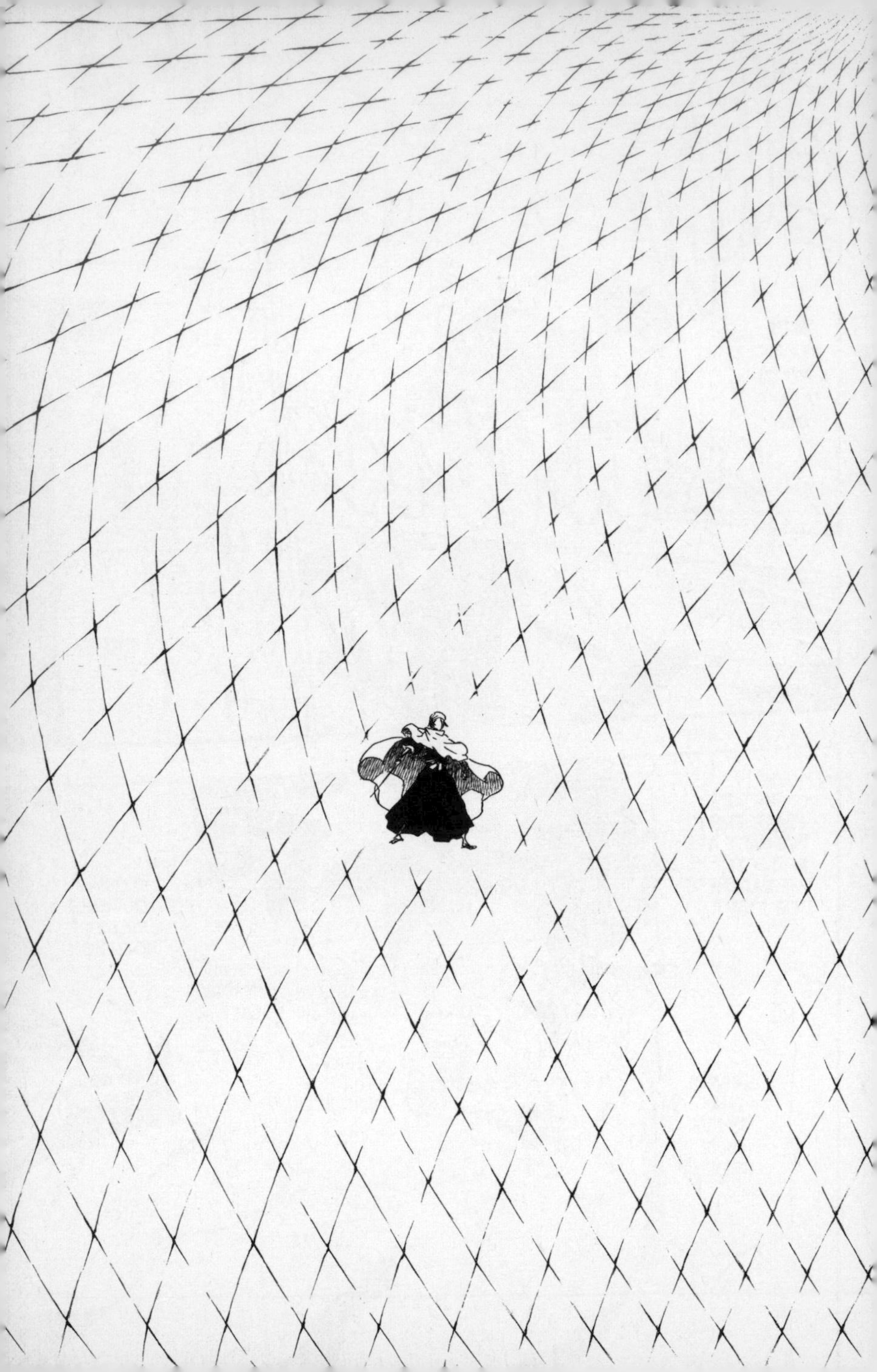

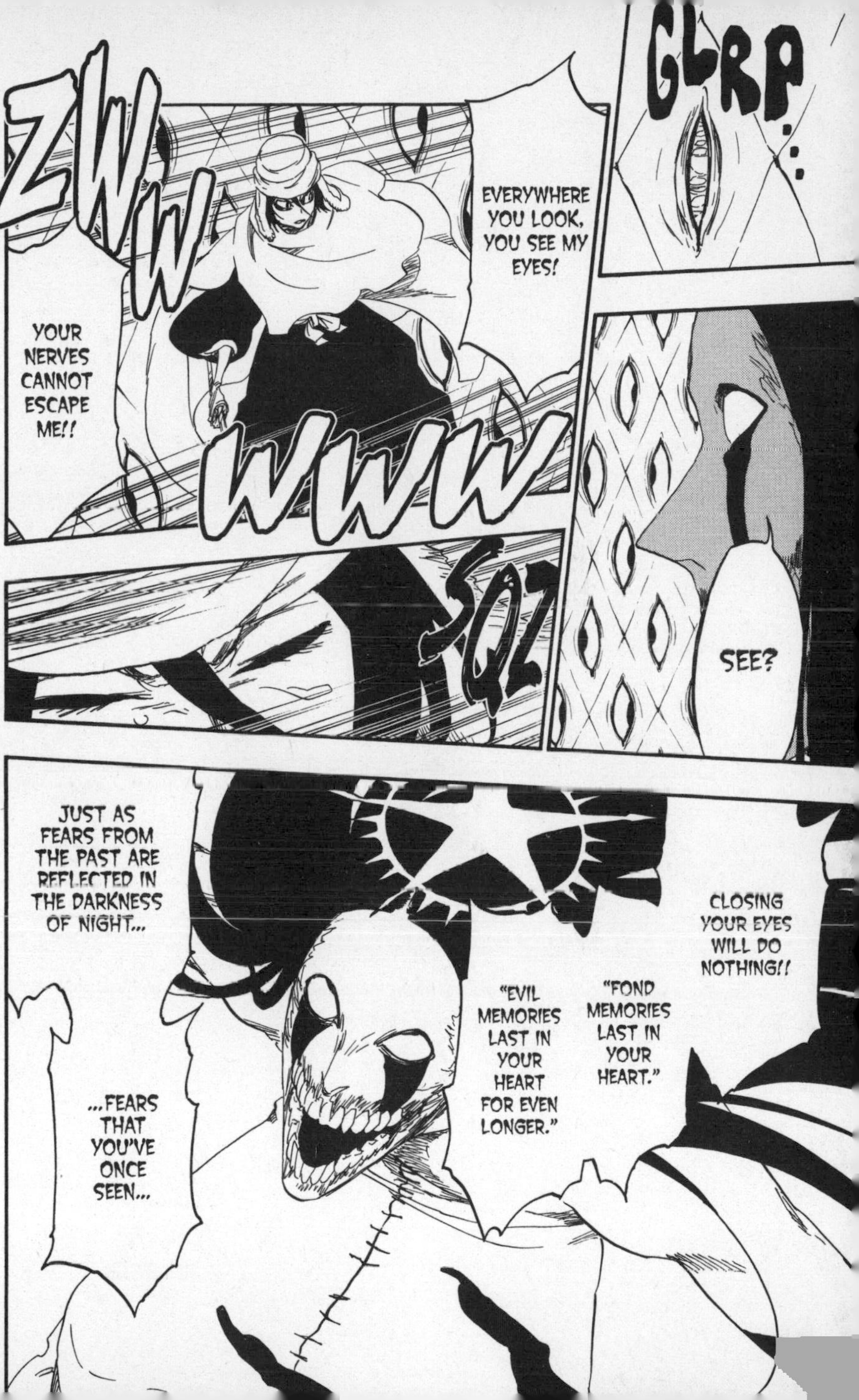
GLRP...
EVERYWHERE YOU LOOK, YOU SEE MY EYES!
SEE?
YOUR NERVES CANNOT ESCAPE ME!!
ZWWW
WWWW
CLOSING YOUR EYES WILL DO NOTHING!!
"FOND MEMORIES LAST IN YOUR HEART."
"EVIL MEMORIES LAST IN YOUR HEART FOR EVEN LONGER."
JUST AS FEARS FROM THE PAST ARE REFLECTED IN THE DARKNESS OF NIGHT...
...FEARS THAT YOU'VE ONCE SEEN...

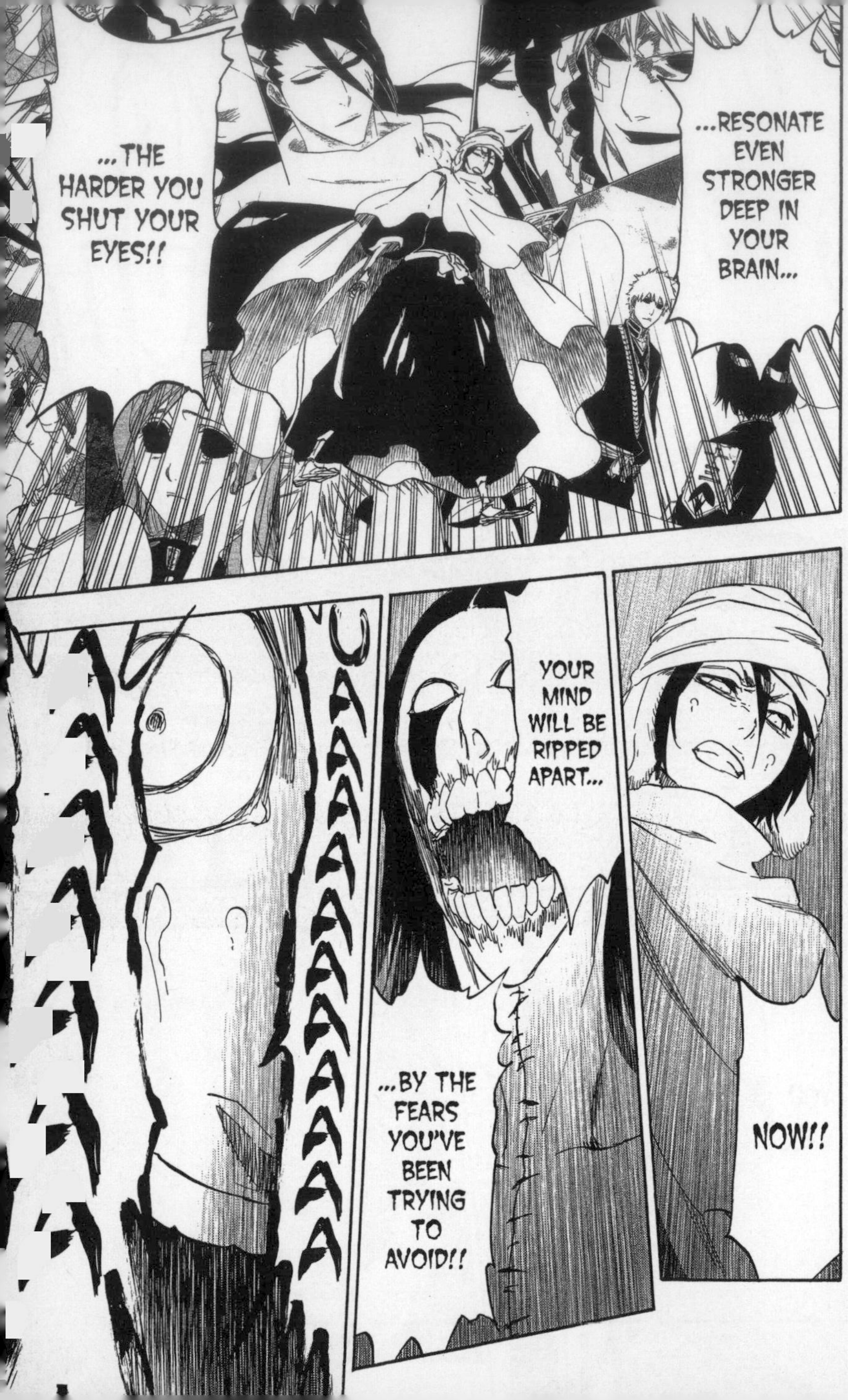
...RESONATE EVEN STRONGER DEEP IN YOUR BRAIN...
...THE HARDER YOU SHUT YOUR EYES!!
NOW!!
YOUR MIND WILL BE RIPPED APART...
...BY THE FEARS YOU'VE BEEN TRYING TO AVOID!!
UAAAAAAAAAAAA

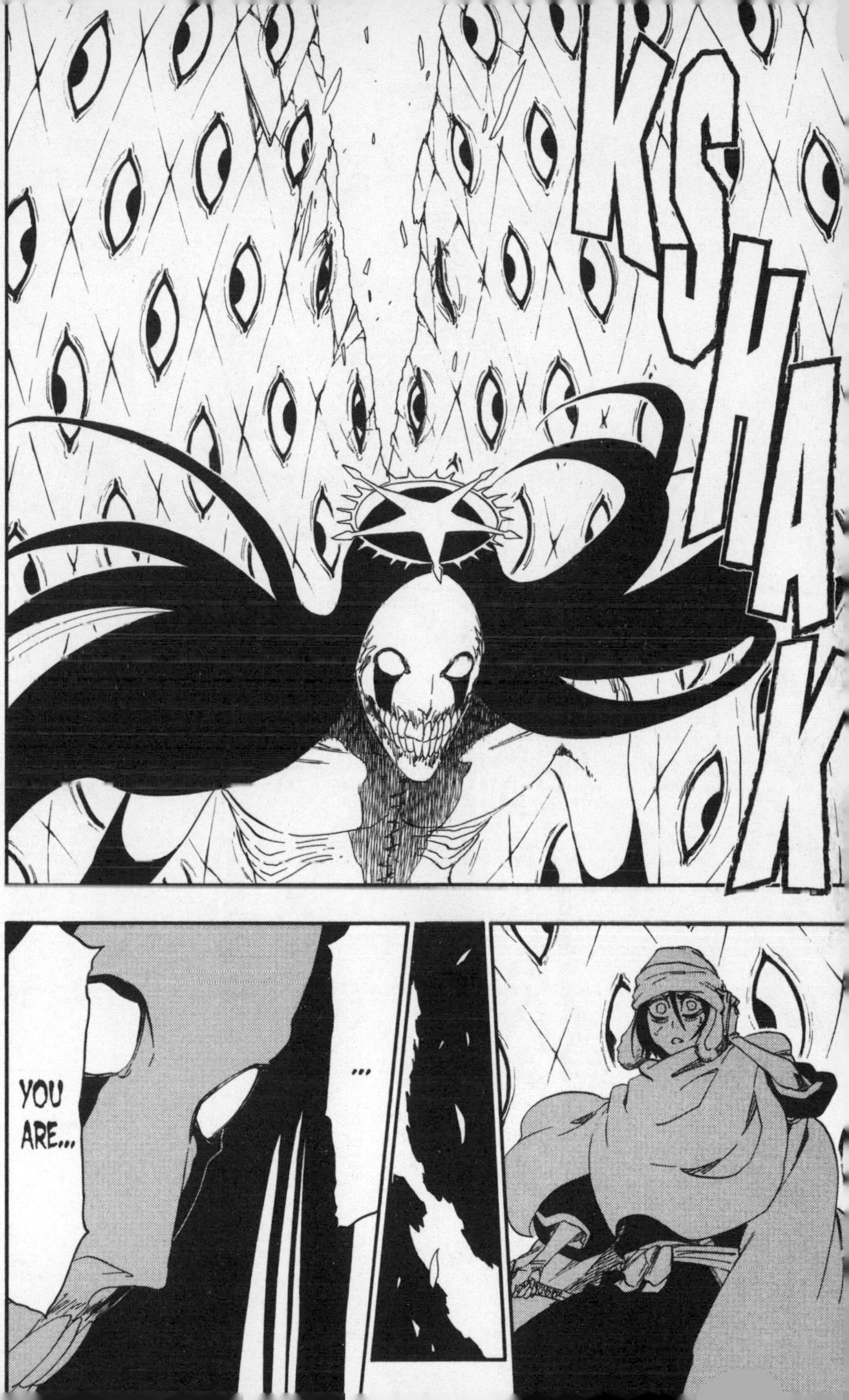
KSHAK
...
YOU ARE...

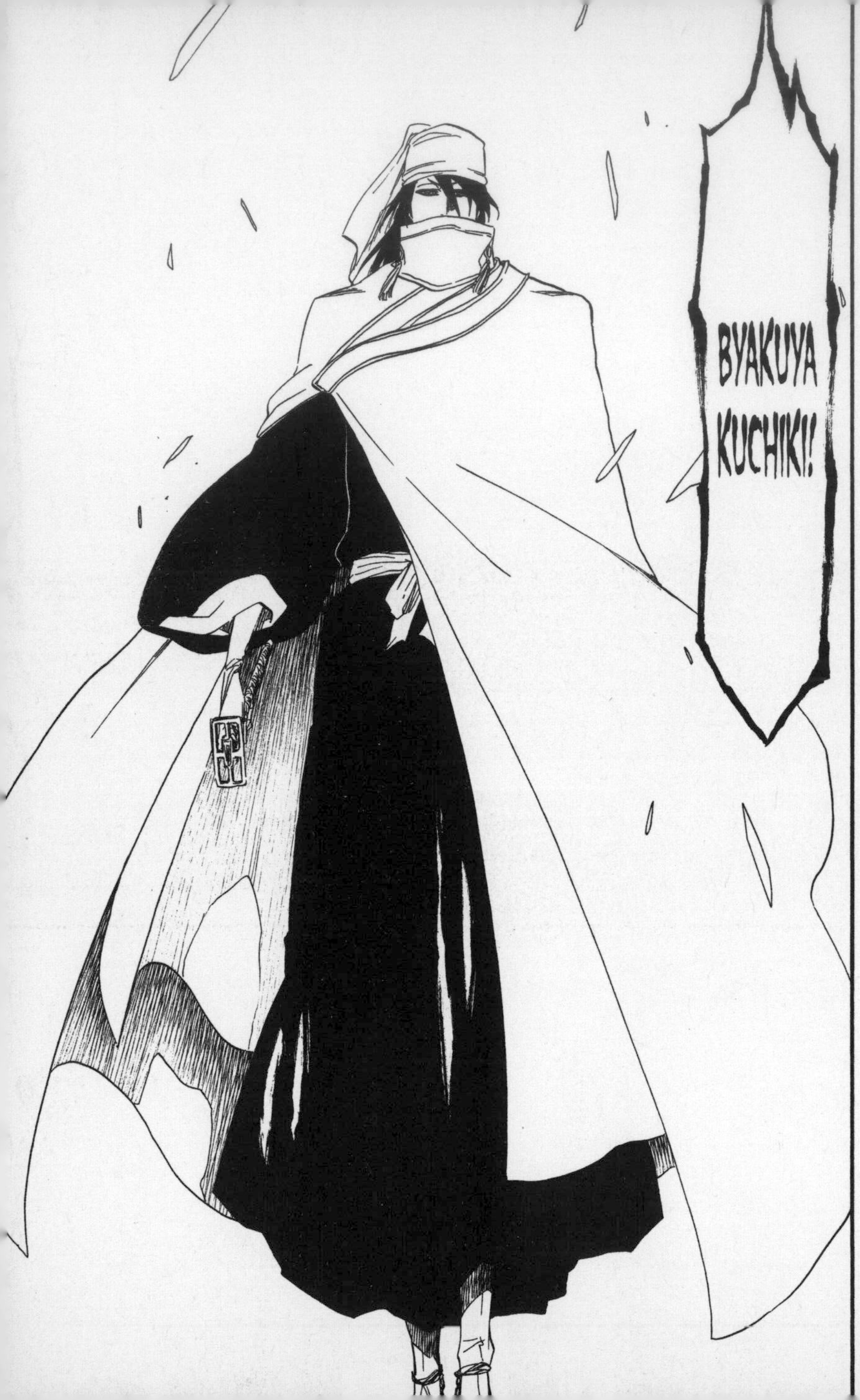
BYAKUYA KUCHIKI!

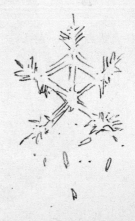

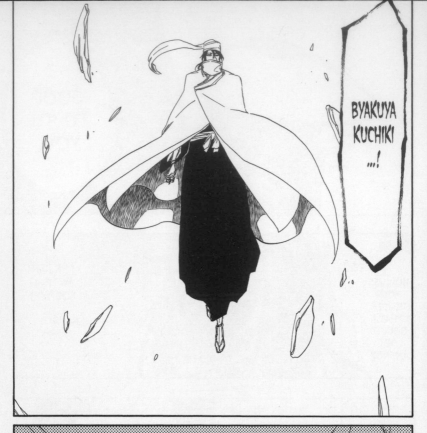

BYAKUYA KUCHIKI ...!

BLEACH 569.

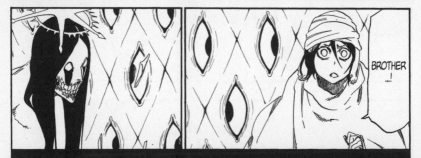

BROTHER ...!

The White Haze

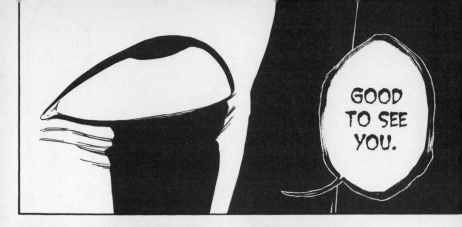

GOOD TO SEE YOU.
I'VE BEEN WAITING FOR YOU.
SO? HOW ARE YOUR INSIDES THAT I GOUGED OUT DOING?
I SCRAPED OUT YOUR ENTIRE STOMACH.
YOU MUST BE HUNGRY FROM NOT BEING ABLE TO EAT.
LOOKS LIKE...
...YOU LOST SOME WEIGHT?

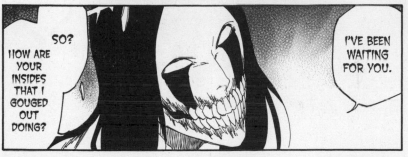

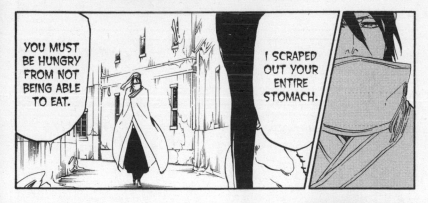

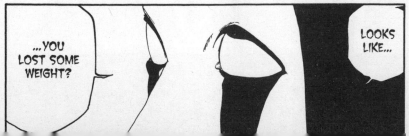

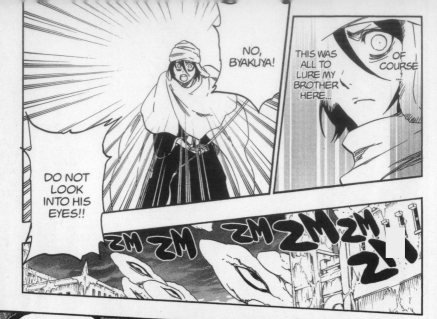

NO, BYAKUYA!

THIS WAS ALL TO LURE MY BROTHER HERE....

OF COURSE...

DO NOT LOOK INTO HIS EYES!!

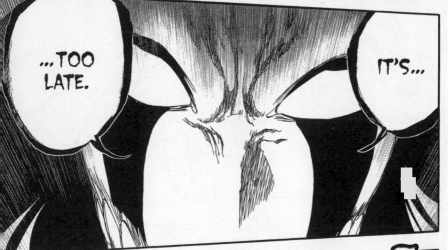

...TOO LATE.

IT'S...

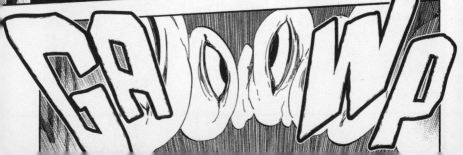

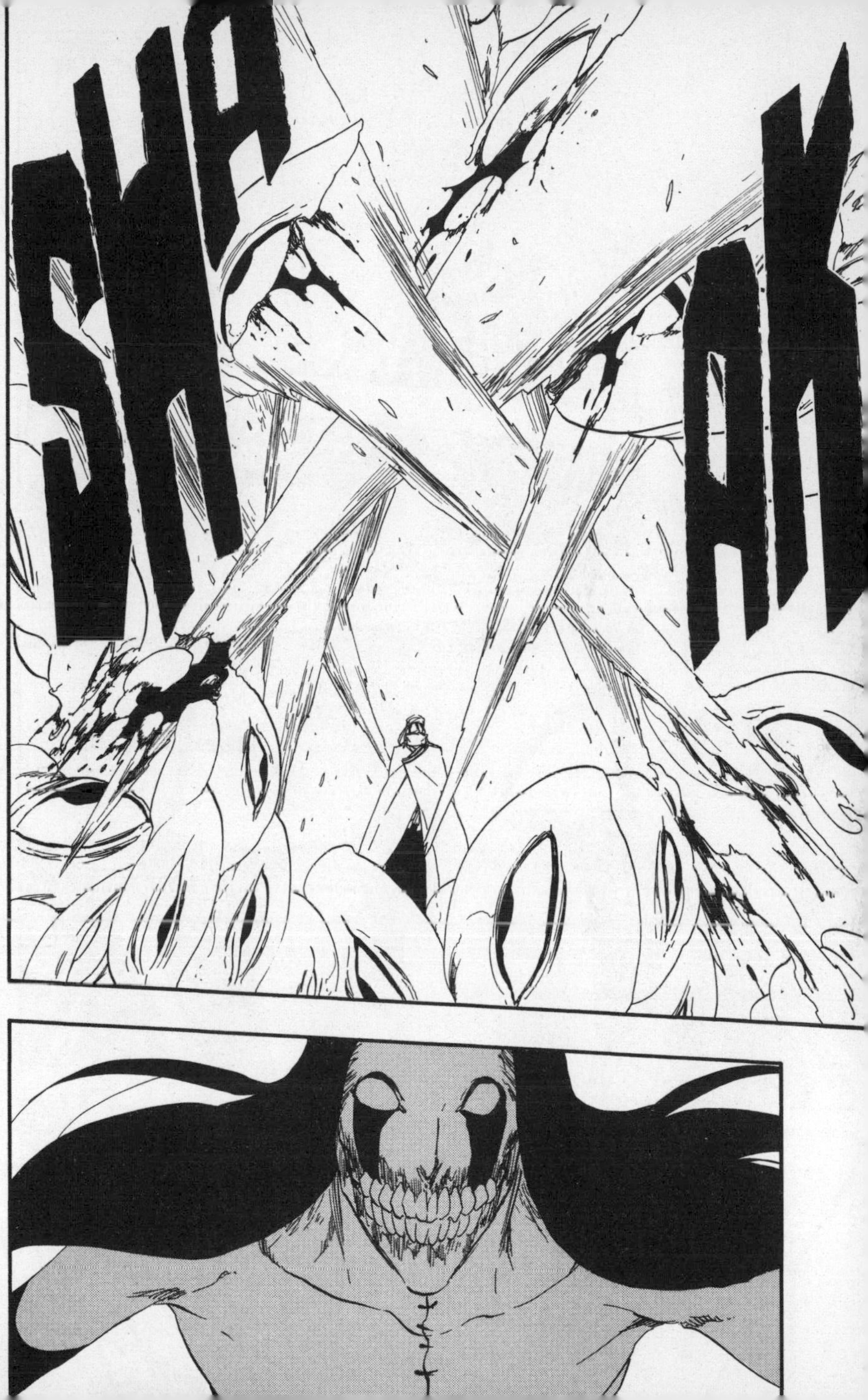
SHRAK

READ THIS WAY

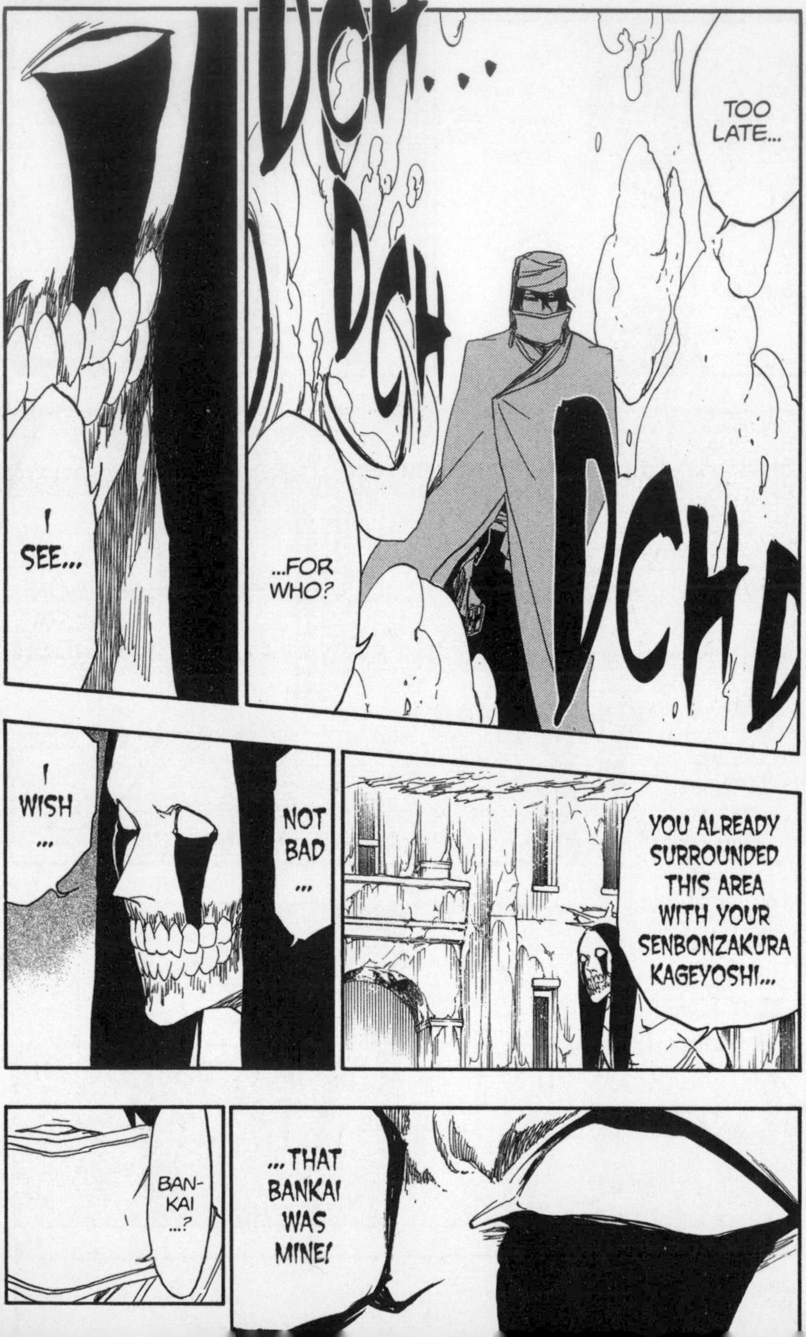
TOO LATE...
DCH...
DCH
DCHD
...FOR WHO?
I SEE...
YOU ALREADY SURROUNDED THIS AREA WITH YOUR SENBONZAKURA KAGEYOSHI...
NOT BAD ...
I WISH ...
...THAT BANKAI WAS MINE!
BAN-KAI ...?

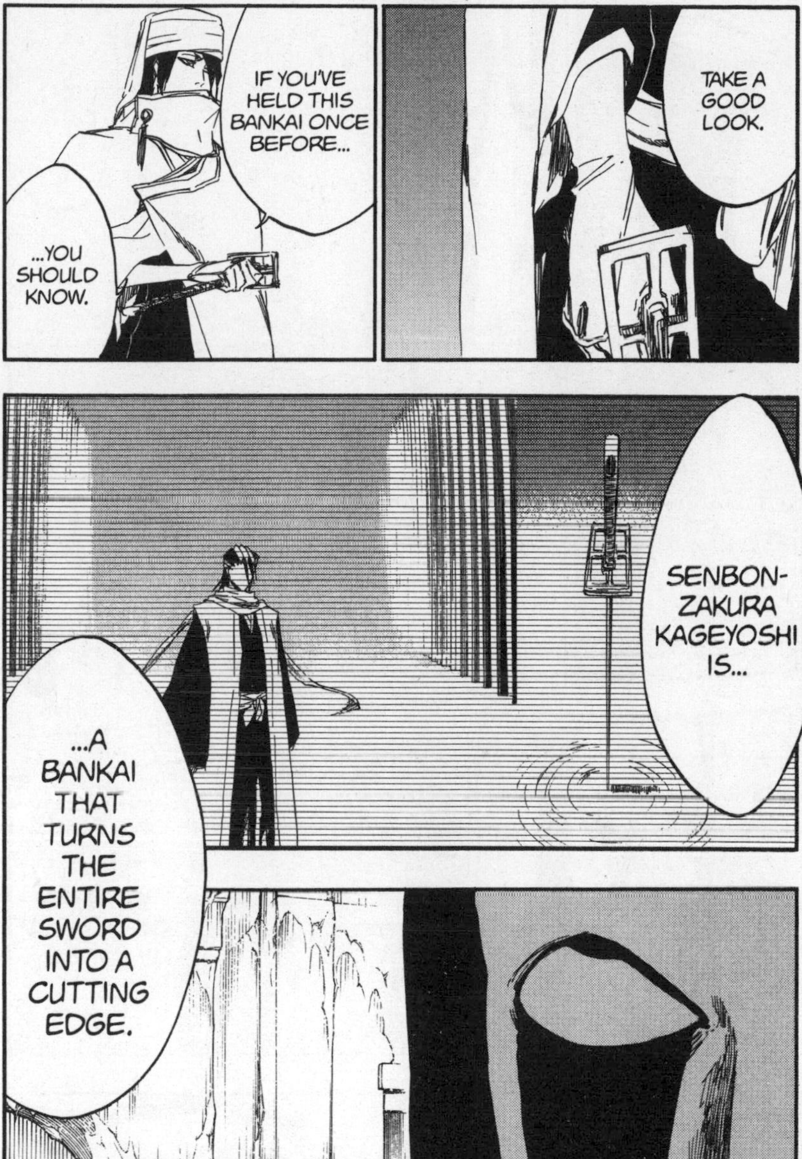
TAKE A GOOD LOOK.
IF YOU'VE HELD THIS BANKAI ONCE BEFORE...
...YOU SHOULD KNOW.
SENBON-ZAKURA KAGEYOSHI IS...
...A BANKAI THAT TURNS THE ENTIRE SWORD INTO A CUTTING EDGE.

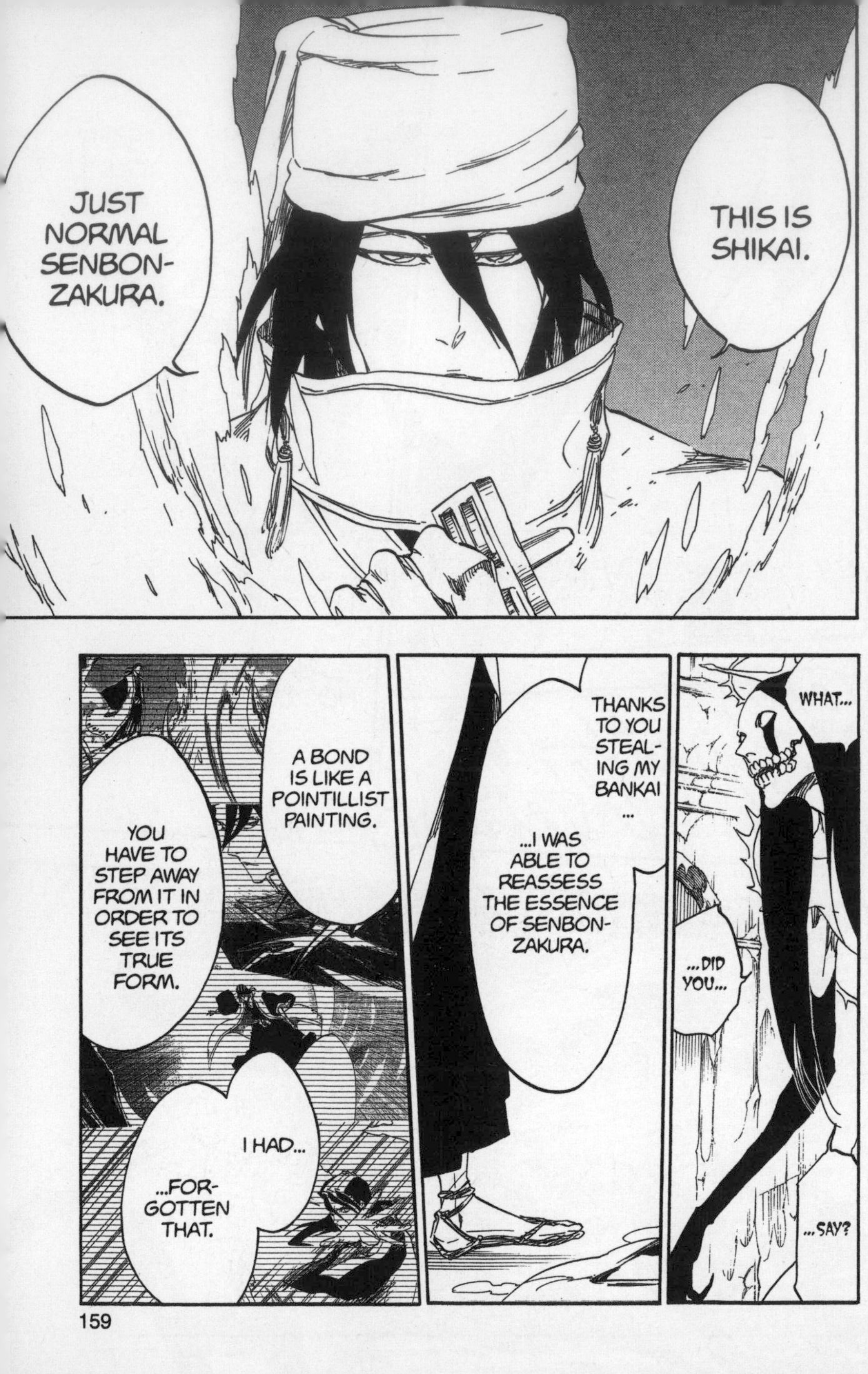
THIS IS SHIKAI.
JUST NORMAL SENBON-ZAKURA.
WHAT...
...DID YOU...
...SAY?
THANKS TO YOU STEAL-ING MY BANKAI ...
...I WAS ABLE TO REASSESS THE ESSENCE OF SENBON-ZAKURA.
A BOND IS LIKE A POINTILLIST PAINTING.
YOU HAVE TO STEP AWAY FROM IT IN ORDER TO SEE ITS TRUE FORM.
I HAD...
...FOR-GOTTEN THAT.

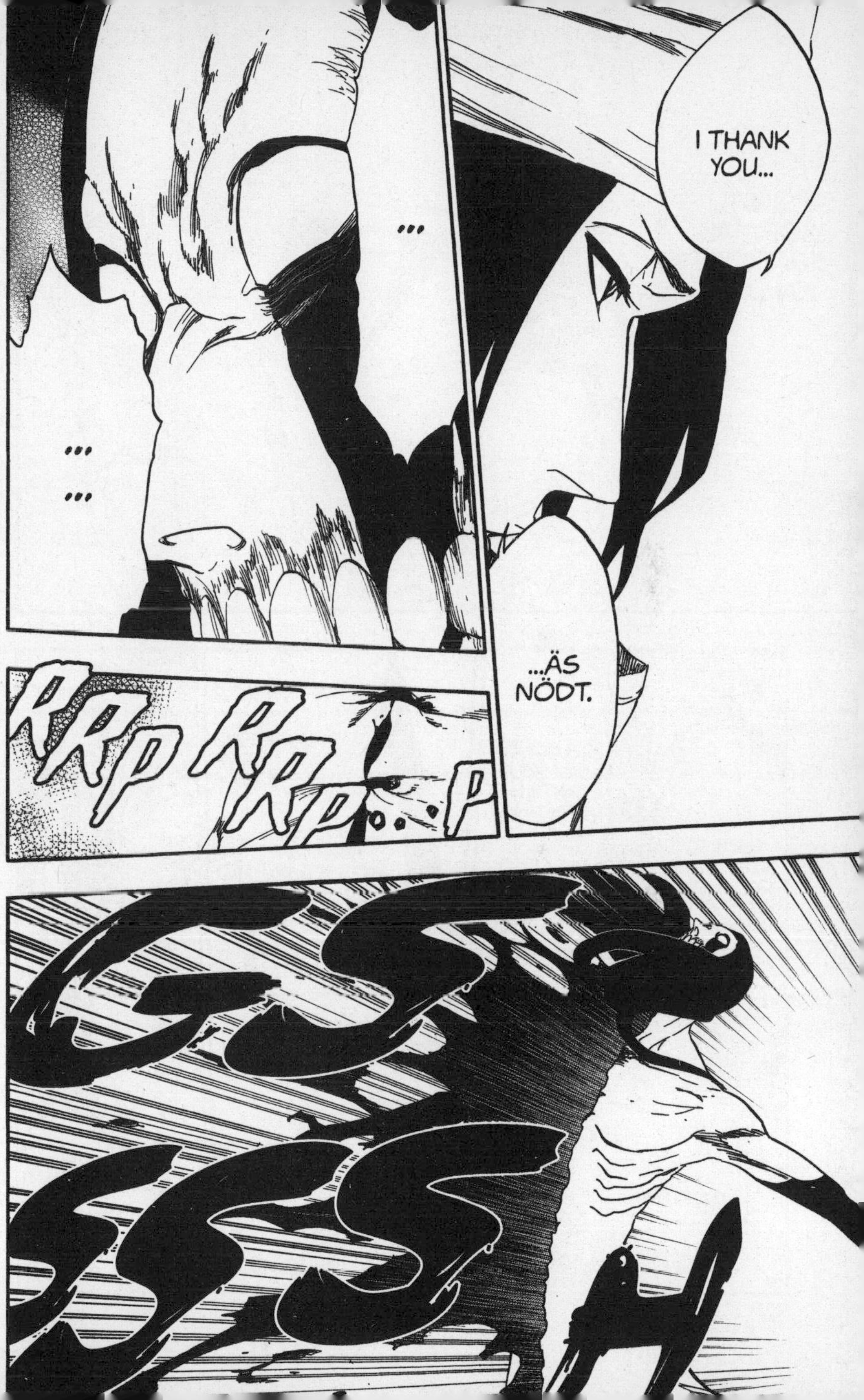
I THANK YOU...
...ÄS NÖDT.
...
...
...
RRP RRP...P

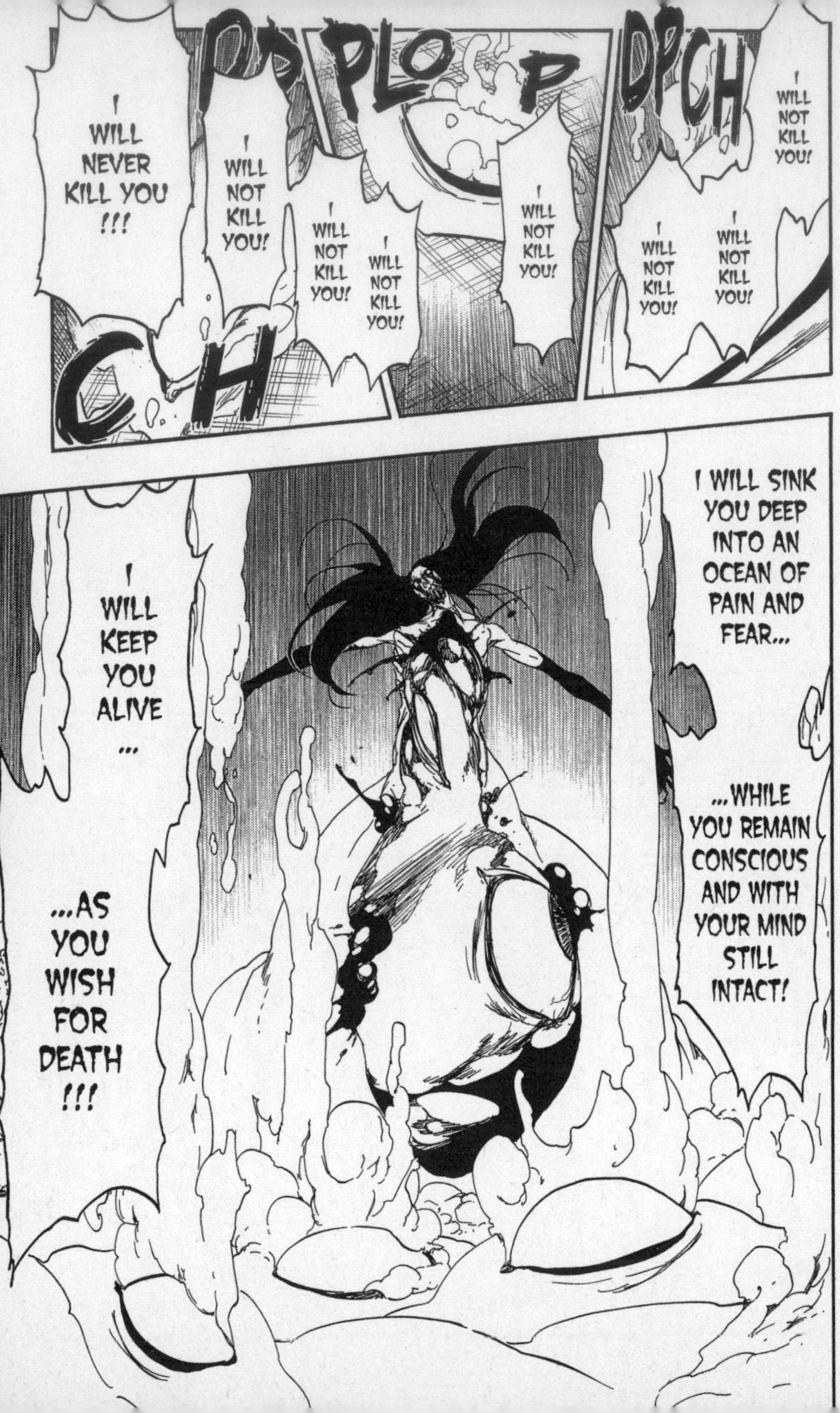
DPCH
I WILL NOT KILL YOU!
I WILL NOT KILL YOU!
I WILL NOT KILL YOU!
PLOP
I WILL NOT KILL YOU!
I WILL NOT KILL YOU!
I WILL NOT KILL YOU!
I WILL NOT KILL YOU!
I WILL NEVER KILL YOU!!!
CH
I WILL SINK YOU DEEP INTO AN OCEAN OF PAIN AND FEAR...
...WHILE YOU REMAIN CONSCIOUS AND WITH YOUR MIND STILL INTACT!
I WILL KEEP YOU ALIVE...
...AS YOU WISH FOR DEATH!!!

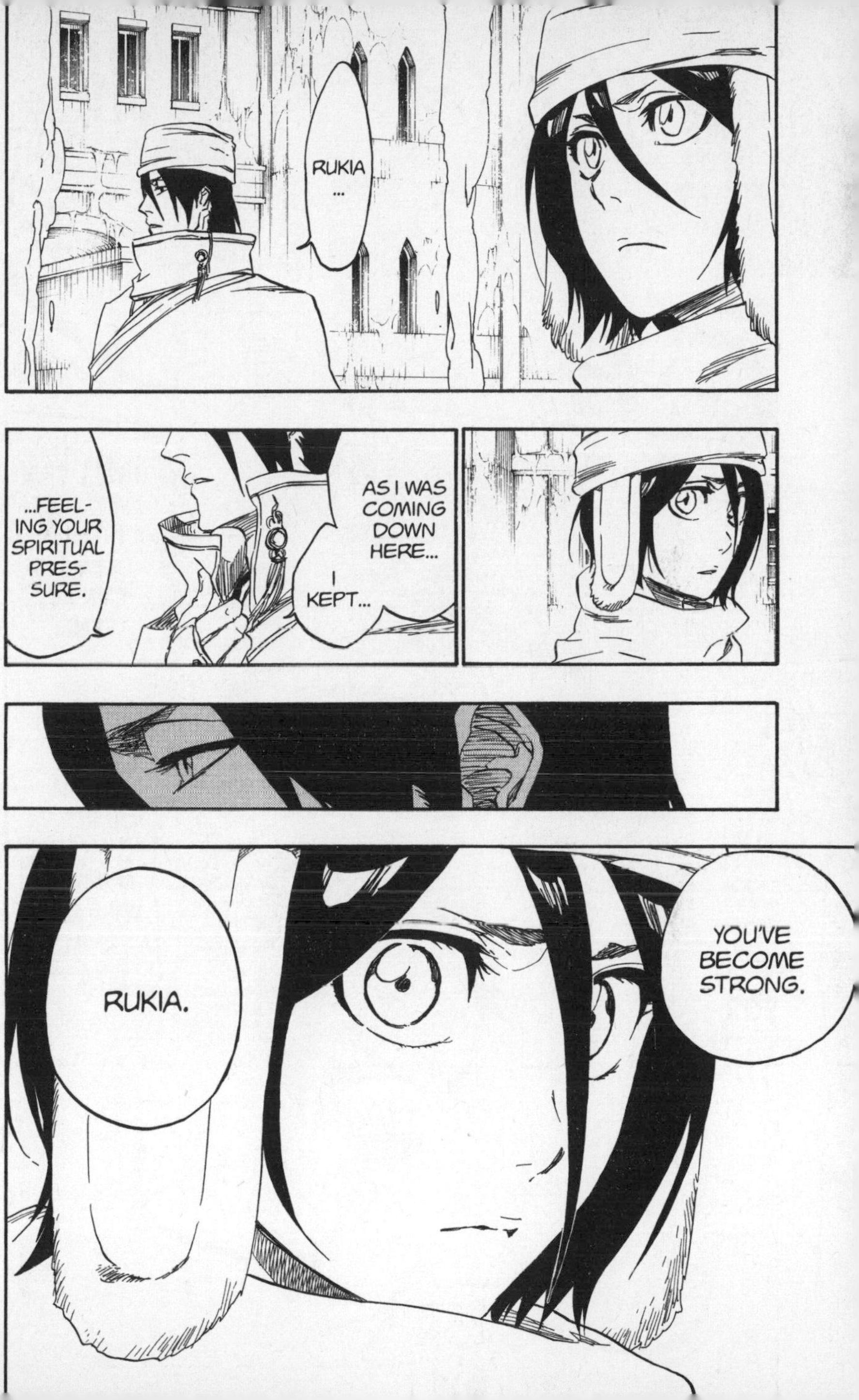
RUKIA ...
AS I WAS COMING DOWN HERE... I KEPT...
...FEELING YOUR SPIRITUAL PRESSURE.
YOU'VE BECOME STRONG.
RUKIA.

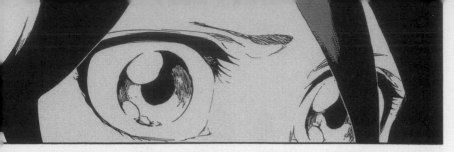

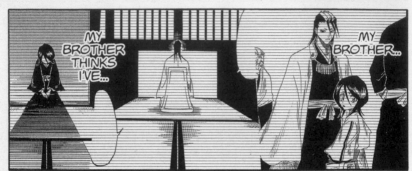

MY
BROTHER
THINKS
I'VE...

MY
BROTHER...

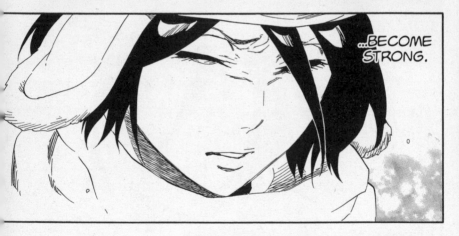

...BECOME
STRONG.

...IS NOT
BORN IN A
VACUUM.

FEAR
...

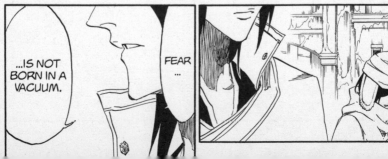

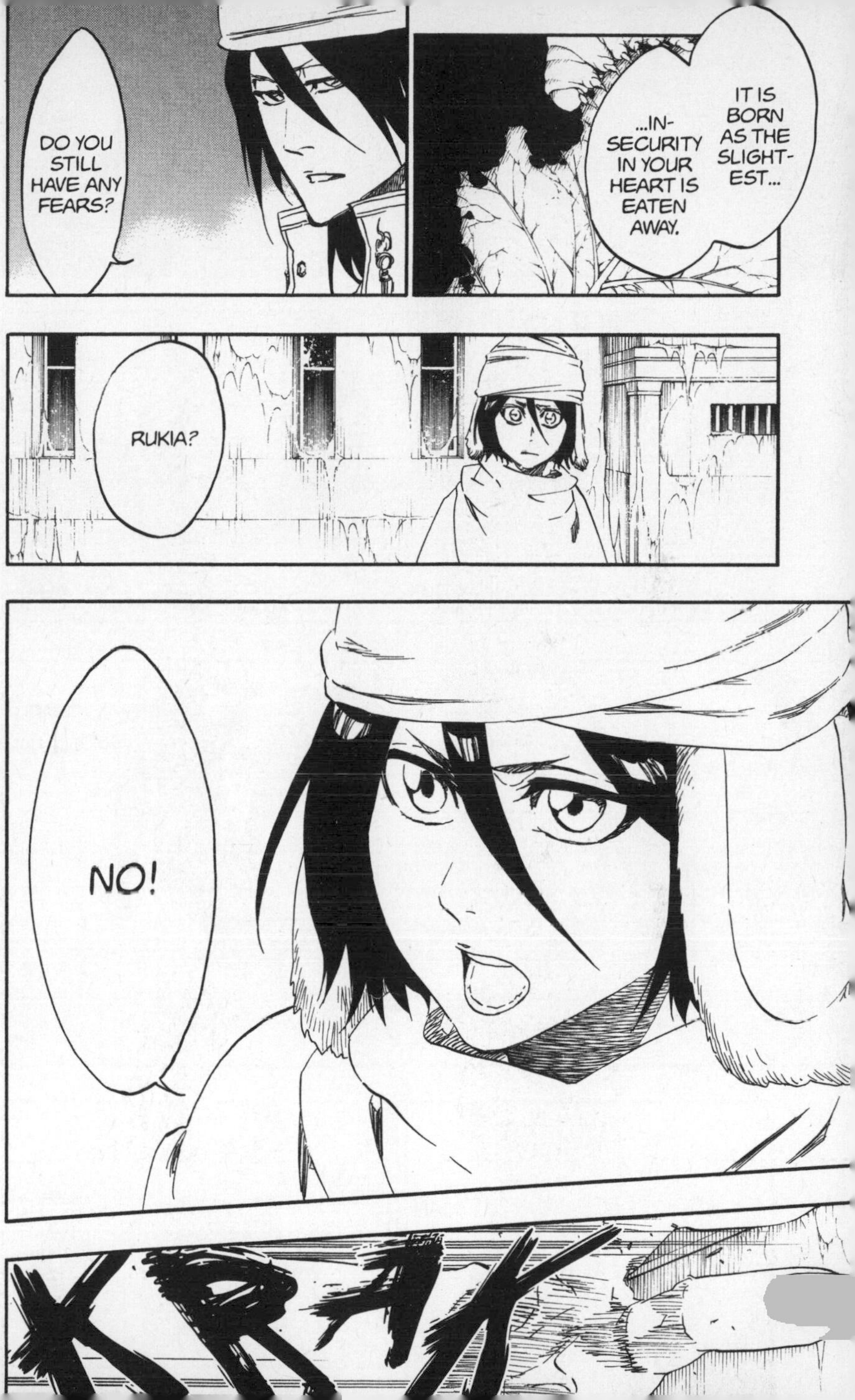
IT IS BORN AS THE SLIGHT-EST...
...IN-SECURITY IN YOUR HEART IS EATEN AWAY.
DO YOU STILL HAVE ANY FEARS?
RUKIA?
NO!
KRAK

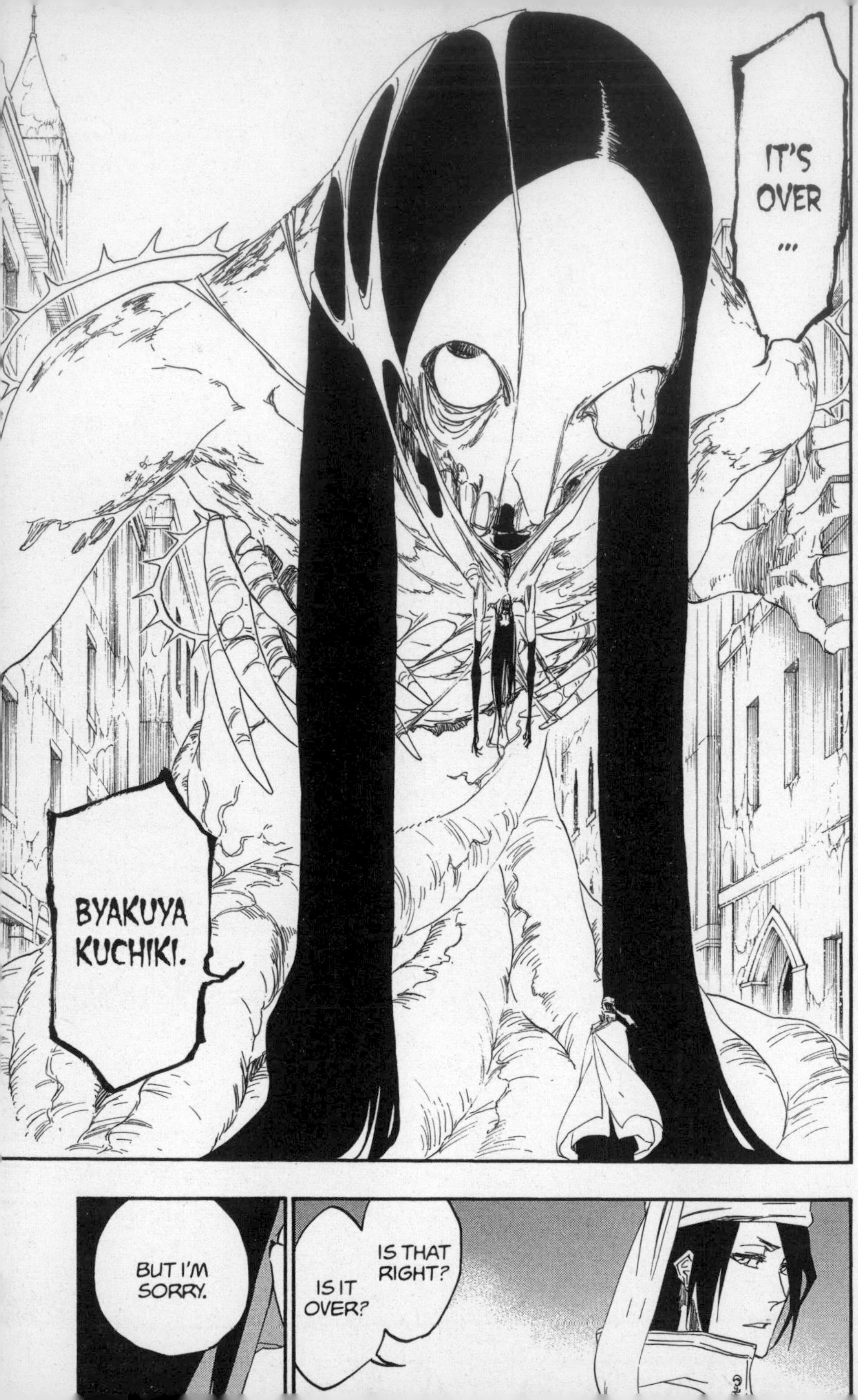
IT'S OVER ...
BYAKUYA KUCHIKI.
IS IT OVER?
IS THAT RIGHT?
BUT I'M SORRY.

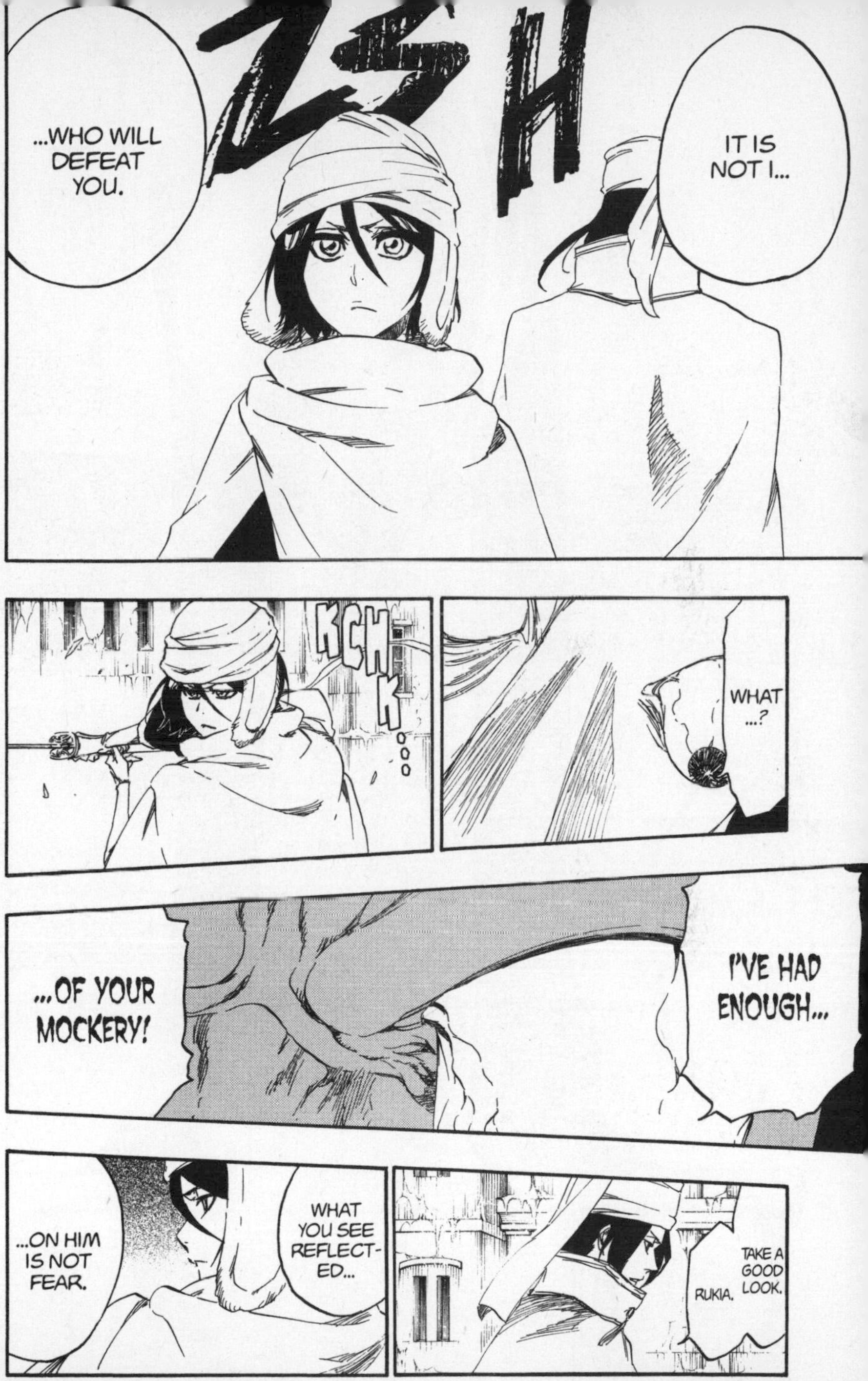
IT IS NOT I...
ZSH
...WHO WILL DEFEAT YOU.
WHAT ...?
KCH-K
I'VE HAD ENOUGH...
...OF YOUR MOCKERY!
TAKE A GOOD LOOK.
RUKIA.
WHAT YOU SEE REFLECTED...
...ON HIM IS NOT FEAR.

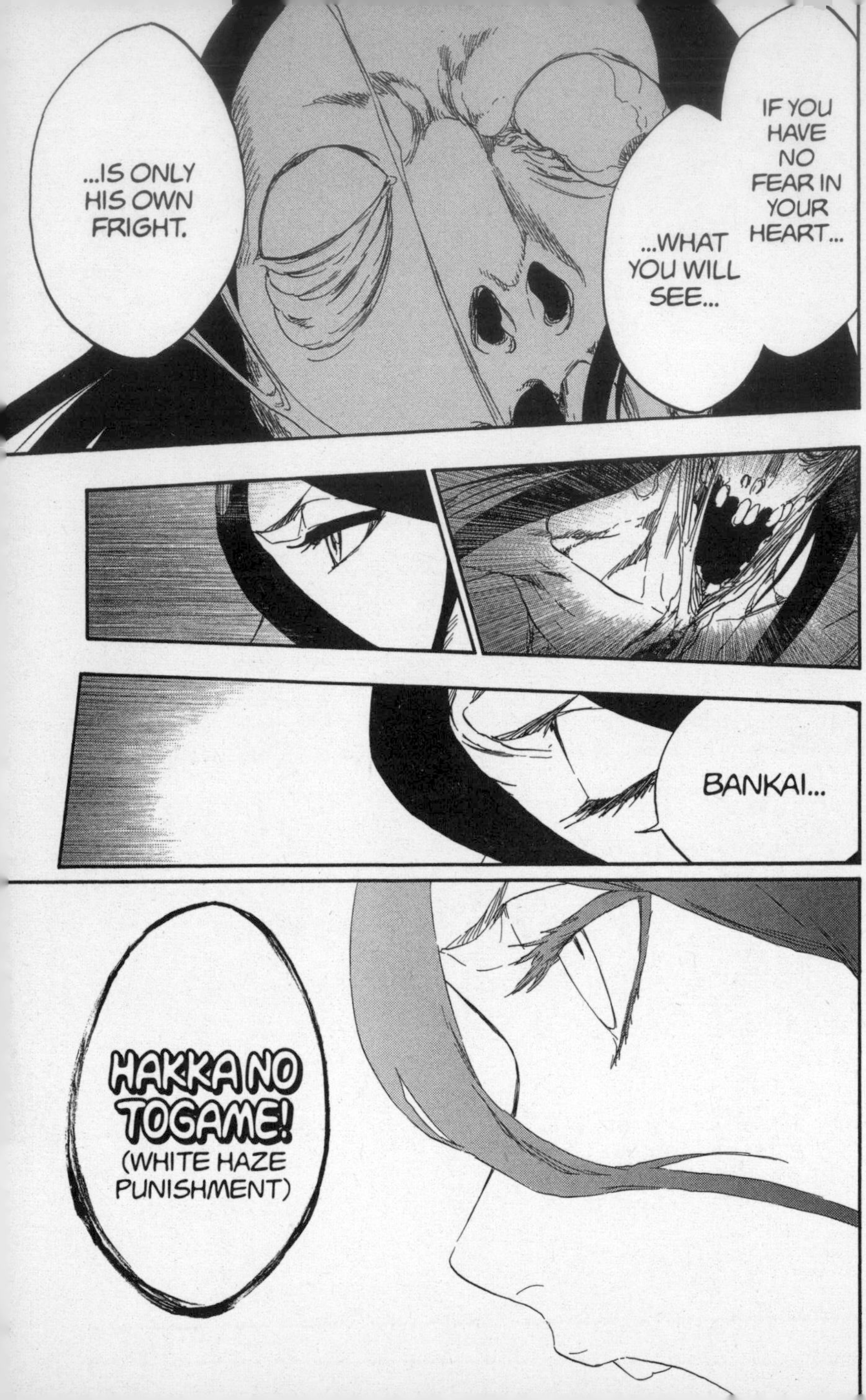
IF YOU HAVE NO FEAR IN YOUR HEART...
...WHAT YOU WILL SEE...
...IS ONLY HIS OWN FRIGHT.
BANKAI...
HAKKA NO TOGAME!
(WHITE HAZE PUNISHMENT)

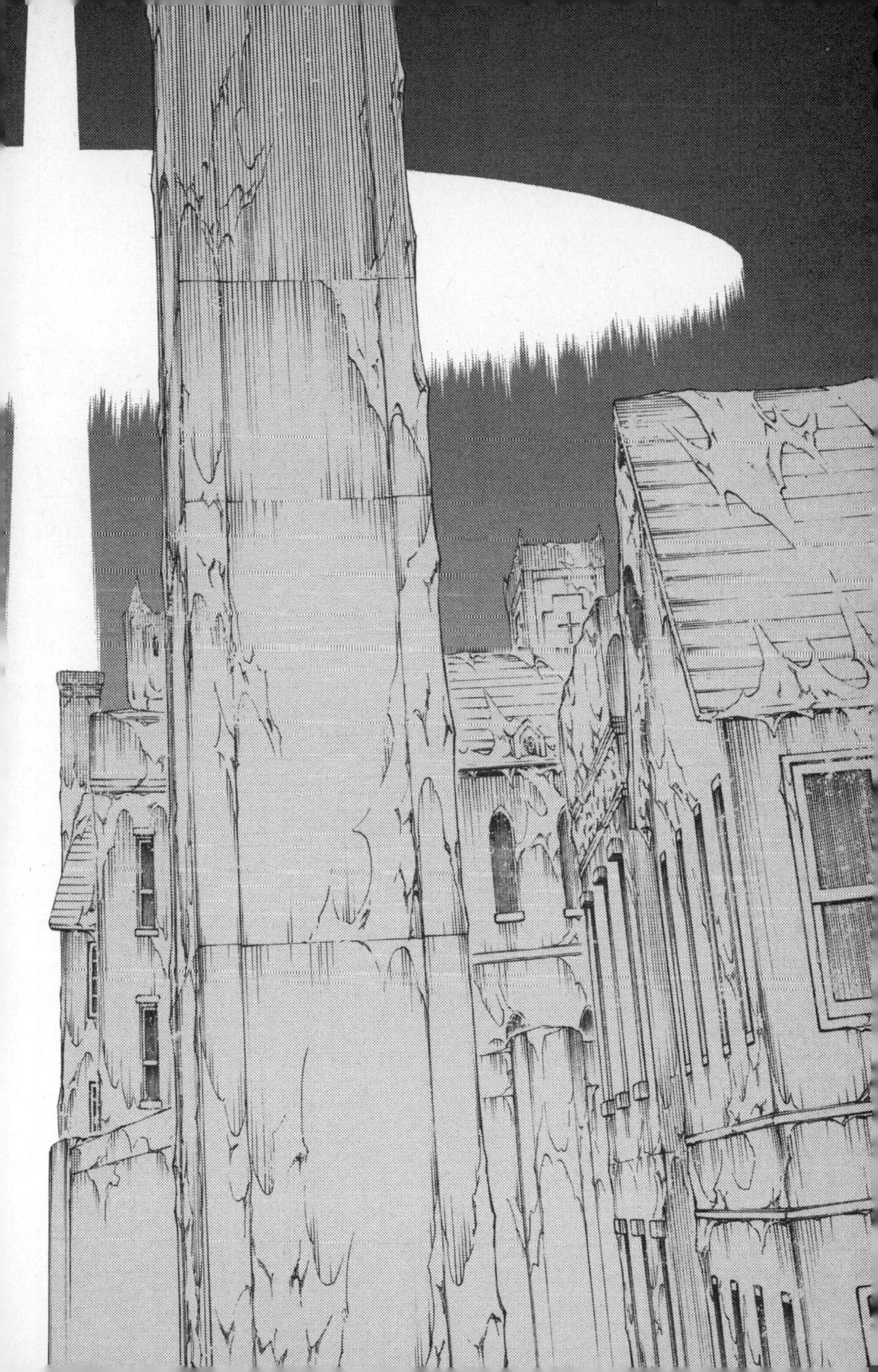

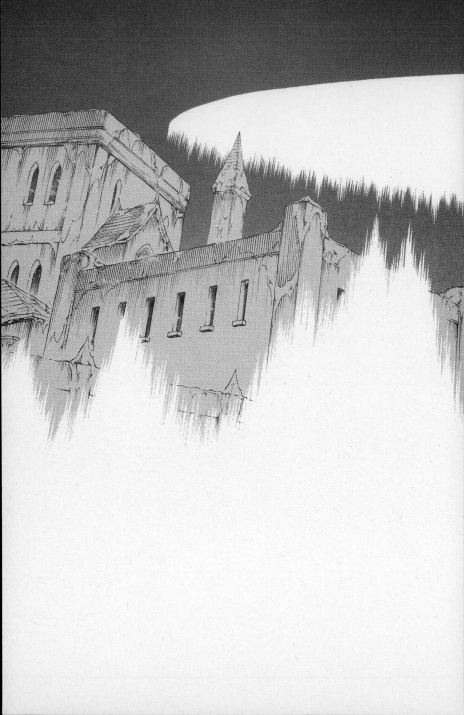

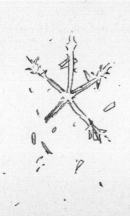

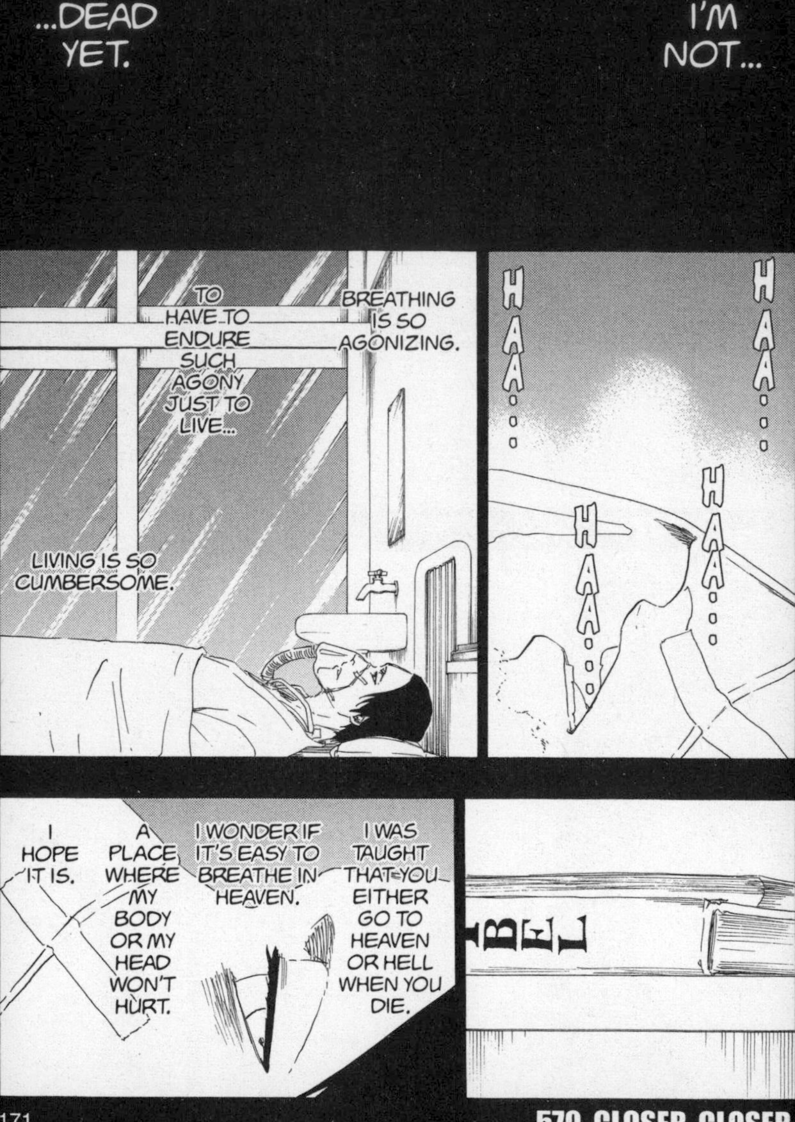
I'M NOT...
...DEAD YET.
HAAA...
HAAA...
HAAA...
HAAA...
BREATHING IS SO AGONIZING.
TO HAVE TO ENDURE SUCH AGONY JUST TO LIVE...
LIVING IS SO CUMBERSOME.
I WAS TAUGHT THAT YOU EITHER GO TO HEAVEN OR HELL WHEN YOU DIE.
I WONDER IF IT'S EASY TO BREATHE IN HEAVEN.
A PLACE WHERE MY BODY OR MY HEAD WON'T HURT.
I HOPE IT IS.

570. CLOSER, CLOSER

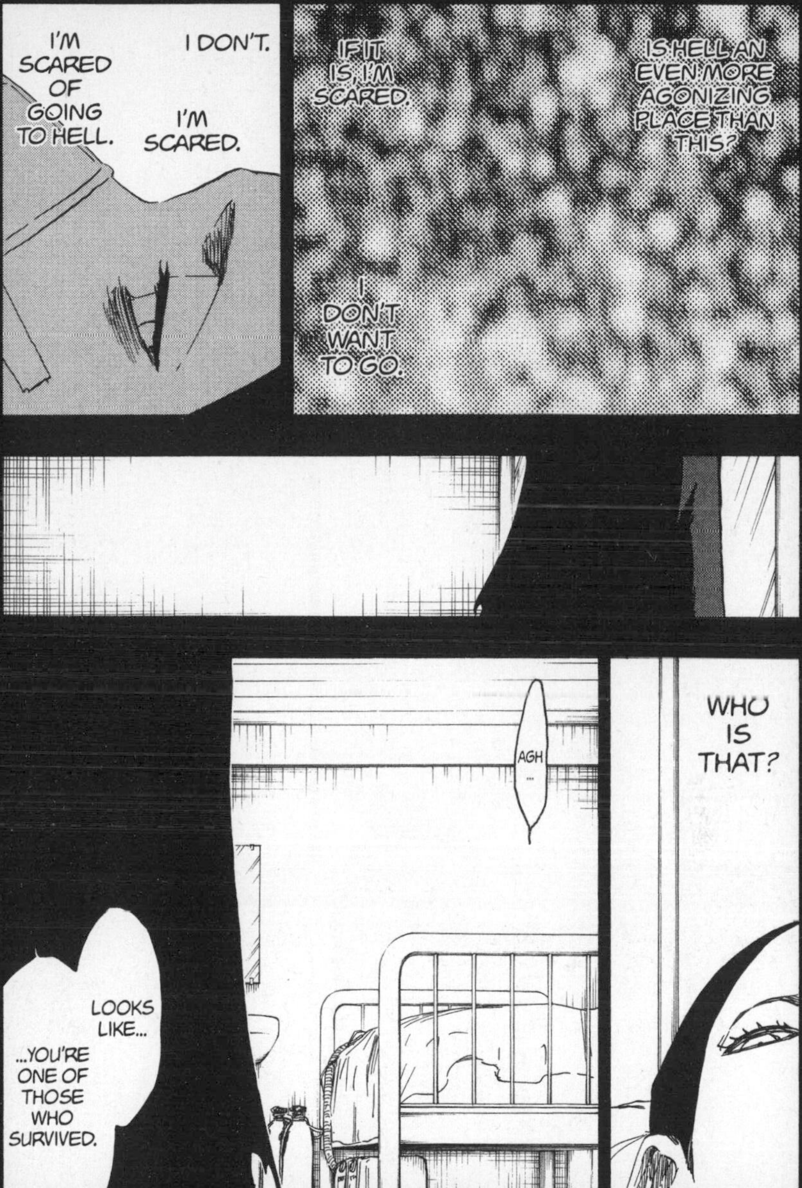
IS HELL AN EVEN MORE AGONIZING PLACE THAN THIS?
IF IT IS, I'M SCARED.
I DON'T WANT TO GO.
I DON'T.
I'M SCARED.
I'M SCARED OF GOING TO HELL.
WHO IS THAT?
AGH...
LOOKS LIKE...
...YOU'RE ONE OF THOSE WHO SURVIVED.

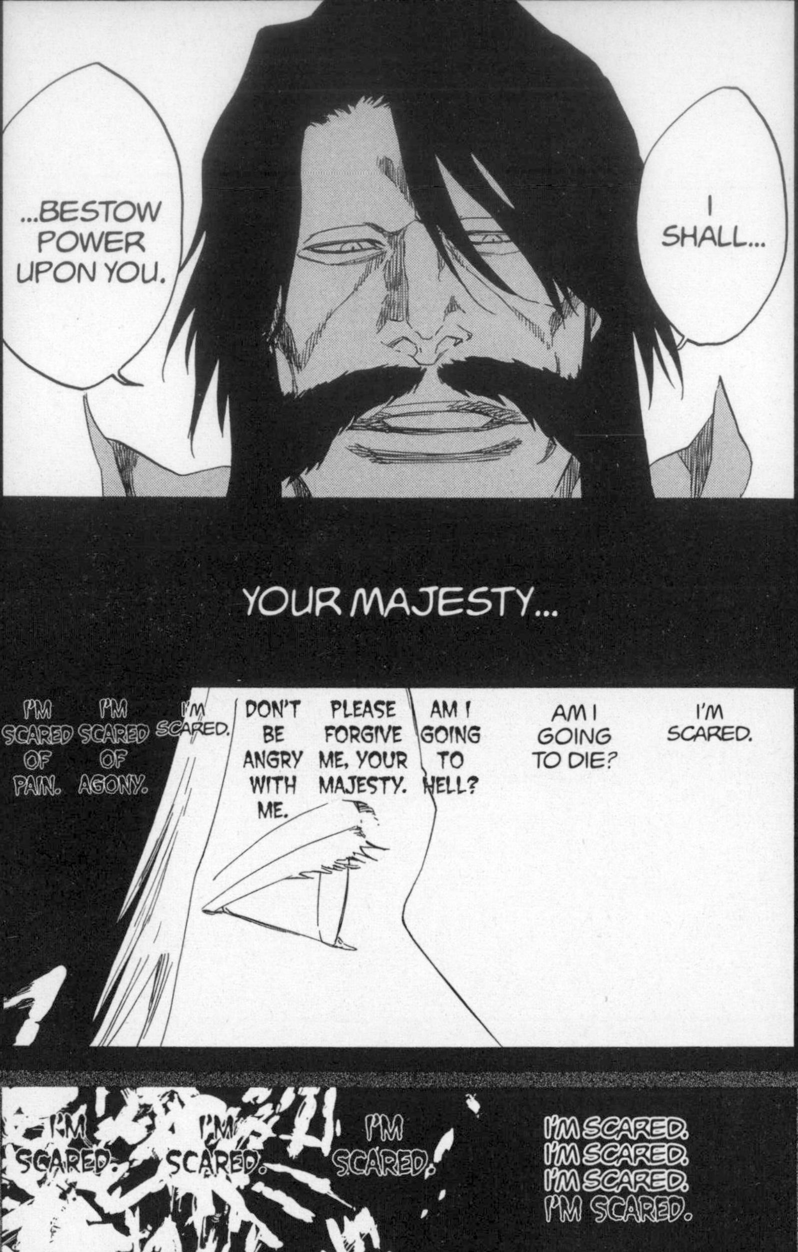
I SHALL...
...BESTOW POWER UPON YOU.
YOUR MAJESTY...
I'M SCARED.
AM I GOING TO DIE?
AM I GOING TO HELL?
PLEASE FORGIVE ME, YOUR MAJESTY.
DON'T BE ANGRY WITH ME.
I'M SCARED.
I'M SCARED OF AGONY.
I'M SCARED OF PAIN.
I'M SCARED. I'M SCARED. I'M SCARED. I'M SCARED.
I'M SCARED.
I'M SCARED.
I'M SCARED.

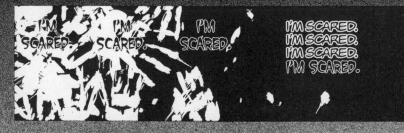

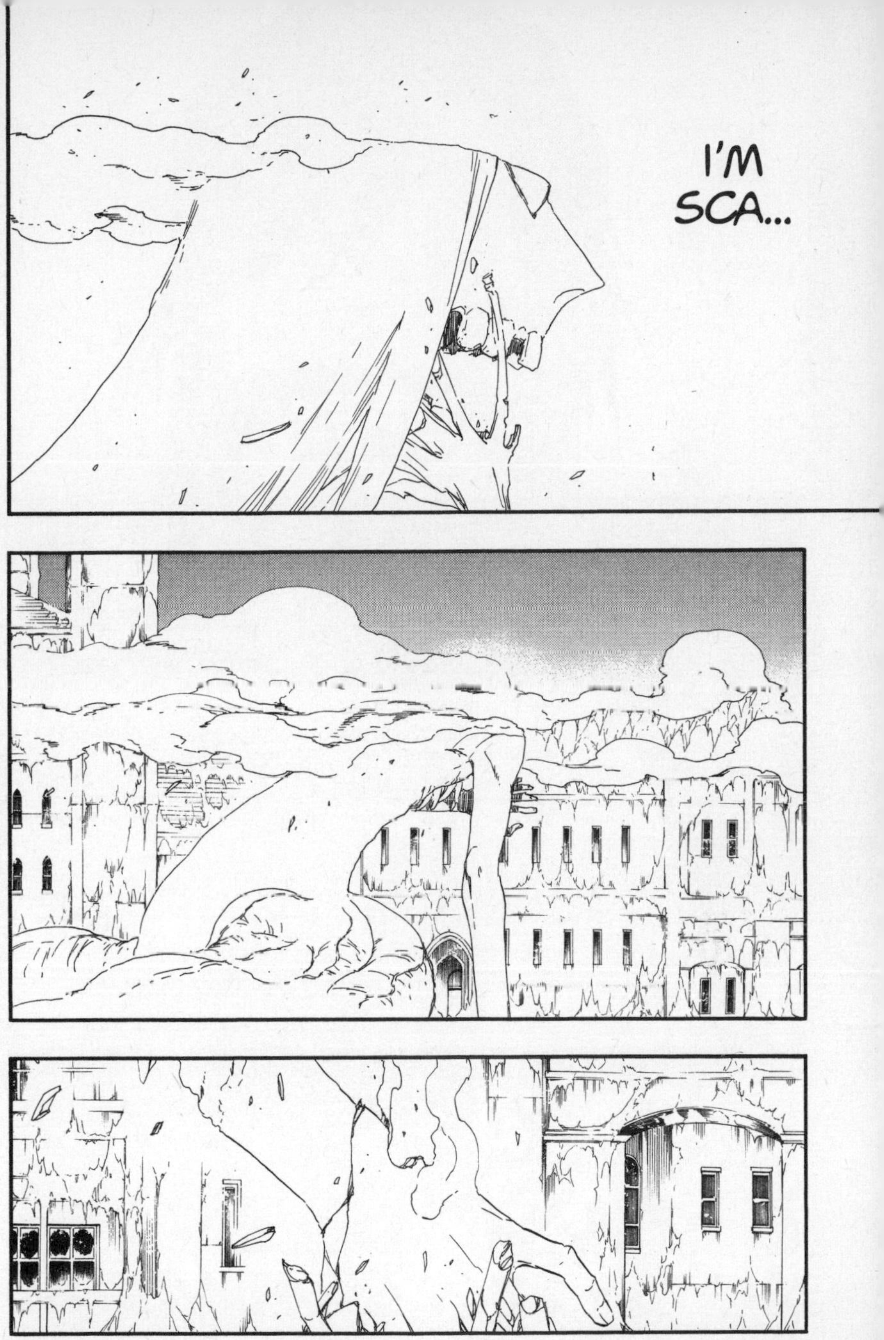
I'M
SCA...

READ THIS WAY

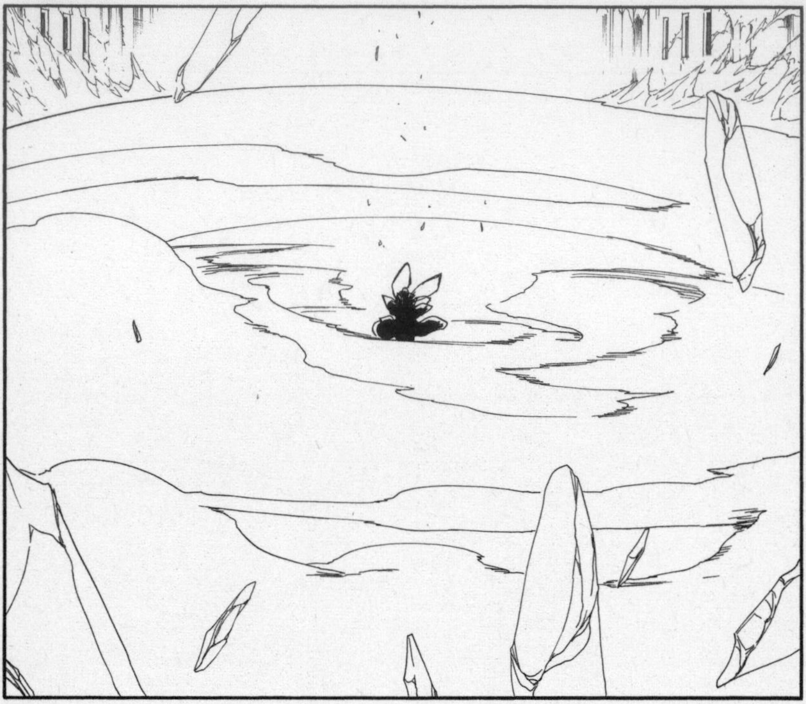

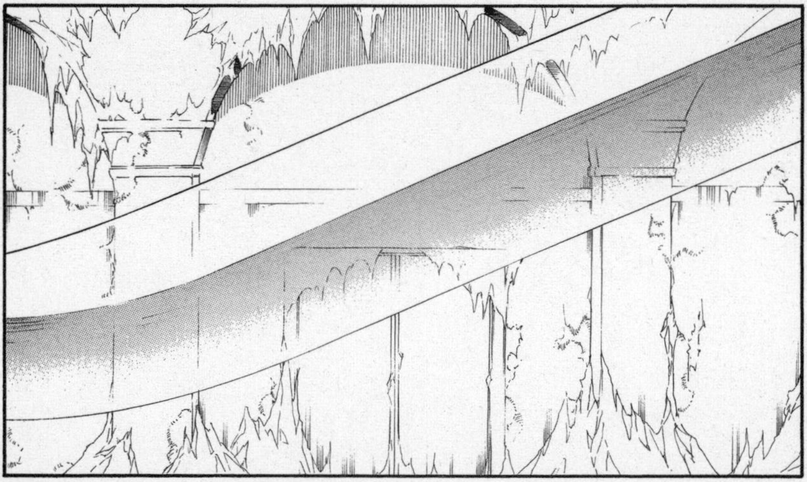

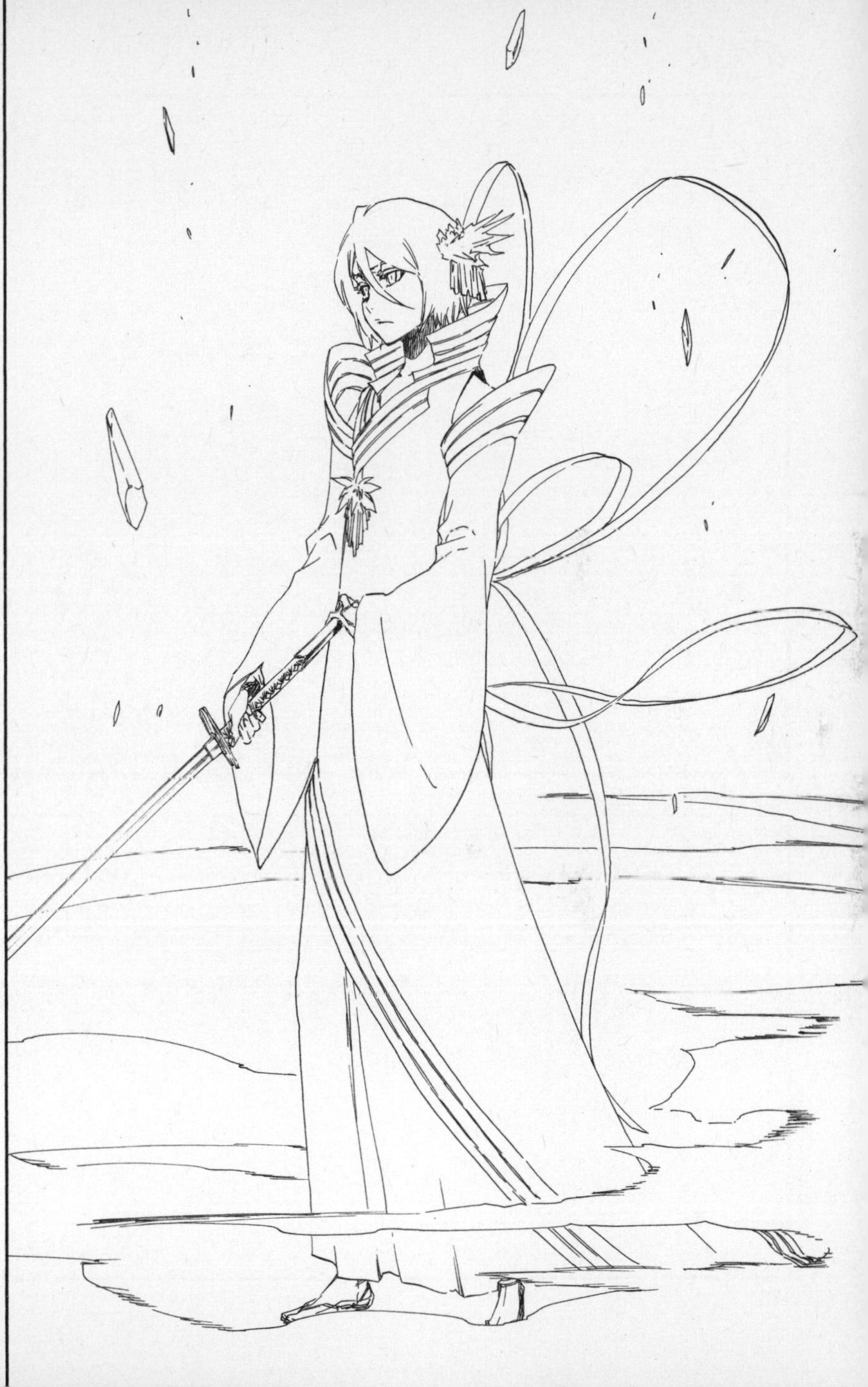

CRK
KRK
CRK
KRCK
KRK...K

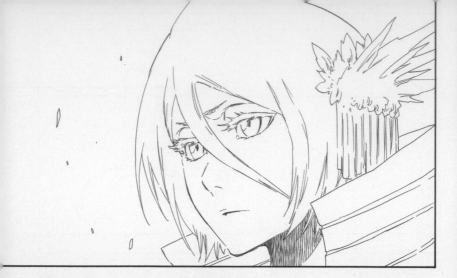

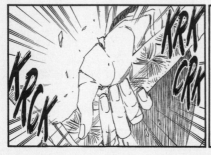

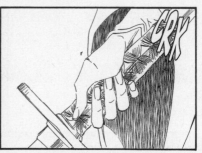

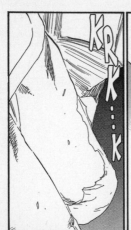

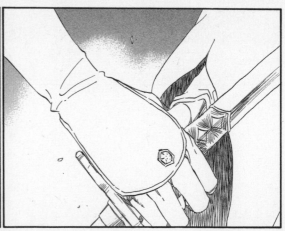

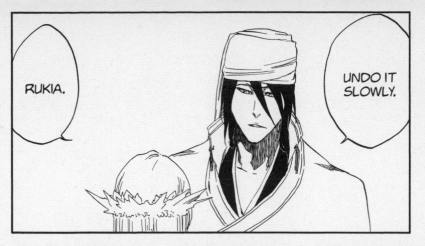

RUKIA.

UNDO IT SLOWLY.

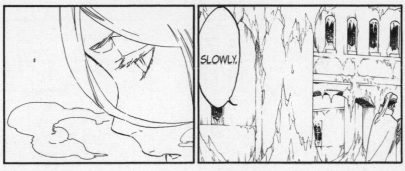

SLOWLY.

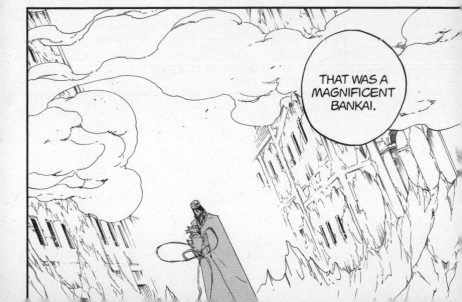

THAT WAS A MAGNIFICENT BANKAI.

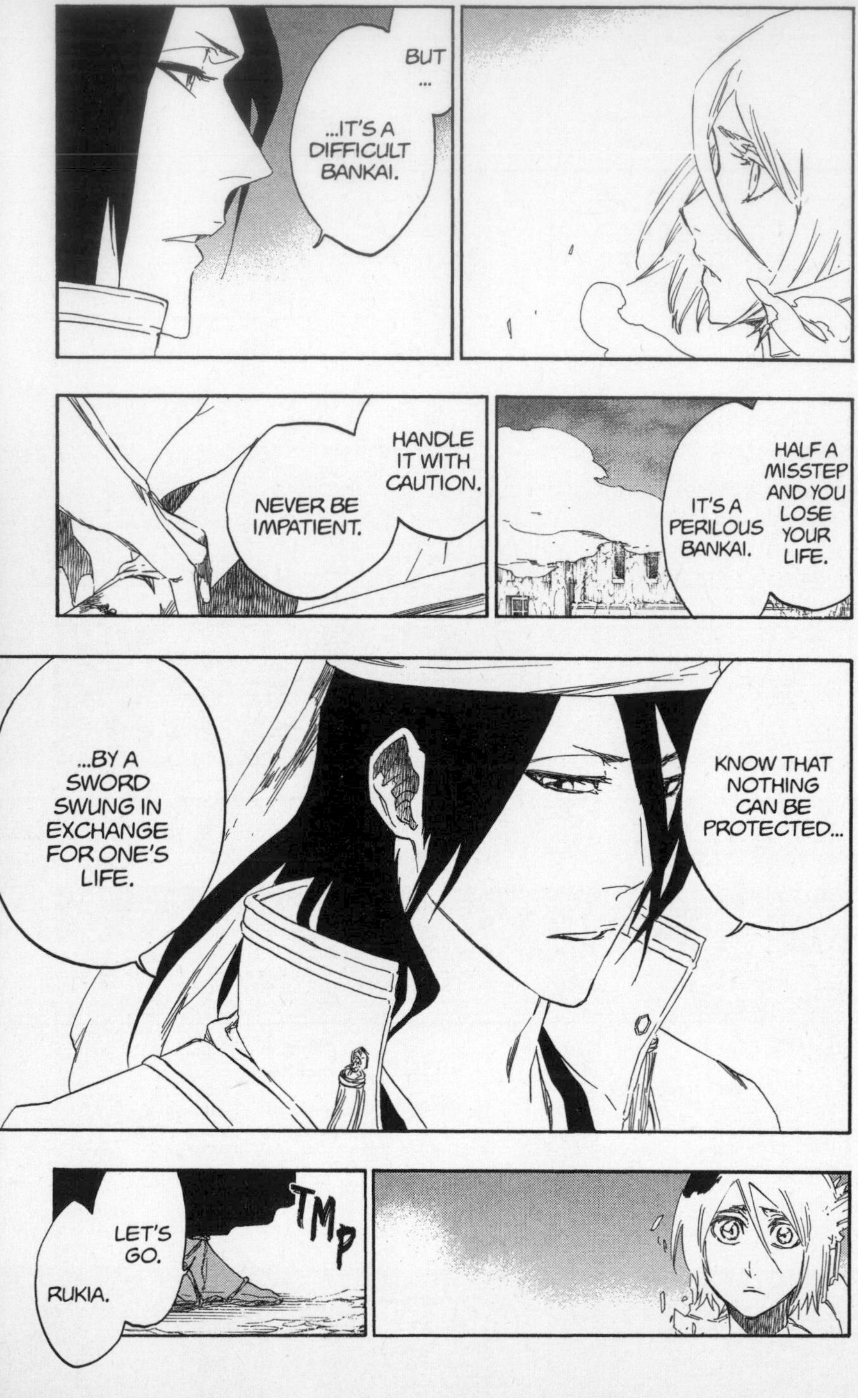
BUT ...
...IT'S A DIFFICULT BANKAI.
HALF A MISSTEP AND YOU LOSE YOUR LIFE.
IT'S A PERILOUS BANKAI.
HANDLE IT WITH CAUTION.
NEVER BE IMPATIENT.
KNOW THAT NOTHING CAN BE PROTECTED...
...BY A SWORD SWUNG IN EXCHANGE FOR ONE'S LIFE.
TMP
LET'S GO.
RUKIA.

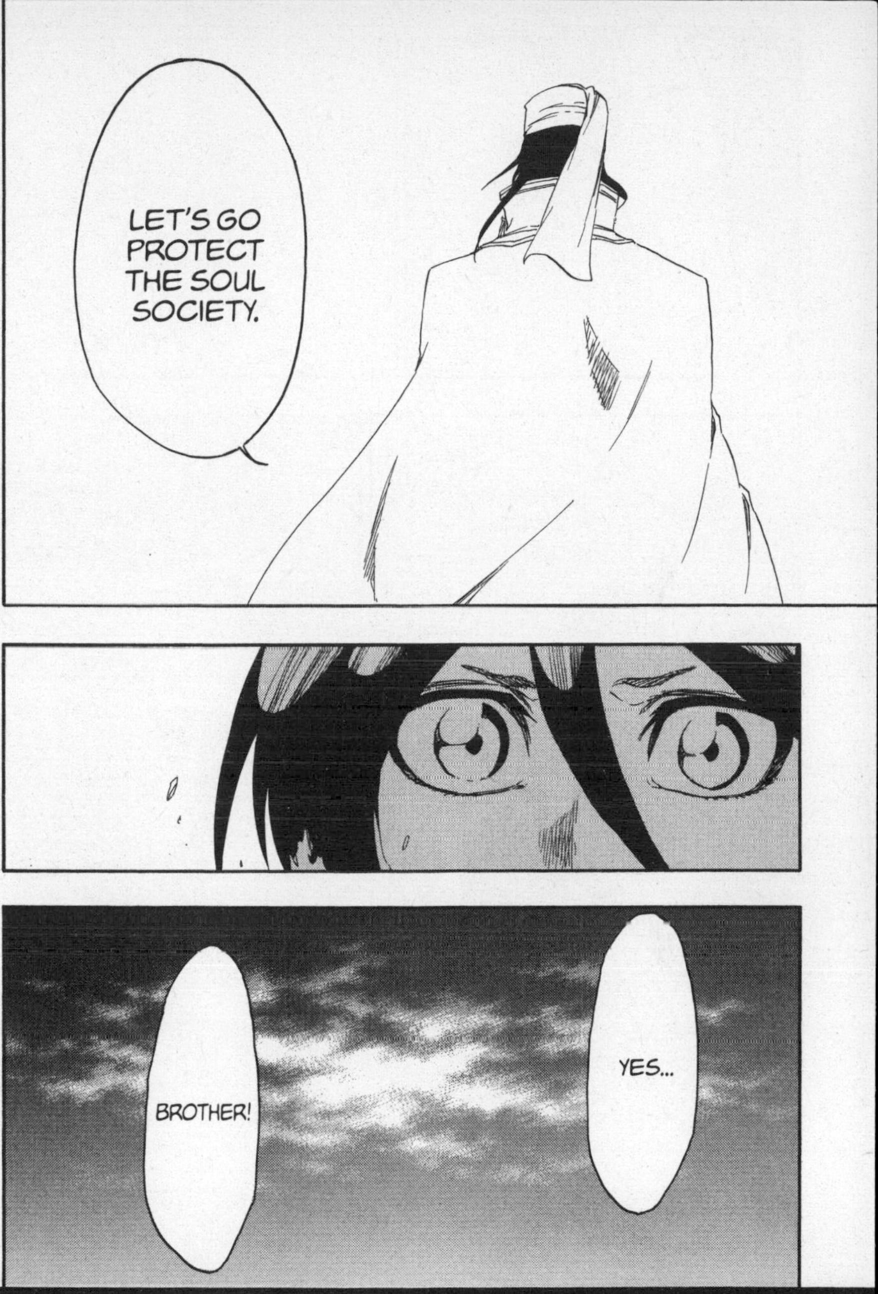
LET'S GO PROTECT THE SOUL SOCIETY.
YES...
BROTHER!

bleach 570.

Closer, Closer

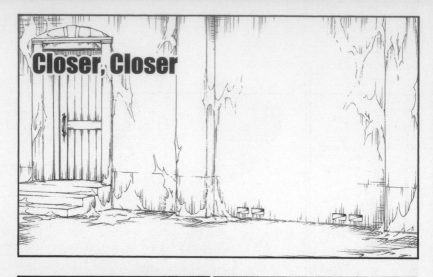

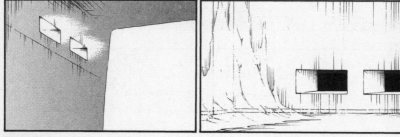

KOTECHIN!

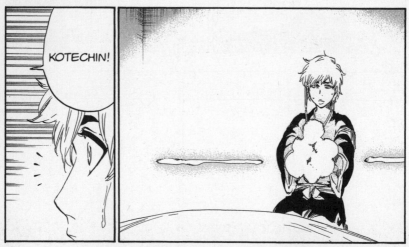

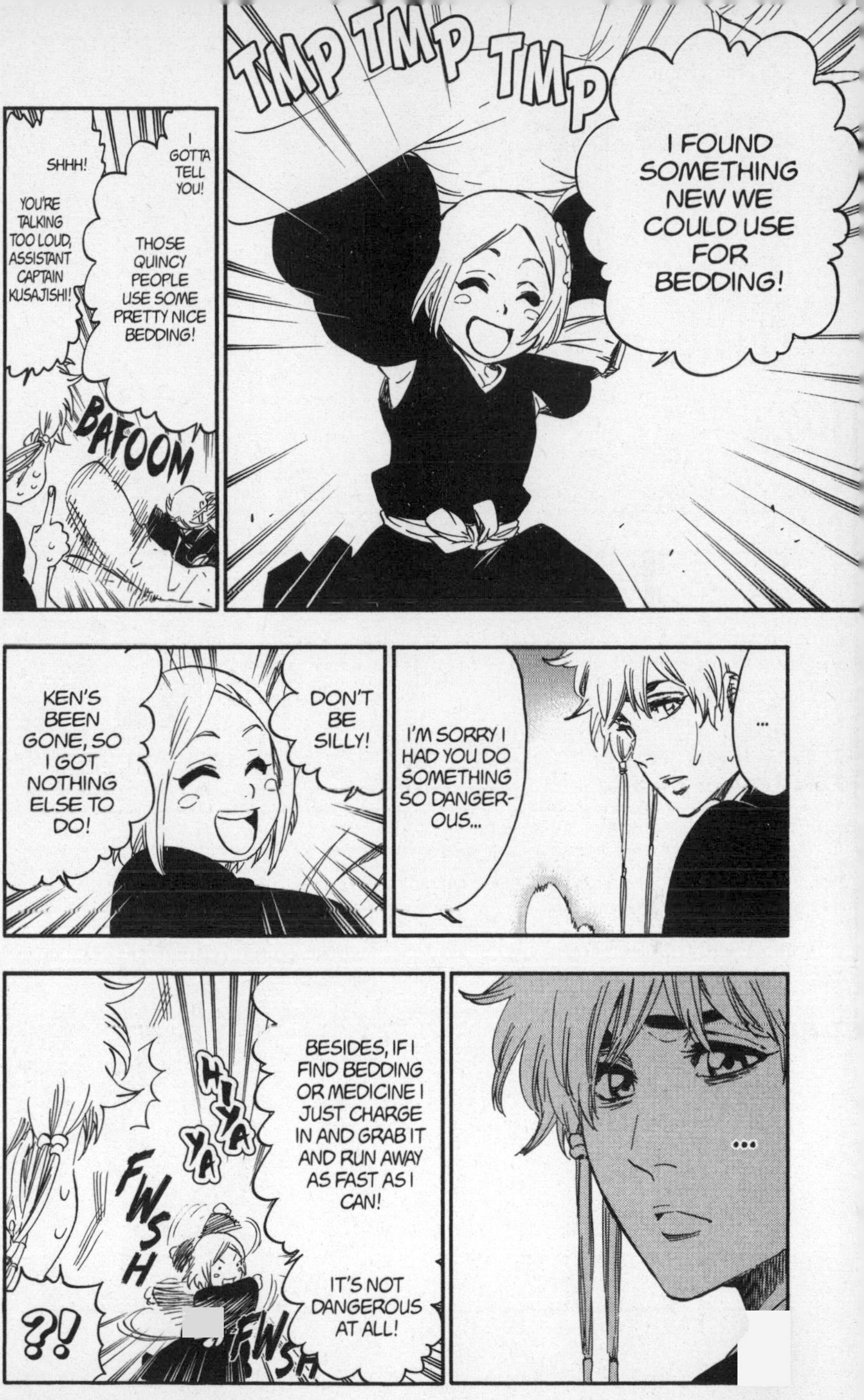
TMP TMP TMP
I FOUND SOMETHING NEW WE COULD USE FOR BEDDING!
I GOTTA TELL YOU!
THOSE QUINCY PEOPLE USE SOME PRETTY NICE BEDDING!
SHHH!
YOU'RE TALKING TOO LOUD, ASSISTANT CAPTAIN KUSAJISHI!
BAFOOM
...
I'M SORRY I HAD YOU DO SOMETHING SO DANGER-OUS...
DON'T BE SILLY!
KEN'S BEEN GONE, SO I GOT NOTHING ELSE TO DO!
...
BESIDES, IF I FIND BEDDING OR MEDICINE I JUST CHARGE IN AND GRAB IT AND RUN AWAY AS FAST AS I CAN!
HIYA YA
FWSH
IT'S NOT DANGEROUS AT ALL!
FWSH
?!

READ THIS WAY

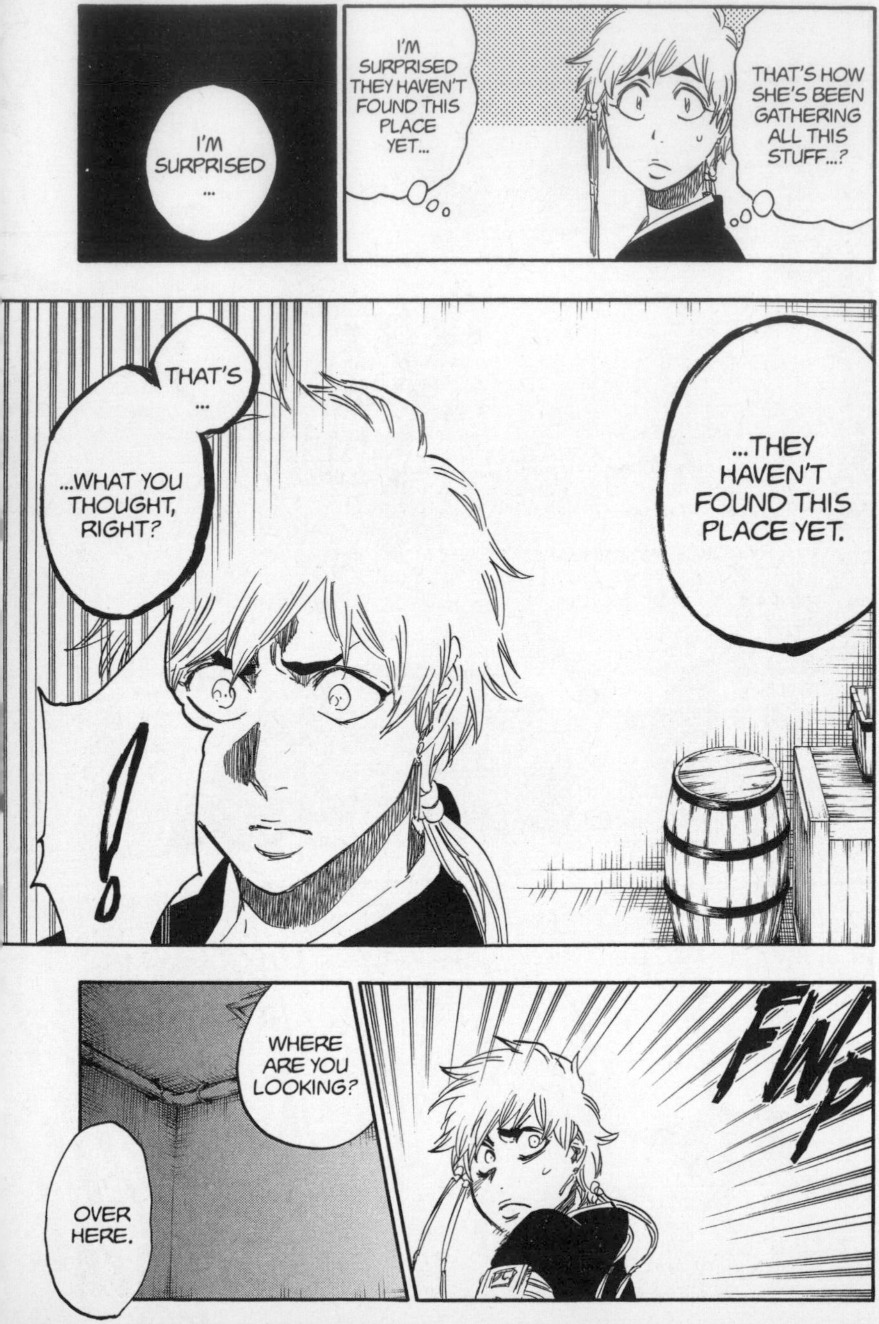
THAT'S HOW SHE'S BEEN GATHERING ALL THIS STUFF...?
I'M SURPRISED THEY HAVEN'T FOUND THIS PLACE YET...
I'M SURPRISED ...
...THEY HAVEN'T FOUND THIS PLACE YET.
THAT'S ... ...WHAT YOU THOUGHT, RIGHT?
FWP
WHERE ARE YOU LOOKING?
OVER HERE.

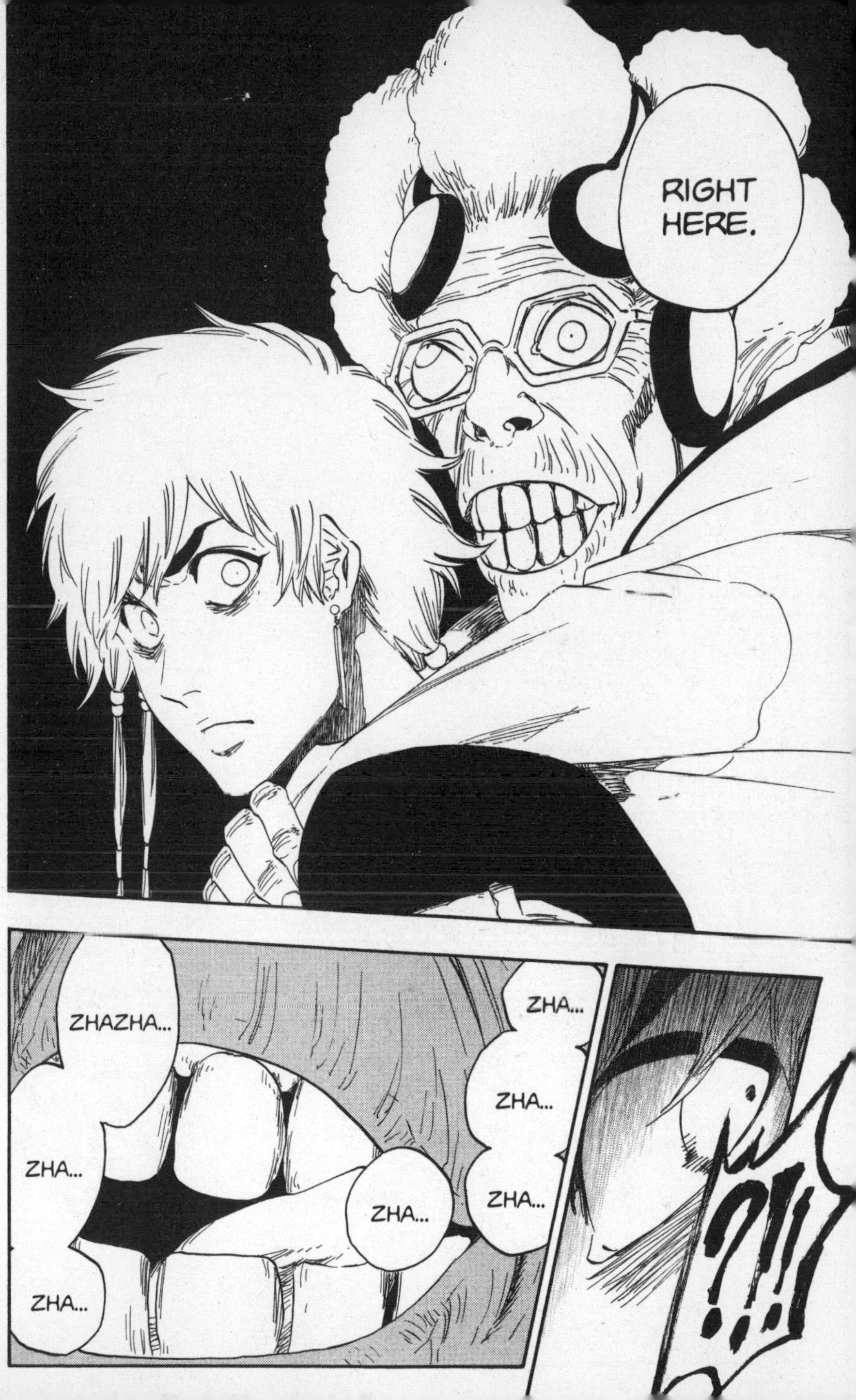
RIGHT HERE.
?!!
ZHA...
ZHAZHA...
ZHA...
ZHA...
ZHA...
ZHA...
ZHA...

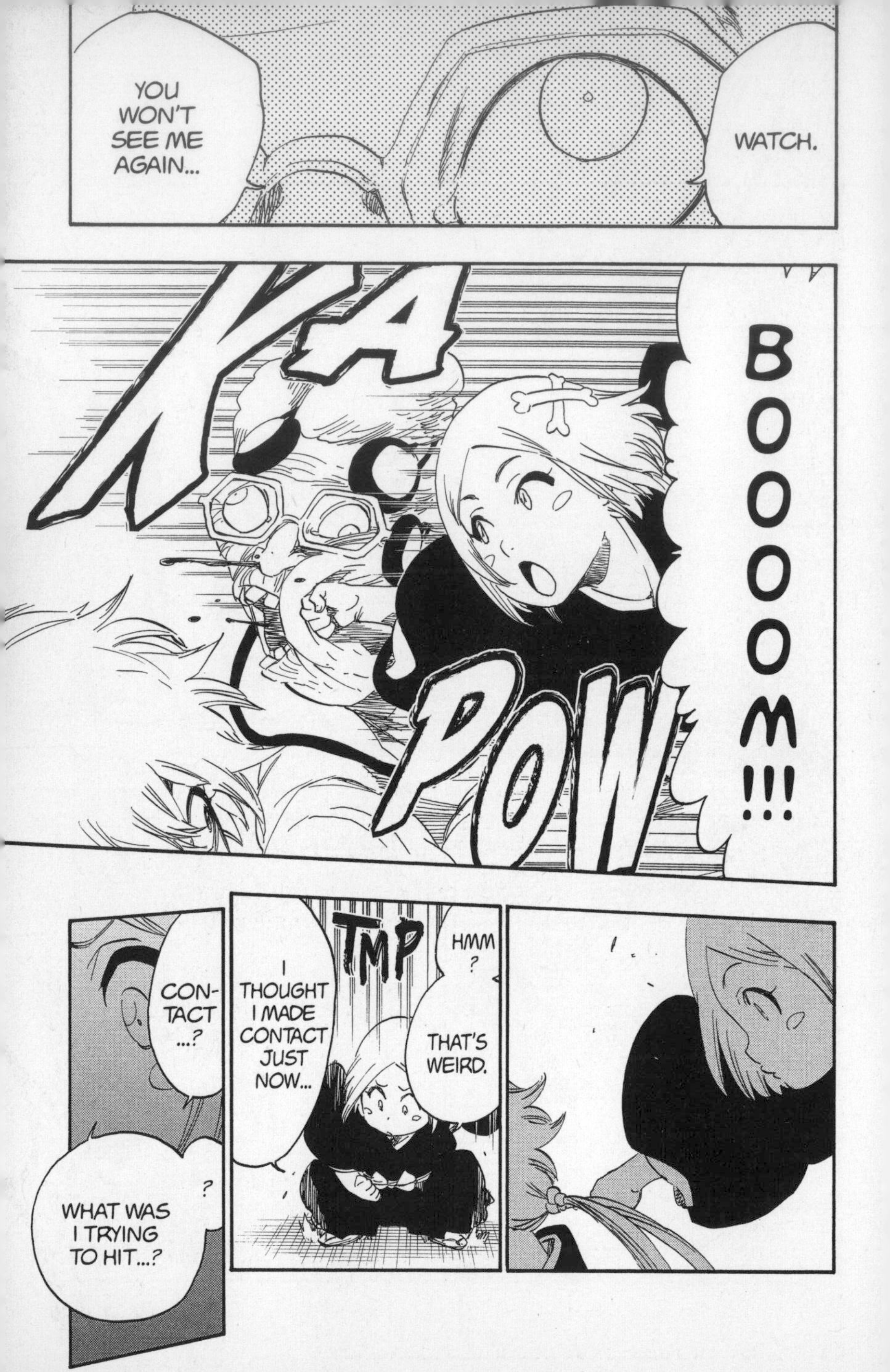
WATCH.
YOU WON'T SEE ME AGAIN...
BOOOOOM!!!
KA
POW
HMM?
TMP
I THOUGHT I MADE CONTACT JUST NOW...
THAT'S WEIRD.
CON-TACT ...?
?
WHAT WAS I TRYING TO HIT...?

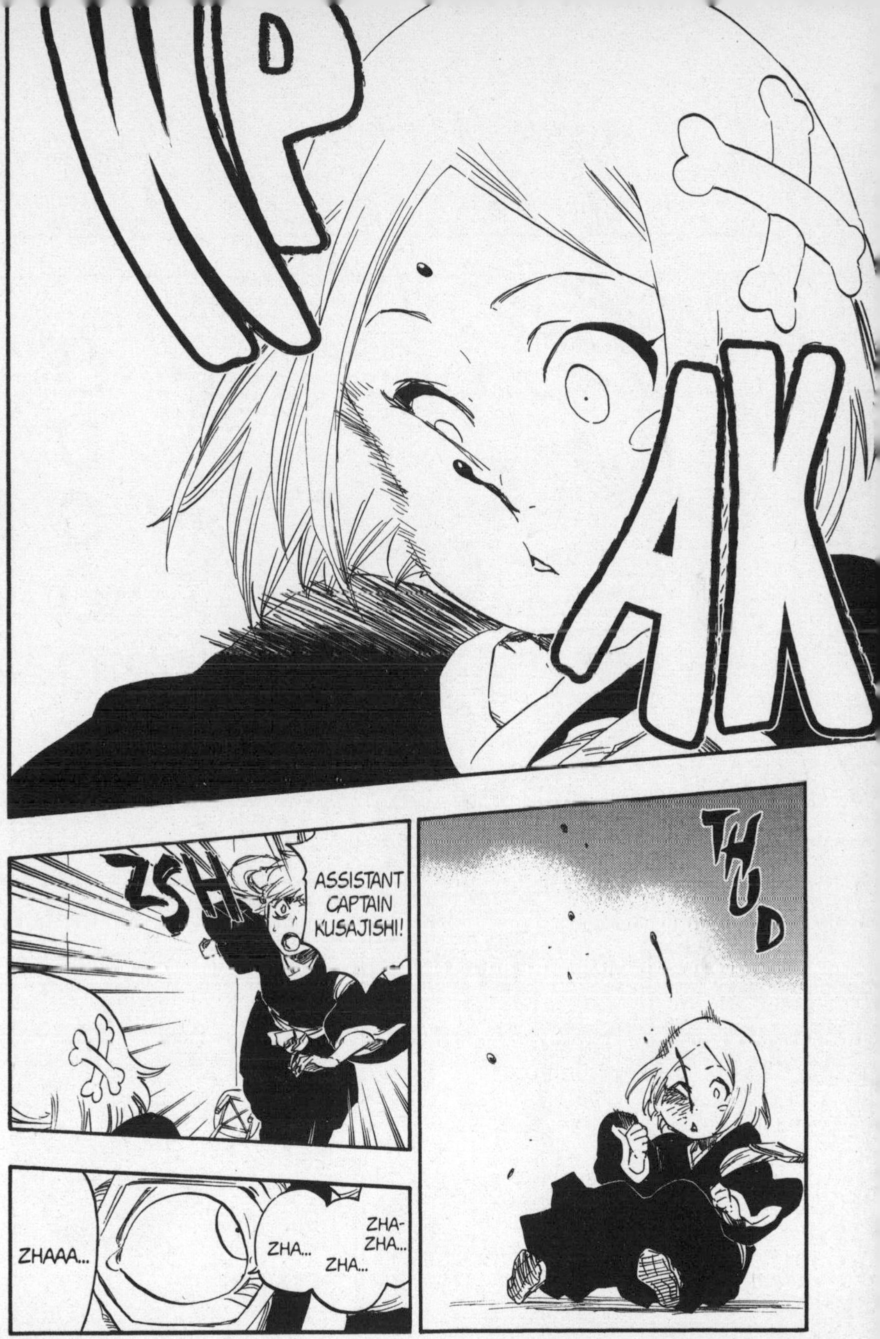
WHP
AK
THUD
ZSH
ASSISTANT CAPTAIN KUSAJISHI!
ZHA-ZHA...
ZHA...
ZHA...
ZHAAA...

READ THIS WAY

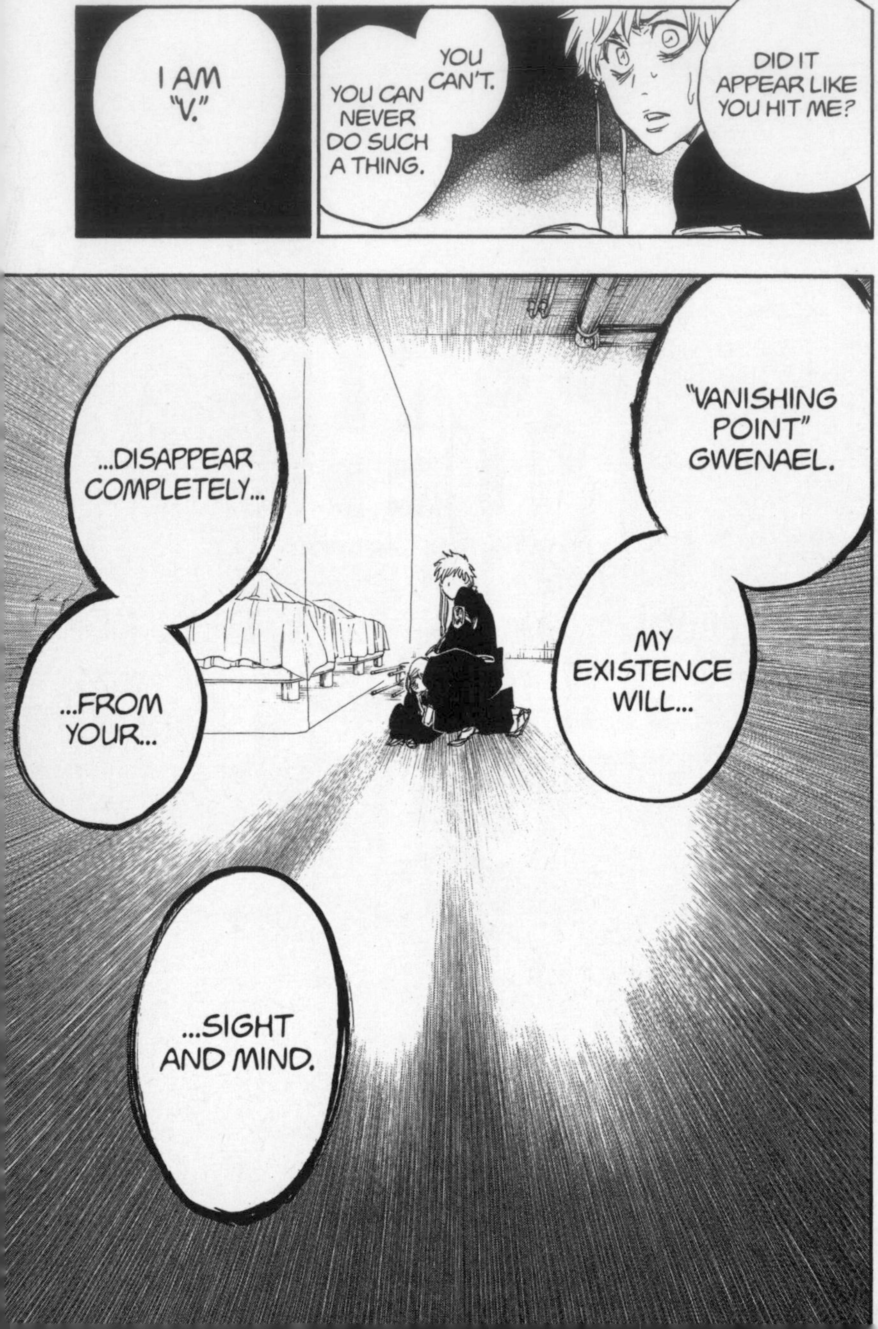
DID IT APPEAR LIKE YOU HIT ME?
YOU CAN'T.
YOU CAN NEVER DO SUCH A THING.
I AM "V."
"VANISHING POINT" GWENAEL.
MY EXISTENCE WILL...
...DISAPPEAR COMPLETELY...
...FROM YOUR...
...SIGHT AND MIND.

CONTI
NUED
IN
BLEACH
64

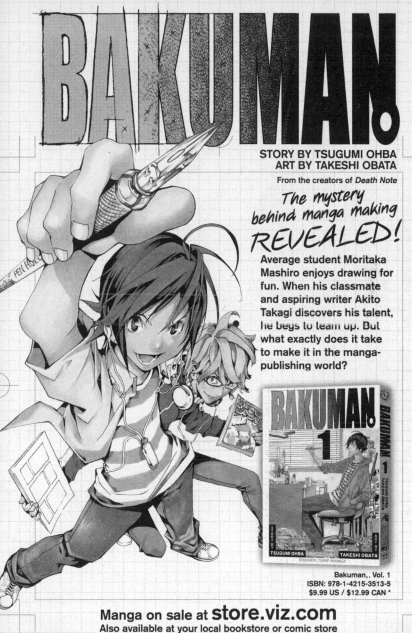

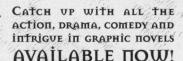
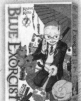

You're Reading in the Wrong Direction!!

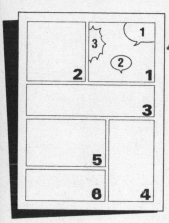

Whoops! Guess what? You're starting at the wrong end of the comic!

...It's true! In keeping with the original Japanese format, **Bleach** is meant to be read from right to left, starting in the upper-right corner.

Unlike English, which is read from left to right, Japanese is read from right to left, meaning that action, sound effects and word-balloon order are completely reversed... something which can make readers unfamiliar with Japanese feel pretty backwards themselves. For this reason, manga or Japanese comics published in the U.S. in English have sometimes been published "flopped"—that is, printed in exact reverse order, as though seen from the other side of a mirror.

By flopping pages, U.S. publishers can avoid confusing readers, but the compromise is not without its downside. For one thing, a character in a flopped manga series who once wore in the original Japanese version a T-shirt emblazoned with "M A Y" (as in "the merry month of") now wears one which reads "Y A M"! Additionally, many manga creators in Japan are themselves unhappy with the process, as some feel the mirror-imaging of their art skews their original intentions.

We are proud to bring you Tite Kubo's **Bleach** in the original unflopped format. For now, though, turn to the other side of the book and let the adventure begin...!

—Editor

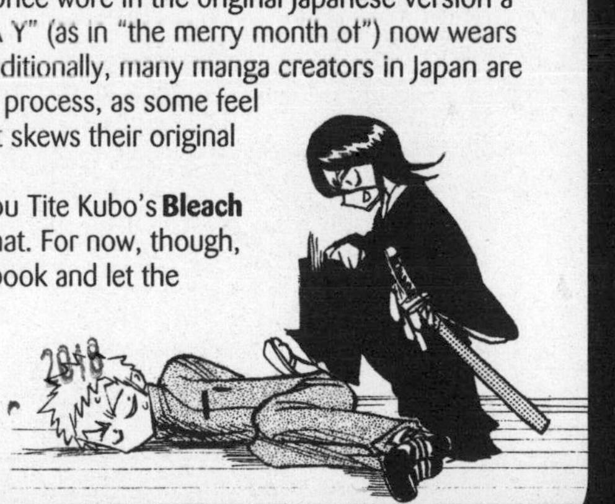